Social*Text* 142

Radical Care
Edited by Hiʻilei Julia Kawehipuaakahaopulani Hobart and Tamara Kneese

Nicole Charles is assistant professor of women and gender studies in the Department of Historical Studies at the University of Toronto Mississauga. Her research engages science and technology studies and transnational and women-of-color feminisms to deconstruct the entwined politics of biomedicine, care, gender, race, and colonialism in the anglophone Caribbean.

Elijah Adiv Edelman is assistant professor in the Department of Anthropology at Rhode Island College in Providence. His work has appeared in *GLQ*, *Journal of Homosexuality*, *Porn Studies*, and *Journal of Sex Research*, as well as in the collections *Queer Necropolitics* (2014), *Queer Excursions* (2014), and *Out in Public* (2009).

Hiʻilei Julia Kawehipuaakahaopulani Hobart is assistant professor of anthropology at the University of Texas at Austin. She is currently writing a history of comestible ice in Hawaiʻi across the nineteenth and twentieth centuries that investigates the sensorial and affective dimensions of Indigenous dispossession.

Tamara Kneese is assistant professor of media studies and director of gender and sexualities studies at the University of San Francisco. Her work considers the affective, embodied, and sacred dimensions of media and technology. She is currently writing a book about the platform infrastructures of digital afterlives.

Micki McGee is associate professor of sociology and American studies at Fordham University. She is the author *Self-Help, Inc.: Makeover Culture in American Life* (2005) and is currently at work on a book about neurodiversity and neoliberalism.

Leyla Savloff is a PhD candidate in the Department of Anthropology at the University of Washington. Her dissertation, "Entre Nosotres: The Social and Political Spheres of Women against Prisons," examines enactments of freedom and creative responses to the criminal justice system by a women's collective in Argentina.

Cotten Seiler is associate professor of American studies at Dickinson College. He is the author of *Republic of Drivers: A Cultural History of Automobility in America* (2009) and is currently at work on a monograph exploring the biopolitics of twentieth-century US liberalism.

Dean Spade is associate professor at the Seattle University School of Law. He is the author of *Normal Life: Administrative Violence, Critical Trans Politics and the Limits of Law* (2015). His video projects and writing are available at deanspade.net. His tool kit on mutual aid is at bigdoorbrigade.com.

Radical Care

Survival Strategies for Uncertain Times

Hi‘ilei Julia Kawehipuaakahaopulani Hobart
and Tamara Kneese

> Caring for myself is not self-indulgence, it is self-preservation, and that is
> an act of political warfare.
> —Audre Lorde, *A Burst of Light*

Care has reentered the zeitgeist. In the immediate aftermath of the 2016
US presidential election, op-eds on #selfcare exploded across media platforms.[1] But for all the popular focus on self-care rituals, new collective
movements have also emerged in which moral imperatives to act—to
care—are a central driving force. In a recent interview, Angela Davis
explicitly tied social change to care: "I think our notions of what counts
as radical have changed over time. Self-care and healing and attention to
the body and the spiritual dimension—all of this is now a part of radical
social justice struggles. That wasn't the case before."[2] Davis points to a
growing awareness that individual impulses and interior lives, the intimate and banal details of family histories and personal experiences, are
directly connected to external forces. Care, then, is fundamental to social
movements. For examples we might look to the way that Indigenous peoples and their allies have rearticulated their positions as protectors rather
than protesters, emphasizing the importance of caring for and being good
stewards of the earth, or how Occupy-style actions emerged at US Immigration and Customs Enforcement detention centers to denounce the
separation of migrant children from their families in "tender age camps"
at the US border, positioning parental care (both to give and to receive it)
as a human right.[3] While the phenomenon of care as political warfare has
a long genealogy (one that we outline below), it has taken on fresh signifi-

Social Text 142 · Vol. 38, No. 1 · March 2020
DOI 10.1215/01642472-7971067   © 2020 Duke University Press

cance since the election of Donald Trump and its global reverberations: the rolling back of civil liberties, government denial of anthropogenic climate change, and human rights abuses serve as reminders that structural inequity and disenfranchisement come with corporeal and emotional tolls that care seeks to remediate.

Of course, the problem is much larger and older than Trump. Brazil's Jair Bolsonaro, Rodrigo Duterte in the Philippines, and Israel's Benjamin Netanyahu all reflect the global rise of an authoritarian right wing that threatens already vulnerable communities. For the purposes of this special issue of *Social Text*, we define radical care as a set of vital but underappreciated strategies for enduring precarious worlds. While radical care is often connected to positive political change by providing spaces of hope in dark times, the articles in this collection simultaneously acknowledge the negative affects associated with care. Because radical care is inseparable from systemic inequality and power structures, it can be used to coerce subjects into new forms of surveillance and unpaid labor, to make up for institutional neglect, and even to position some groups against others, determining who is worthy of care and who is not. Even so, in the face of state-sanctioned violence, economic crisis, and impending ecological collapse, collective care offers a way forward. In this issue, we look to histories of radical care in the United States and beyond in order to better understand how radical care is intervening in social and political movements today.

More than a Feeling

Broadly speaking, *care* refers to a relational set of discourses and practices between people, environments, and objects that approximate what philosophers like Adam Smith and David Hume identify as "empathy," "sympathy," or "fellow feeling."[4] Theorized as an affective connective tissue between an inner self and an outer world, care constitutes a feeling with, rather than a feeling for, others. When mobilized, it offers visceral, material, and emotional heft to acts of preservation that span a breadth of localities: selves, communities, and social worlds. Questions of who or what one might care for, and how, can be numerous.[5] While recognizing the pervasive use of care as an imperative for any number of social and personal concerns, our focus here is on the instances where care is employed against immediate crises and precarious futures.

Our framing of care as a critical survival strategy responds to two emergent strains of care discourses that are coincident but vastly different. On the one hand, self-care is both a solution to and a symptom of the social deficits of late capitalism, evident, for example, in the way that remedies for hyperproductivity and the inevitable burnout that follows are commoditized in the form of specialized diets, therapies, gym memberships, and schedule management.[6] On the other hand, a recent surge of academic interest in care and its metonyms across multiple disciplines and subfields through recent or forthcoming volumes, symposia, conference panels, and keynote addresses—all announced between the time this issue's call for papers went out and the drafting of this introduction—considers how our current political and sociotechnical moment sits at the forefront of philosophical questions about who cares, how they do it, and for what reason.[7] Following recent theoretical interventions into the importance of self-care despite its susceptibility to neoliberal co-optation, calls to vapid consumption, and association with a wellness ideology, this issue extends the potentialities of self-care outward to include other forms of care that push back against structural disadvantage.[8]

This issue examines the care strategies used by individuals and groups across historical periods and in different parts of the world when institutions and infrastructures break down, fail, or neglect. Reciprocity and attentiveness to the inequitable dynamics that characterize our current social landscape represent the kind of care that can radically remake worlds that exceed those offered by the neoliberal or postneoliberal state, which has proved inadequate in its dispensation of care.[9] This may sound like a naive proposition, particularly given the precarious circumstances that are culminating in our current moment: anthropogenic climate change, infrastructural ruin, mass extinction, growing wealth inequality, geopolitical failure, and others cataloged by this journal's recent special issue titled "Collateral Afterworlds."[10] When crisis and disaster are the relentlessly pervasive frameworks through which, for some, "redemption is not recognized as immanent or expected as forthcoming," despondence and disorientation are rational outcomes.[11] Despite such unavoidable circumstances, we find hope in locating spaces and enactments of care. Specifically, mobilizations of care allow us to envision what Elizabeth Povinelli describes as an *otherwise*.[12] It is precisely from this audacity to produce, apply, and effect care despite dark histories and futures that its radical nature emerges. Radical care can present an otherwise, even if it cannot completely disengage from structural inequalities and normative assumptions regarding social reproduction, gender, race, class, sexuality, and citizenship. To that end, the articles in this collection locate and analyze the mediated boundaries of what it means for individuals and groups to feel and provide care, survive, and even dare to thrive in environments that challenge their very existence.

Care of the Self and Others: Collectivism and Commercialism

By the time people began turning to self-care as a mechanism for coping with postelection political despair in 2016, a robust industry of neoliberal wellness ideology trends offered individualized solutions to structural problems. Digital health technologies, such as fitness and productivity apps, and personal devices, such as Fitbits and smartphones, allow individuals to practice forms self-management embedded within neoliberal logics. Furthermore, by incentivizing health behaviors through insurance discounts, corporations can nudge their employees to stop smoking or exercise more; corporate ideologies regarding self-management align with new technologies intended to promote self-care.[13] Through such technologies, self-care is reduced to the habitual and individual level: have you attended to your own well-being by walking enough steps or eating enough vegetables today? As a form of self-help, these technologies allow individuals to maintain productivity in the face of adversity and exhaustion, offering a New Age salve in a fresh iteration of the Weberian Protestant work ethic. It is no accident that patients' self-care is now a mandatory part of medical treatment plans, including hygiene, prescription drug monitoring, proper sleep, and sex.

In the United States, where so many are without adequate health insurance plans, cancer patients and accident survivors may outsource their care to crowdfunding platforms, where individuals depend on the kindness of internet strangers to help them meet their financial goals before they can receive treatment.[14] In turn, potential wellness solutions are presented through new technologies, such as self-tracking wearables: a mode of care that one must buy into that keeps the onus of care on individuals and often requires the sharing of personal data.[15] A person's life is reduced to metrics, such as counted steps, heart rate, hydration status, weight, and oxygen levels. Self-care is thus popularly associated with self-optimization, or a way of preparing individuals for increased productivity in demanding workplaces when, in reality, things like chronic illness are incompatible with capitalist productivity and even visible forms of activism: it is difficult to join street protests if you are a caretaker, suffer from depression or anxiety, or cannot get out bed.[16] Those who fail to practice self-care may indeed be labeled "noncompliant" and thus less deserving of care.

In this way, the neoliberal model of care as one of moralized self-management produces the body as a site in which idealized citizenship coalesces as an unachievable goal that, simultaneously, glosses over the political, economic, and ideological structures that do the work of marginalization.[17] For example, Lana Lin describes her discomfort with survivorship as a circumscribed identity, wherein the language of cancer survivorship places the impetus on survivors to take care of themselves and losing one's "battle" with cancer becomes a mark of failure.[18] Read through the framework of Michel Foucault's theories about discipline and the care of the self, technologically mediated health practices might be seen as an extension of modern biopolitics, in which neoliberal subjectivity at once resists and reinscribes the power of the state.[19] Importantly, this formulation of the self operates under a false assumption of agency and choice rather than an acknowledgment that such practices are a key locus that produces some bodies as nonnormative and then, in turn, articulates them as a problem.[20]

Histories of Radical Care

Since the time Audre Lorde wrote *A Burst of Light* (1988), from which we draw our epigraph, her words have become a mantra, or perhaps a way of reminding ourselves that self-care is necessary for collective survival within a world that renders some lives more precarious than others. Within the larger passage where Lorde describes her fight against cancer, she conjures up images of Black activists coursing through her veins as they fight against colonial powers; she connects the anonymity of cancer to governmental neglect; and she jettisons the individualism of Foucault's self-care in favor of coalitional survival.[21] The fact that this quote is often presented without its original context in its popular usage tells us much about the difference between radical and neoliberal self-care. Radical care is not, as Inna Michaeli explains, the kind of self-care that has been co-opted by neoliberal imperatives to "treat yourself" but is, instead, a way of understanding "a self which is grounded in particular histories and present situations of violence and vulnerability."[22] A genealogy of radical care is thereby aligned with the emergence of self-care, but certainly not contained by it: within this formulation, the self is not a generic, philosophical self but a situated self engaged in complex sets of relations. Disabilities studies scholars dovetail with these arguments when they point to the importance of recognizing subjects as inherently networked and interdependent. When Laura Forlano, for example, describes the assemblages of human and nonhuman caretaking devices that allow a disabled cyborg body to function, she states that "in caring for myself, I am enlisted into a practice of actively participating in, maintaining, repairing and caring for multiple medical technologies (rather than using them passively)."[23] This section reconciles the historiography of care through two trajectories that we see as overlapping and complementary: on the one hand, feminist self-care, and on the other, Black and brown activist care work, both of which have aimed to fill in the gaps between structural breakdown, failure, and neglect.

The notion of feminist self-care emerged from the need for medical practitioners—particularly therapists or other professionals who dealt with trauma patients—to maintain a capacity to care for others and for patients to better care for themselves. In her ethnography of faith-based workers in New Zealand and Uganda, for example, anthropologist Susan Wardell focused on the ways that clergy members and other religious non-profit workers thought of self-care as a way of replenishing the individual after giving too much to others or as a way of keeping care for others sustainable.[24] Arthur Kleinman, an instrumental proponent of self-care, argued that "inasmuch as caregiving (and receiving) is done by individuals who themselves are complex and divided and who inhabit local worlds that are also plural and divided, it needs to be understood as a process that is affected by emotional, political, and economic realities."[25] In other words, care does not happen in a vacuum; rather, care of the self promised to sustain the social and personal costs of caregiving.

At the same time that self-care became important to the business of caregiving, a pivot toward self-care as a radical praxis emerged as one that was particularly attentive to the gendered power dynamics embedded within "women's work." In the early 1970s, autonomist Marxist feminists associated with the Italian anticapitalist Left pushed for the recognition of domestic and reproductive labor in the Wages for Housework campaign, during which Silvia Federici argued that "by denying housework a wage and transforming it into an act of love, capital has killed many birds with one stone."[26] The movement, which spread internationally, critiqued the atomization and invisibility of women's care work within the domestic sphere that made it difficult for women to collectively organize like other workers. By pushing for recognition in the public sphere, the individualized care performed for a spouse, child, or home became tied to a larger collective action.

Principles of collective care through self-care applied to antiracist and feminist political movements. During the women's movement and civil rights era of the 1960s and 1970s, physical health became central to maintaining community resiliency against racism, sexism, colonialism, classism, and homophobia. In the United States, projects like *Our Bodies, Ourselves* (1970) distributed information about women's reproductive health through pamphlets and meetings in intimate spaces like living rooms.[27] Around the same time, the Black Panther Party implemented key programs that sought to fortify community strength and power by linking health advocacy and activism, including a free breakfast program that fed over ten thousand school children per day and free medical clinics that administered preventative health care, as well as housing and social services.[28] These efforts reverberated transnationally, giving rise to global consciousness about the important connections between physical well-being and antiracism work. For example, Maria John has shown how the establishment of urban Indigenous health clinics, from Seattle, Washington, to Sydney, Australia (both formed in the early 1970s), echoed the practical and ideological model of the Black Panthers.[29] To this day, grassroots medical and dietary health support services remain a cornerstone of political movements that critique state and environmental racism, as evidenced in the free clinics and kitchens established by water protectors at Standing Rock to protest the construction of the Dakota Access Pipeline in 2016, food justice programs like Soul Fire Farm that make explicit the connections among dietary health, environmental justice, and state racism by framing self-care as a liberatory imperative, and the women's group Las Patronas in Mexico, which prepares and distributes food to migrants speeding by atop freight trains bound for the United States.[30]

Gaps in Care: Institutional Failure and the Co-optation of Care

Our interpretation of radical care comprises underlying tensions. The first, referred to above, is the symbiotic and at times contradictory relationship between self-care and care for others. The second tension reveals the normative assumptions baked into care: it is both essential for social reproduction and yet often invisible or undervalued, which means it is ripe for exploitation and co-optation. Finally, a third tension within care is the expression of solidarity versus charity, or the way that care is mobilized as a response to neglect or catastrophe. In this section, we lay out these considerations against the political and financial economies that shape normative assumptions about who and what drive a practice of care.

Shannon Mattern suggests that the work of care can be easily overlooked because of how its impact is cumulative: a process that requires attentiveness and fortitude over innovation. Mattern also addresses the possible pitfalls of romanticizing both maintenance and care, which are often caught up in globalized development and urban renewal projects:

> Across the many scales and dimensions of this problem, we are never far from three enduring truths: (1) Maintainers require care; (2) caregiving requires maintenance; and (3) the distinctions between these practices are shaped by race, gender, class, and other political, economic, and cultural forces. Who gets to organize the maintenance of infrastructure, and who then executes the work? Who gets cared for at home, and who does that tending and mending?[31]

Crucially, the process of extending self-care outward and building a collective capacity for substantive political change requires hard work. So often this work is performed below the line, ignored by the media or narratives about political leaders and social change agents. Following Michelle Murphy's cautioning "against the conflation of care with affection, happiness, attachment, and positive feelings as political goods,"[32] we acknowledge the ways that fragile communities operationalize care toward liberatory ends despite, through, and alongside unequal power structures by focusing our attention on the work of caring, but we also notice who is uncared for, who receives care and who does not, and who is expected to perform care work, with or without pay. Care is profoundly present for those performing its labor and—not uncoincidentally—those most easily overlooked by the politically and socially privileged. Herein lie some of the central tensions that surface in colloquial articulations of care, which presume individualism, benevolence, or moral purity despite the fact that distributions of resources, such as social services, fresh and affordable foods, or clean water, shape the conditions by which emotional and physical capacities for care are supported.

Finally, because care can be mobilized as a way to privilege some groups at the expense of others, the "radical" aspect of care can bleed into right-wing and white supremacist politics as much as it upholds leftist utopian visions. In describing her current book project on machine learning and segregation, *Discriminating Data: Neighborhoods, Individuals, Proxies,* media theorist Wendy Hui Kyong Chun argues that social networking platforms rely on a logic of homophily: birds of a feather flock together, so you will want to date, love, and be neighborly with those who are just like you, who share your fundamental values and interests.[33] The problem with care attached to fellow feeling or sympathy is that all too often it means that care is reserved for those deemed worthy. As Cotten Seiler's article in this issue underscores, radical care is also potentially dangerous: affective feelings of compassion and empathy toward poor whites during the Great Depression, for instance, could be used as justification for caring for fellow whites over others, despite the state-backed care offered by the New Deal. What happens when images of suffering or violence fail to inspire warm feelings and subsequent charitable action? Care is unevenly distributed and cannot be disentangled from structural racism and inequality.

In addition to the kind of commercialized co-optation of neoliberal self-care we describe above, political leaders also take advantage of stereotypes about caregiving to extract unpaid labor from citizens. Care is a collective capacity to build an alternative to colonialism and capitalism, but those in power can also instrumentalize empathy and care to their own ends. For example, Andrea Muehlebach has shown how the post-Fordist Italian state valorizes and manipulates compassion in order to absolve itself of responsibility to its most marginalized citizens.[34] In the context of the United States, the American health care and childcare systems are kept afloat by a vast corpus of unpaid or devalued domestic work performed by poor immigrant women and kin members.[35] Domestic workers are some of the most exploited workers, not just in the United States but globally; in Saudi Arabia, Indonesia, and Bangladesh they are often poor migrant women and are without labor unions or other protections, often subjected to sexual assault and other forms of violence.[36]

To be clear, the problems that radical care seeks to remedy are not just a product of neoliberal policy or the election of Donald Trump and other authoritarian leaders. Older histories of settler colonialism and centuries of exploitation inform the inequalities entangled with care today. As Leanne Betasamosake Simpson and Dionne Brand put it, "The monster has arrived, and the monster was always here."[37]

Conclusion: Solidarity Not Charity

As global capitalism breaks down in various sites across the globe, we see radical care emerge through collective action. While care is often fraught, we end with a more hopeful depiction of radical care by highlighting the work of some organizations that offer examples of what we theorize above. Often the answer is through coalitional work: rather than looking out only for those in your same social positions, coalitions inspire people to work together across class, race, ethnicity, religious, and state boundaries toward a common cause.

After state governments implemented austerity measures in the wake of the 2008 global financial crisis, people organized to care for those who were left in the cold. In Spain, the Plataforma de Afectados por la Hipoteca provides access to fair housing and social rents through mutual aid. The organization was spurred by the collapse of the real estate market and provides emotional as well as economic support to those who cannot pay their mortgages. In Canada, austerity inspired a new wave of disability rights activism that focused on allowing people with disabilities to directly hire their attendants through the Direct Funding Program.[38] Communities come together and use radical care to provide assistance to those who are overlooked by the state and other institutions.

Relief collectives provide supplies and offer labor on a grassroots level in response to the devastation wrought by hurricanes, intensified by climate change. Occupy Sandy is one example of the collective organizing that emerges from catastrophe. Rather than merely donating supplies, relief efforts included building more sustainable communities, bolstering local businesses, and employing skill-sharing techniques. The work of Mutual Aid Disaster Relief, which employs the slogan "Solidarity Not Charity," describes what radical care looks like:

> Disaster survivors themselves are the first responders to crisis; the role of outside aid is to support survivors to support each other. The privileges associated with aid organizations and aid workers—which may include access to material resources, freedom of movement, skills, knowledge, experience, and

influence—are leveraged in support of disaster survivors' self-determination and survival in crisis, and their long-term resilience afterwards, ultimately redistributing these forms of power to the most marginalized.[39]

Charity relies on neoliberal discourses of moral obligation and individual character. Solidarity, however, relies on working with communities and asking them what they need rather than making paternalistic assumptions. Instead of following neoliberal, colonialist development models around innovation and the mining of hope, mutual aid offers space for true collaboration.[40]

Through examples of neglect and exploitation across manifold communities and places, care contains radical promise through a grounding in autonomous direct action and nonhierarchical collective work. Instead of only acting as a force for self-preservation, care is about the survival of marginal communities because it is intimately connected to modern radical politics and activism. As Maria Puig de la Bellacasa notes, caring is "an ethically and politically charged *practice*."[41] During moments of crisis, radical care allows communities to live through hardship. Despite the different time periods and cultural contexts covered in this special issue, the articles develop key points of connection that can begin the work of assessing disparate histories of care and their implications today and to ask what we can learn from previous mistakes or contemporary injustices when it comes to radical care. Importantly, the articles in this issue provide complicated, critical depictions of radical care rather than simply romanticizing care.

The first article provides a historical perspective on how care became racialized within nineteenth- and early twentieth-century thought. Using the iconic image of Dorthea Lange's *Migrant Mother*, Cotten Seiler shows how New Deal–era deployments of eugenics emerged within social welfare programs in the United States. To do so, he carefully unpacks Charles Darwin's and Jean-Baptiste Lamarck's popular theories of evolution and follows them through policy making that employed white supremacist discourses of care, in which sympathy came to be aligned with affective modes of whiteness. In turn, these discourses had implications for government policy, which embedded ideas of deservedness (and, by extension, produced the ideal subjects of care) into social welfare programs. By connecting a history of ideas to their ongoing and violent material effects, Seiler importantly foregrounds the inverse of a politically utopian form of radical care: a care that is "radical" in its alliance with right-wing, white supremacist forces. Seiler calls this "'white care': a surround of institutions and infrastructure dedicated to the education, health, security, mobility, and comfort of the white citizenry," and in doing so shows how romanticizing radical care is dangerous, because it can be used to exclude and subject some groups to institutional neglect.

When Seiler's article is paired with Micki McGee's article on the "care problem" of the capitalist economy, the failures of institutional care (or, rather, care's institutionalization) become painfully clear. The phenomenon that we know as the "care economy" comprises an overlooked bedrock of patriarchal capitalism: without an army of low- or no-wage care workers to support the cleaning, coddling, organizing, and mending of homes, children, the elderly, and the underserved, our fragile systems of productivity would collapse. She turns to self-help and "life-hacking" literatures that shift the burden of care onto the individual rather than attending to the structural challenges that unfairly burden women (and even more so women of color) in order to reveal how women in academia who "expose a problem . . . pose a problem" (to use the words of Sara Ahmed) through uncompensated and labor-intensive child-rearing.[42] Indeed, while putting together this special issue of *Social Text*, each of the editors conceived, birthed, and nursed new babies, requiring each to channel specific forms of care across our personal and early-career professional lives.

Child-rearing and motherhood alternatively become exploitative props for negligent institutions or become sites for creative forms of radical care. Through her ethnographic study of Argentinean women who are serving their sentences under a special house arrest program for pregnant women or women who are the caretakers of young children, Leyla Savloff identifies radical care as a tactic for dealing with a punitive state apparatus. Women under house arrest are oppressed through normative assumptions about motherhood as well as the carceral logics of the prison system. Through this program, the home becomes a site of incarceration that allows limited forms of creative freedom. Savloff shows how domestic and reproductive care can be instrumentalized and appropriated by the state, which subjects women under house arrest to new forms of labor, coercion, and surveillance. At the same time, the women's collective YoNoFui provides women with opportunities for forming community and learning how to craft, offering a space for radical care rather than reproducing neoliberal individualism. YoNoFui not only provides opportunity for skill sharing and individual empowerment but also actively mobilizes for prisoners' rights and against institutional violence.

Collective responses to institutional neglect are also reflected in Elijah Adiv Edelman's ethnographic research of the DC Trans Coalition Needs Assessment. Opening with the case study of one woman's death, Edelman examines how trans life is constituted through necropolitics: living a life worth living, and a death worth dying. Barbara's death contrasts with the experiences of many trans activists, who are often estranged from birth family members or die violent deaths. Edelman uses her story "not because her death exemplifies or directly contrasts with trans lives and deaths but because it is often through the messy and frequently traumatic incoherence of death and loss that we experience the full potential of radical care." Using a concept of "trans vitalities," Edelman provides a perspective of radical care that disrupts normative depictions of the good life. For members of the coalition, "the personal and political transformative power of coalition-based trans social justice work functions as a form of radical care and productive life force." Edelman complicates notions of normative care, risk, and resilience that are often attached to trans bodies and experiences.

As highlighted in Edelman's study of trans coalitional activism, those with risky bodies endure coercive forms of care. Care in the form of aid is complicated by the agency of its recipients: when is it strategically and politically sound to resist care itself? Nicole Charles examines how Barbadians treat human papillomavirus (HPV) vaccines as suspicious technologies within a postcolonial state. Charles shows how the impetus to care, or the structural or moral positions that encourage people to offer care, affect recipients' reactions. Rather than blindly accepting biomedical aid, risk and prevention are negotiated instead by refusals of the HPV vaccine. In acts of refusal, parents exhibit care by protecting their children from an untrustworthy medical establishment. Charles uses the legacies of slavery and colonialism in Barbados and the broader Caribbean to contextualize resistance against HPV vaccines in the twenty-first century, considering them as "entangled factors of care, profit, science, black female sexuality, and risk." Through history and qualitative interviews with parents in Barbados, Charles shows how vaccine suspicion and refusal are forms of radical care, as parents push back against biomedical narratives that might label their children sexually promiscuous: "Suspicion embodies a radical potential to teach of a care rooted in deep witnessing and reflection as a precursor to prescription, mediation, and medical innovations." Medical professionals, public health officials, and scholars of science, technology, and society should all reconsider their assumptions about care and vaccine acceptance.

Finally, Dean Spade approaches the topic of radical care through mutual aid, examining community responses to climate catastrophe and immigration raids. His contribution offers a practical primer in collective organizing strategies. Mutual aid projects, including the Oakland Power Project, which trains community members to perform health care without calling 911, and Mutual Aid Disaster Relief, which provides relief to those living in the aftermath of natural disasters, are examples of situated care networks. Spade pays particular attention to mutual aid as the least visible or celebrated kind of work in the context of capitalism, white supremacy, and patriarchy because it is essentially reproductive labor. We have been taught to valorize and glamorize other activities—giving speeches, passing legislation, bringing lawsuits, organizing marches—and to discount, not notice, not care about care labor. Schüll argues that mutual aid is necessary to mobilize large numbers of people, to build infrastructure for survival that matters now and will matter more in coming disasters and breakdown, and that engaging in mutual aid projects teaches us essential skills that are denied in white patriarchal capitalism, such as collaboration, feedback, and participatory decision making. Mutual aid projects can easily become appropriated in neoliberalism, so those engaged in them are actively trying to resist this co-optation, advocating for solidarity rather than charity.

Taken together, these articles work through the meaning of care as a set of acts, ideologies, and strategies that offer possibilities for living through uncertain times. With care reentering the zeitgeist as a reaction to today's political climate, radical care engages histories of grassroots community action and negotiates neoliberal models for self-care. Studies of care thereby prompt us to consider how and when care becomes visible, valued, and necessary within broader social movements. Rather than romanticizing care or ignoring its demons, radical care is built on praxis. As the traditionally undervalued labor of caring becomes recognized as a key element of individual and community resilience, radical care provides a roadmap for an otherwise.

Notes

1. Kisner, "Politics of Conspicuous Self-Care."
2. Quoted in van Gelder, "Radical Work of Healing."
3. Goodyear-Kaʻōpua, "Protectors of the Future."
4. Fennell, *Last Project Standing*, 22.
5. Martin, Myers, and Viseu, "Politics of Care in Technoscience."
6. Bloom, "How 'Treat Yourself' Became a Capitalist Command."
7. A short list, as most recent instances, includes the 2019 conference "Interrogating Self Care: Bodies, Personhood, and Movements in Tumultuous Times," sponsored by the Consortium for Graduate Studies in Gender, Culture, Women, and Sexuality (see www.gcws.mit.edu/gcws-events-list/selfcaregradconference); Maile Arvin's 2018 plenary talk for the Critical Ethnic Studies Association conference that implored the audience, "We have to work less" (Arvin, "CESA 2018 Plenary Talk"); and a forum on "Ethics, Theories, and Practices of Care" in Gold and Klein, *Debates in the Digital Humanities 2019*. See also Puig de la Bellacasa, "Matters of Care in Technoscience"; and Forlano, "Maintaining, Repairing, and Caring."
8. Ahmed, "Self-Care as Warfare"; Penny, "Life Hacks of the Poor and Aimless."
9. Simpson and Brand, "Temporary Spaces of Joy and Freedom."
10. See Wool and Livingston, "Collateral Afterworlds."
11. Wool and Livingston, "Collateral Afterworlds," 2. Also see Buck, "Pleasure and Political Despondence."
12. Povinelli, "Routes/Worlds."

13. Hull and Pasquale, "Toward a Critical Theory of Corporate Wellness."
14. Berliner and Kenworthy, "Producing a Worthy Illness."
15. Schull, "Data for Life."
16. Gregg, *Counterproductive*; Hedva, "Sick Woman Theory."
17. Guthman and DuPuis, "Embodying Neoliberalism."
18. Lin, "Queer Art of Survival."
19. Dilts, "From 'Entrepreneur of the Self' to 'Care of the Self.'"
20. Guthman and DuPuis, "Embodying Neoliberalism."
21. Lorde, *Burst of Light*, 130.
22. Michaeli, "Self-Care," 53.
23. Forlano, "Maintaining, Repairing, and Caring," 33.
24. Wardell, *Living in the Tension*.
25. Kleinman, "Caregiving as Moral Experience," 1551.
26. Federici, *Wages against Housework*, 2–3.
27. Murphy, "Immodest Witnessing."
28. Heynen, "Bending the Bars of Empire"; Nelson, *Body and Soul*.
29. John, "Sovereign Bodies," 28.
30. Estes, *Our History Is the Future*; Penniman, *Farming While Black*; Icaza, "Decolonial Feminism and Global Politics."
31. Mattern, "Maintenance and Care."
32. Murphy, "Unsettling Care," 719.
33. Chun, "We're All Living in Virtually Gated Communities." In this short article, Chun presents a major argument from her current book project, noting that algorithms group people into online communities based on affinity or shared interest, which leads to further segregation.
34. Muehlebach, "On Affective Labor in Post-Fordist Italy."
35. Chang, *Disposable Domestics*; Armstrong, Armstrong, and Scott-Dixson, *Critical to Care*; Winant, "Trumpcare."
36. Falconer and Kelly, "Global Plight of Domestic Workers."
37. Simpson and Brand, "Temporary Spaces of Joy and Freedom."
38. Hande and Kelly, "Organizing Survival and Resistance in Austere Times."
39. Mutual Aid Disaster Relief, "Core Values."
40. Irani, *Chasing Innovation*.
41. Puig de la Bellacasa, "Matters of Care in Technoscience," 90.
42. Ahmed, *Living a Feminist Life*, 37.

References

Ahmed, Sara. *Living a Feminist Life*. Durham, NC: Duke University Press, 2017.
Ahmed, Sara. "Self-Care as Warfare." *feministkilljoys* (blog), August 25, 2014. feminist killjoys.com/2014/08/25/selfcare-as-warfare/.
Armstrong, Pat, Hugh Armstrong, and Krista Scott-Dixon. *Critical to Care: The Invisible Women in Health Services*. Toronto: University of Toronto Press, 2008.
Arvin, Maile. "CESA 2018 Plenary Talk by Maile Arvin." Plenary talk for the Critical Ethnic Studies Association Conference, September 17, 2018. www.critical ethnicstudiesjournal.org/blog/2018/9/17/cesa-2018-plenary-talk-by-maile-arvin.
Berliner, Lauren, and Nora Kenworthy. "Producing a Worthy Illness: Personal Crowdfunding amidst Financial Crisis." *Social Science and Medicine* 187 (2017): 233–42.
Bloom, Ester. "How 'Treat Yourself' Became a Capitalist Command." *Atlantic*, Novem-

ber 19, 2015. www.theatlantic.com/business/archive/2015/11/how-treat-yourself
-became-a-consumerist-command/416664/.

Buck, Marie. "Pleasure and Political Despondence." *Poetry Foundation Blog*, January 2018. www.poetryfoundation.org/harriet/2018/01/pleasure-and-political-despondence.

Chang, Grace. *Disposable Domestics: Immigrant Women Workers in the Global Economy*. 2nd ed. Chicago: Haymarket Books, 2016.

Chun, Wendy Hui Kyong. "We're All Living in Virtually Gated Communities and Our Real-Life Relationships Are Suffering." *Wired UK*, April 13, 2017. www
.wired.co.uk/article/virtual-segregation-narrows-our-real-life-relationships.

Dilts, Andrew. "From 'Entrepreneur of the Self' to 'Care of the Self': Neo-liberal Governmentality and Foucault's Ethics." *Foucault Studies*, no. 12 (2011): 130–46.

Estes, Nick. *Our History Is the Future: Standing Rock versus the Dakota Access Pipeline, and the Long Tradition of Indigenous Resistance*. London: Verso, 2019.

Falconer, Rebecca, and Annie Kelly. "The Global Plight of Domestic Workers: Few Rights, Little Freedom, Frequent Abuse." *Guardian*, March 17, 2015. www.the
guardian.com/global-development/2015/mar/17/global-plight-domestic-workers
-labour-rights-little-freedom-abuse.

Federici, Silvia. *Wages against Housework*. Bristol, UK: Falling Wall, 1975.

Fennell, Catherine. *Last Project Standing: Civics and Sympathy in Post-Welfare Chicago*. Minneapolis: University of Minnesota Press, 2015.

Forlano, Laura. "Maintaining, Repairing, and Caring for the Multiple Subject." *Continent* 6, no. 1 (2017): 30–35.

Gold, Matthew K., and Lauren F. Klein, eds. *Debates in the Digital Humanities 2019*. Minneapolis: University of Minnesota Press, 2019.

Goodyear-Kaʻōpua, Noelani. "Protectors of the Future, Not Protestors of the Past: Indigenous Pacific Activism and Mauna a Wākea." *South Atlantic Quarterly* 116, no. 1 (2017): 184–94.

Gregg, Melissa. *Counterproductive: Time Management in the Knowledge Economy*. Durham, NC: Duke University Press, 2018.

Guthman, Julie, and E. Melanie DuPuis. "Embodying Neoliberalism: Economy, Culture, and the Politics of Fat." *Environment and Planning D: Society and Space* 24 (2006): 427–48.

Hande, Mary Jean, and Christine Kelly. "Organizing Survival and Resistance in Austere Times: Shifting Disability Activism and Care Politics in Ontario, Canada." *Disability and Society* 30, no. 7 (2015): 961–75.

Hedva, Johanna. "Sick Woman Theory." *Mask*, January 2016. maskmagazine.com/not
-again/struggle/sick-woman-theory.

Heynen, Nik. "Bending the Bars of Empire from Every Ghetto for Survival: The Black Panther Party's Radical Antihunger Politics of Social Reproduction and Scale." *Annals of the Association of American Geographers* 99, no. 2 (2009): 406–22.

Hull, Gordon, and Frank Pasquale. "Toward a Critical Theory of Corporate Wellness." *BioSocieties* 13, no. 1 (2018): 190–212.

Icaza, Rosalba. "Decolonial Feminism and Global Politics: Border Thinking and Vulnerability as Knowing Otherwise." In *Critical Epistemologies of Global Politics*, edited by Marc Woons and Sebastian Weier, 26–45. Bristol: E-International Relations, 2017.

Irani, Lilly. *Chasing Innovation: Making Entrepreneurial Subjects in Modern India*. Princeton, NJ: Princeton University Press, 2019.

John, Maria. "Sovereign Bodies: Urban Indigenous Health and the Politics of Self-Determination in Seattle and Sydney, 1950–1980." PhD diss., Columbia University, 2016.

Kisner, Jordan. "The Politics of Conspicuous Self-Care." *New Yorker*, March 14, 2017. www.newyorker.com/culture/culture-desk/the-politics-of-selfcare.

Kleinman, Arthur. "Caregiving as Moral Experience." *Lancet* 380, no. 9853 (2012): 1550–51.

Lin, Lana. "The Queer Art of Survival." *WSQ* 44, nos. 1–2 (2016): 341–46.

Lorde, Audre. *A Burst of Light*. Ithaca, NY: Firebrand Books, 1988.

Martin, Aryn, Natasha Myers, and Ana Viseu. "The Politics of Care in Technoscience." *Social Studies of Science* 45, no. 5 (2015): 625–41.

Mattern, Shannon. "Maintenance and Care." *Places*, November 2018. placesjournal.org/article/maintenance-and-care/.

Michaeli, Inna. "Self-Care: An Act of Political Warfare or a Neoliberal Trap?" *Development* 60, nos. 1–2 (2017): 50–56.

Muehlebach, Andrea. "On Affective Labor in Post-Fordist Italy." *Cultural Anthropology* 26, no. 1 (2011): 59–82.

Murphy, Michelle. "Immodest Witnessing: The Epistemology of Vaginal Self-Examination in the U.S. Feminist Self-Help Movement." *Feminist Studies* 30, no. 1 (2004): 115–47.

Murphy, Michelle. "Unsettling Care: Troubling Transnational Itineraries of Care in Feminist Health Practices." *Social Studies of Science* 45, no. 5 (2015): 717–37.

Mutual Aid Disaster Relief. "Core Values." mutualaiddisasterrelief.org/core-values/ (accessed August 16, 2019).

Nelson, Alondra. *Body and Soul: The Black Panther Party and the Fight against Medical Discrimination*. Minneapolis: University of Minnesota Press, 2011.

Penniman, Leah. *Farming While Black: Soul Fire Farm's Practical Guide to Liberation on the Land*. White River Junction, VT: Chelsea Green, 2018.

Penny, Laurie. "Life Hacks of the Poor and Aimless." *Baffler* (blog), July 8, 2016. thebaffler.com/war-of-nerves/laurie-penny-self-care.

Povinelli, Elizabeth A. "Routes/Worlds." *e-flux journal*, no. 27 (2011). www.e-flux.com/journal/27/67991/routes-worlds/.

Puig de la Bellacasa, Maria. "Matters of Care in Technoscience: Assembling Neglected Things." *Social Studies of Science* 41, no. 1 (2011): 85–106.

Schüll, Natasha Dow. "Data for Life: Wearable Technology and the Design of Self-Care." *BioSocieties* 11, no. 3 (2016): 317–33.

Simpson, Leanne Betasamosake, and Dionne Brand. "Temporary Spaces of Joy and Freedom." *Literary Review of Canada*, June 2018. reviewcanada.ca/magazine/2018/06/temporary-spaces-of-joy-and-freedom/.

van Gelder, Sarah. "The Radical Work of Healing: Fania and Angela Davis on a New Kind of Civil Rights Activism." *Yes!*, February 18, 2016. www.yesmagazine.org/issues/life-after-oil/the-radical-work-of-healing-fania-and-angela-davis-on-a-new-kind-of-civil-rights-activism-20160218.

Wardell, Susan. *Living in the Tension: Care, Selfhood, and Wellbeing among Faith-Based Youth Workers*. Durham, NC: Carolina Academic Press, 2018.

Winant, Gabriel. "Trumpcare Could Bring Back an Epidemic of Abuse." *New York Times*, June 28, 2017. www.nytimes.com/2017/06/28/opinion/trumpcare-senior-abuse-nursing-obamacare.html.

Wool, Zoë H., and Julie Livingston. "Collateral Afterworlds: An Introduction." In "Collateral Afterworlds: Sociality besides Redemption." Special issue, *Social Text*, no. 130 (2017): 1–15.

The Origins of White Care

Cotten Seiler

> Care for the race . . . this must be the keynote of our future.
> —Henry Fairfield Osborn, *Man Rises to Parnassus*, 1928

Critics have hailed Dorothea Lange's iconic 1936 photograph *Migrant Mother, Nipomo, California* as both an encapsulation of the human crisis of the Great Depression and a spur to the egalitarian reforms of the New Deal. Although Progressive-era reformers had deployed documentary photographs to mobilize political support, it was in the 1930s, as technological and industrial enhancements enabled more effective reproduction and dissemination to a mass audience, that the photograph emerged fully as a formidable political instrument. Immediately after its appearance in the *San Francisco News*, Lange's image of the beleaguered farmworker Florence Thompson and her children began to circulate widely in public culture, complementing the thousands of Farm Security Administration (FSA) photographs of the "forgotten man" invoked in center-left political rhetoric. Exemplified in Lange's own 1933 *White Angel Breadline* and 1934 *Man Beside Wheelbarrow* and John Vachon's 1938 *Unemployed Man*, this figure, in Lange's words, "with his head down, with his back against the wall, with his livelihood . . . overturned," pervaded Depression-era cultural production.[1]

Such representations imbued their white subjects "simultaneously [with] a sense of individual worth and class victimage."[2] One crafter of such images, John Steinbeck, valorized the white Dust Bowl migrants in the West as desperate but nonetheless "resourceful and intelligent Americans who have gone through the hell of the drought." In contrast to the "peon class" origins of the earlier migrants to the region, the more recent diaspora derived from "the best American stock" and thus could be expected, if aided and treated fairly, to "be citizens of the highest type."[3] Although the FSA photographs and other propaganda art of the 1930s also imaged people of color, they deliberately leveraged white immiseration to elicit viewers' support for the ameliorative programs and policies of the New Deal.[4] *Migrant Mother* and the countless images of "downcast mostly white people patiently, lawfully, awaiting relief" traded in a beset, consanguine whiteness that would resonate with, and motivate to care-oriented political action, audiences conditioned by hegemonic conceptions of race.[5]

This article argues that the effectiveness of these twentieth-century representations of white abjection, which importuned their viewers to demand recuperative action by the state, owed to a nineteenth-century conceptualization of racialized whiteness that foregrounded empathy as whites' signal evolutionary achievement and the font of their potential. This conceptualization emerged from post-Darwinian or, more properly speaking, anti-Darwinian evolutionary theory that articulated whiteness as an acquired disposition to *care*, as both noun and verb. This deep context helps us account for the rise of a statist, ameliorative new liberalism at the turn of the century and the building of a midcentury apparatus of white care: a surround of institutions and infrastructure dedicated to the education, health, security, mobility, and comfort of the white citizenry.

The New Deal and the care-oriented liberalism of the midcentury United States recruited political subjects to a mode of care that was radical in two ways: its departure from US norms of governmentality and its stark circumscription by race. White care entailed a biopolitical project predicated on what Michel Foucault called "state racism." This principle licenses the modern state to "make live" elements of the national population who are deemed favorable and "let die" those cast as deleterious.[6] White supremacy, rather than a general humanitarianism, underwrote and propelled the egalitarian, reformist, redistributive politics of a transformed liberalism.

Given the traditional animus to the power of a centralized state in mainstream US political culture, New Deal liberalism required for its realization both a clearly specified population of consanguine white Americans and a catastrophe—or a series of them—sufficiently threatening to that population to justify the apparatus of care.[7] As the state directed itself to the reformers' agenda in the New Deal and beyond, its policy making drew on a reservoir of thought that testified to the differing evolutionary viability of the human races and imbued whiteness with the civilization-building qualities of sympathy, benevolence, and justice. Florence Thompson (phenotypically white despite her Cherokee lineage) and her children would be made to live through a range of interventions by the biopolitical state.

"They Had Developed Wings in Attempting to Fly": The Neo-Lamarckian Evolutionary Narrative

The decade following Charles Darwin's 1859 *On the Origin of Species by Means of Natural Selection, or, The Preservation of Favoured Races in the Struggle for Life* saw the hypothesis of the transmutation of species over long expanses of time displace the authoritative doctrine of special creation, which held that species were created in their fixed form, ran their course, died out, and were replaced by other species, all via successive "mental operations of the Creator."[8] Transmutationists prior to Darwin, such as Jean-Baptiste Lamarck and Darwin's grandfather Erasmus Darwin, had regarded evolution as a teleological process of ascent, the precise mechanisms of which remained speculative: either supernaturally implanted forces in the organism transformed it along a predetermined course, or external stimuli compelled the organism to improve itself, or both. More perfect species arose when organisms obtained characteristics that enhanced their chances of survival and, somehow, passed these traits on to their offspring. Twentieth-century thinkers would deride Lamarck's 1809 account of giraffes achieving their elongated necks over many generations of stretching to reach the leaves of trees, but the story was likely enough before the advent of genetics, and its stress on the organism's efforts and God's will as the drivers of species change comforted those who, even as they abandoned the doctrine of special creation, still sought design and teleology in evolution.

Darwin's theory of natural selection thwarted such conceptions. *Origin* emphasized simply that new traits appeared and, when sustained in subsequent generations, became the "materials for natural selection to act on and accumulate."[9] Perpetually shifting environments made all perfection transient and organisms' efforts futile: only by a diversity of traits could a species hope to survive the natural violence of the world, and only then by becoming, over generations, something different. "Not one living species," Darwin wrote, "will transmit its unaltered likeness to a distant futurity."[10]

Darwin's insistence on contingency became particularly rankling when confronting human origins, which Darwin's 1871 *Descent of Man* traced to lower forms and primates. Many devout monotheists militated against this genealogy (and still do), but commentators of more secular stripes also excoriated Darwinism for rendering humanity bestial and the universe rudderless.[11] Even Darwin's allies demurred on natural selection as the forge of the human mind and soul.

Disagreement over human descent did not, however, prevent transmutationist evolutionism from suffusing the natural and social sciences, as well as the humanities and popular culture in the late nineteenth-century

Atlantic world. Yet this ascendant evolutionism "deserted materialism," in the words of one approving contemporary, for the more dulcet song of "what may be called scientific theology, or theologic science."[12] The era thus witnessed a "non-Darwinian revolution" that dislodged special creationism from its authoritative perch even as it "succeeded in preserving and modernizing the old teleological view of things."[13] By the turn of the century only a handful of diehard neo-Darwinians insisted on the natural selection of randomly generated, heritable traits as the crucial mechanism of species change, and observers spoke credibly of the deathbed of Darwinism.

In the United States, a loosely affiliated American School of Evolution blended Darwin's ideas with those of Lamarck to confect a more ideologically useful evolutionary narrative. In this endeavor they drew from the English polymath Herbert Spencer, who in the 1840s had begun advocating what he called interchangeably the theory of evolution and the theory of Lamarck. Spencer spent the next five decades extrapolating from that theory a synthetic philosophy that united all organic phenomena in a vast process of refinement and advance. Although Spencer countenanced a role for natural selection, he continued to favor Lamarck's principle of "functionally-acquired modifications, transmitted and increased," as the essential mechanism of species change.[14]

Building on Spencer's popular ideas, the American School of Evolution developed and retailed its neo-Lamarckian evolutionism in academic scholarship, lectures, and lay journals. Putting the transmission of acquired traits "at the very base of our theories," in the words of one member, the paleontologist Henry Fairfield Osborn, the American School offered its audiences an institutionally sanctioned scientific discourse that reinscribed teleology and tempered Darwinism's tout court animalization of humanity.[15] Their theories informed the evolutionary imagination of most Americans well into the twentieth century, when it was overwritten by the modern evolutionary synthesis that reaffirmed Darwinian claims.[16]

The neo-Lamarckians of the American School exceeded their European colleagues—indeed, Lamarck himself—in asserting that organisms performed deliberate evolutionary labor. "Wings were not given to birds to enable them to fly," wrote Osborn, conveying the pith of neo-Lamarckism, "but they had developed wings in attempting to fly."[17] Such changes, averred Osborn's mentor, the celebrated paleontologist Edward Drinker Cope, "depend on the will." Cope traced what he called "the origin of the fittest" to an organism's deployment of "mind" to activate its own morphological change. "Science proves," Cope announced in an 1887 lecture, "that mind is the creator of organisms."[18] Thus the American School stalwartly asserted, to the enthrallment of audiences, what

Darwin had found risible in Lamarck: "Adaptations by the slow willing of animals."[19]

Yet the neo-Lamarckians of the American School also proposed that a supernaturally implanted "ancestral form of life-energy" or "God-element within" might impel the organism's transformation along pre-scribed lines.[20] Hence, what could be attributed to the organism's efforts, such as birds' wings, could simultaneously be construed as the manifest will of a deity who helped those who helped themselves. Evolution thus occurred aristocratically, as a small vanguard of organisms within each species responded to supernatural imperatives and deployed, in Cope's words, "intelligent choice" to make their own evolutionary luck; mean-while, the laggard members of the species remained inert—perhaps dis-pleasing the deity and certainly consigning themselves to oblivion.[21]

Race as Capacity for Evolutionary Labor

Neo-Lamarckian accounts of transmutation resonated powerfully as allegories of human evolutionary ascent. The geologist Joseph Le Conte averred that "man's conscious voluntary effort is the chief factor in his own evolution." The theist T. H. Eddy mused, "If through a monkey race, as Darwin supposes, then with pride may we look back and point to the fact that from an humble beginning, through the efforts of *the human mind*, we have evolved ourselves to be what we now are?" "We are re-creating ourselves," declared the naturalist William Dickey Gunning; "we have worked the downward slant out of the bodily eye, and we are working it out of the spiritual eye." Moreover, this evolutionary striving did not go unaided: the proper understanding of evolution, wrote the philosopher John Fiske, "makes [human life] seem more than ever the chief object of Divine care."[22] More important, neo-Lamarckian tales of bootstrap-ping and divinely elected species functioned as powerful props to white supremacy, ranking races based on their evident record of evolutionary labor and their viability for further ascent.

As the transmutation hypothesis came into currency after 1840, it pressed against the unity controversy that had mired inquiry into human origins and the causes of visible physical difference since the seventeenth century. The array of human types Europeans encountered in their expe-ditionary ventures enfeebled the biblical orthodoxy of monogenesis, which held that humanity descended from an originally created man and woman and that variations in skin tone and other traits had been produced by dif-ferent environments over countless postdeluge generations. The insurgent theory, polygenesis, attributed to God multiple creations, some of which were experimental or even botched. Enslavers and their allies flocked to polygenesis despite its heresy, as the theory's signal move was to elaborate the humanoid to whom inhumane things could be done clean-handedly.[23]

The immediacy of the unity debate receded with abolition, and Darwin's assertion of *Homo sapiens*' primate descent seemed to hollow out its very premises. "The foot of the ape being proved to be the same as man's," observed an acidic 1863 commentator, "it is of no use now to show that the feet of the ape and the negro are identical."[24] Yet such demonstrations of nonwhite races' "approximations to the simian type," in Cope's words, continued to abound and, in fact, enabled the hypothesis of human descent to gain traction.[25] "Those who adopt the Darwinian hypothesis and believe that we are first cousins of the ape," another 1863 voice proposed, "may perhaps with some consistency go on to represent the African as not only a different but an essentially inferior race."[26] Into postbellum human biology and the new fields of ethnology, sociology, and anthropology slithered a secularized polygenesis that substituted narratives of racial development, stasis, and retardation for those of multiple creations. Ensconced in the neo-Lamarckian framework that stressed evolution as a progressive condition earned by striving, elect organisms, the conceptualization of race as a continuum of animality mitigated the affront that the thesis of primate descent leveled against "civilized" whites, whose social, political, and economic supremacy the disdained Darwinian narrative judged to be, like every evolutionary outcome, haphazard. By contrast, the neo-Lamarckian narrative delivered a bildungsroman of the emergence and rarification of humanity's white portion.

Postbellum evolutionists thus became preoccupied with chronicling the formation of the races, an enterprise that explicated and confirmed the profundity of present-day racial difference. Disseminated in university classrooms and by scholarly journals, popular magazines, literature, museum exhibitions, and fairs, accounts that stressed the antiquity of the races reconciled the "perpetual challenge to the dogma of unity" posed by nonwhites by positioning and tracking the latter along a spatiotemporal "progress from brute to man."[27] Although evolutionists acknowledged the "Rubicon" that separated *Homo sapiens* from its primate cousins, they held that a wider chasm cleaved the civilized from the primitive races.[28] Many suggested that races be classified as species, so ancient and distinct was their "race plasma."[29]

Claims that *longue duree* racial formation had produced differences that were now insurmountable both vied with and issued from what Kyla Schuller has called "impressibility discourse," whereby racialists evaluated each group on "the degree to which [its] hereditary material was embedded in time and retained the capacity to be affected in the future."[30] Physiological features as well as behavior and culture indexed each race's capacity for receiving, absorbing, and warding off impressions from the natural world and human society, and for transmitting refinements to its offspring. Schuller argues that this Lamarckian discourse, which emphasized the mutability rather than the fixity of bodies, characterizes the nineteenth-century racial imagination.

Scientists' assessments of groups' impressibility, like the evaluations of their evolutionary labor, could render certain races "outcasts from evolution" with a finality that matched polygenetic apologia for slavery or, later, hard-hereditarian eugenics.[31] As neo-Lamarckian racialism flattered white audiences that their evolutionary journey amounted to, as the English author Samuel Butler put it, "transmitted perseverance in well-doing," it also reassured them that nonwhites were frozen in a self-inflicted and likely permanent evolutionary stagnation.[32] "The germ-cells are so well protected," Cope wrote, "that long periods of time and long-continued influences are required to produce appreciable changes of character in a family or a race."[33] Calling in 1890 for the expulsion of African Americans from the United States, Cope reminded his readers that "evolution is not possible under all circumstances," and warned of the threat to the republic posed by the Black presence "as it appears to the student of species-characters in body and mind."[34] He pleaded agnostic as to "what the negro may become after centuries of education" but remarked that "he has had as much time in the past as any race, and he has not improved it, or been improved by it"; in his limited educability "he is like other members of the animal kingdom."[35]

However, Cope also affirmed that "growth in intelligence and ethical knowledge and practice" could occur "even in the most ill-favored of the Indo-European stock, if they only have the chance; for it is in the race." The innate "fine nervous susceptibility [and] mental force" in whites derived from their "hundreds of centuries of toil and hardship." The biocultural achievements of this population merited protection, Cope insisted, the most pressing act of which was the quarantine to Africa of the liminally human mass of "dead material in the very centre of our vital organism."[36]

Sympathy as White Evolutionary Accomplishment

Neo-Lamarckians heralded whites' rarefied "ethical knowledge and practice" as the most transformative of their evolutionary achievements. They argued that this particular excellence tracked with the growth of "representative capacity," a faculty that enabled, in Fiske's words, the "resuscitating [and] combining relations not present to the senses."[37] Whites' development of representative capacity had won them intellectual superiority over other races but also generated new "psychical" faculties that drew on but were distinct from mere ratiocination: sympathy, benevolence, justice. Cope regarded the capacity for sympathy "an outgrowth of natural mental constitution" and perforce differently "distributed in the different types of mankind." Race reliably predicted "what to expect of men in an ethical direction"; only whites could inhabit "the ethical life [that] expresses the highest development of humanity."[38]

Fiske attributed whites' exceptional psychical traits to their "gradual prolongation of a period of infancy," which exempted children from performing subsistence labor and thus enabled the fuller expansion of their representative capacity via observation and imaginative play. Moreover, the "sympathetic feelings" routinized and hypertrophied by a long infancy, during which one either received (as a child) or gave (as a parent) care absolutely, would then extend to objects beyond the reproductive family unit, eventually "generat[ing] an abstract moral sense . . . free from the element of personality." "Without the circumstances of infancy." Fiske wrote, "we should never have comprehended the meaning of such phrases as 'self-sacrifice' or 'devotion.'"[39] Experiences of care, repetitively performed and lodged in the race plasma, had aggregated to whites' evolutionary advantage.

According to the neo-Lamarckians, experiences of and dispositions toward care had also crystallized in modern institutions and the modes of sociality with which they were built and maintained. Spencer marveled at the "new emotions making their appearance in the most advanced divisions of our race" and how modernity seemed to accelerate their spread. Among whites, he wrote in 1864,

> there has been a development of those gentle emotions of which inferior races exhibit but the rudiments. Savages delight in giving pain rather than pleasure—are almost devoid of sympathy. While among ourselves philanthropy organizes itself in laws, establishes numerous institutions, and dictates countless private benefactions. . . . We know that emotional characteristics, in common with all others, are hereditary; and the differences between civilized nations descended from the same stock show us the cumulative results of small modifications hereditarily transmitted. And when we see that between savage and civilized races, which diverged from each other in the remote past, and have for a hundred generations followed modes of life becoming ever more unlike, there exist still greater emotional contrasts; may we not infer that the more or less distinct emotions which characterize civilized races, are the organized results of certain daily-repeated combinations of mental states which social life involves?[40]

Practices of sociality, which effected a heritable "increase of fellow-feeling," amounted to the most crucial evolutionary labor whites could perform: such "daily-repeated combinations of mental states" produced "the difference between the cruelty of the barbarous and the humanity of the civilized."[41] The quantity and force of the "altruistic sentiments resulting from sympathy"—pity, generosity, and justice—in each race foretold its "possibility of social progress."[42] The abundance of these traits in whites did not just favor the latter "in a contest with another race destitute of such feelings."[43] Rather, what Fiske isolated as "the tender and unselfish feelings, which are a later product of evolution," would secure whites' passage across the next Rubicon.[44]

Like all useful fictions of race, the conception of the evolutionarily achieved moral and ethical superiority of whites required immense work across a range of institutional sites to both flesh it out and conceal its ideological impetus. It circulated in turn-of-the-century literature, popular culture, politics, religion, and social science. It suffused, for example, the anthropological and medicopsychological literature of marriage and sexuality, which plumbed the outsized capacities of whites for love in its many forms. And love, from the sexual to the filial, was ultimately what *made* civilization, according to the sexologist Ernest Crawley. Love's "relative intensity decreases from the sexual to the social," he wrote, "but, as this decreases, extension increases, and more and more persons are comprehended. . . . In all its forms love plays a part in society only less important than that of the instinct to live. It brings together the primal elements of the family, it keeps the family together, and it unites in a certain fellow-feeling all members of a race or nation." And the "primitive races" possessed "forms of love both less intense and less complex" than those that animated and bound civilized whites.[45] Modern medical and psychological authorities prescribed, as the literary scholar Julian Carter has argued, a normative white erotics of care as healthy and conducive to citizenship as well as companionate marriage. Carter shows how the refined sympathetic feelings Fiske traced to white child-rearing informed the conjugal bed's "truly white sex," which "required the evolutionary achievement of tender concern for one's mate."[46]

White capacities for sympathy also entered into everyday parlance, as in one compliment that registered the speaker's gratitude for another's magnanimity: "That's mighty/awfully/damn white of you," which etymological accounts trace to the US South in the early 1900s.[47] Belief in the rarefied "intelligence and morale" that Osborn and others imputed to whiteness informed the work of Charlotte Perkins Gilman and other feminists, the popular literature of Edgar Rice Burroughs, and a range of drama, music, and film.[48] Some texts emphasized white affective superiority by plumbing the depths of its inverse, biological Blackness. These asserted the latter to be "infinitely lacking in the high mental, moral, and emotional qualities that are especially characteristic of the Anglo-Saxon."[49] Tragic stories of mixed-race characters in particular affirmed a view of the different moral valences of white and nonwhite race plasma.

The 1902 novel *Blood Will Tell*, for example, concludes with its pheno-typically white protagonist lamenting that he possesses "every outward and visible sign but the inward and spiritual grace of the white race is not and can never be mine." He soliloquizes his own abject embodiment of a Blackness "togged out in the dignity, education, and culture of the white race, but . . . only aping the natural, self-evolved civilization and culture of the whites."[50]

Neo-Lamarckism and the New Liberalism

"Races not arrested in their growth, and becoming emancipated from the thrall [of nature]," rhapsodized William Dickey Gunning, "will reach the cerulean heights and create a heaven of earth."[51] Such extravagant rhetoric expressed the utopian progressivism of neo-Lamarckian thought and its capacity to restore for its adherents, after the Darwinian assault on teleology and agency, "full scope and sweep of vision" for "the emotional and imaginative side of man."[52] Its uplifting tale of evolution as the organism's conscious manipulation of self and environment as it propelled itself toward perfection fairly cried out for a corollary politics. If, as Fiske predicted, "the development of the sympathetic side of human nature will doubtless become prodigious . . . as the sphere for [its] exercise is enlarged," might the state enable that enlargement?[53] Indeed, in the neo-Lamarckian framework that makes biocultural advance a matter of will, mind, and capacity, we can sight a through line to the twentieth-century statist liberalism of the New Deal and beyond. Neo-Lamarckism offered the imaginative means by which the state might exert a progressive evolutionary force through the provision of care for the population—or, rather, for the most evolutionarily vigorous subset of the population.

By contrast, no intelligible politics could be articulated on the foundations laid by Darwin: even if the theory of natural selection could be made to speak in terms of something as evanescent as a population, it dismissed the prospect of managing or transforming that population toward some preferred evolutionary end: some new selective pressure, some shift in the environment, would always thwart such plans. Thus, the ideology of social Darwinism, which (mis)interpreted the narrative of natural selection as a guide to how state power ought to be deployed, stood as neo-Lamarckism's opposite number in extrapolating a politics from the prescriptive vacuum that Darwinian theory represented.

Most neo-Lamarckians condemned the vulgar selectionist program of social Darwinism that had gathered force by the last decade of the nineteenth century and that prescribed the demise—by active destruction, neglect, or some mixture thereof—of the disabled, nonwhite, poor, and other populations seen as injurious to the flourishing of the species.

A strain of social Darwinism, the hard-hereditarian eugenics pioneered in the 1880s by Darwin's cousin Francis Galton, sought to regulate reproduction—artificially selecting for the "fittest" varieties of "germ plasm"—and breed a better species. After 1890, selectionists' rejection of the possibility of societal evolution on a mass scale through nurturing environments grew more authoritative, buttressed first by a largely European neo-Darwinism, which denied absolutely the heritability of acquired characteristics, and then with greater force in the next decade by Mendelian genetics.

Peter Bowler has noted that Lamarckians' rhetoric grew increasingly sunny in the early twentieth century, a shift that saw their traditional "concern for consciousness and design" in evolution "converted into a more humanistic optimism related mainly to social problems."[54] We must see this pivot of neo-Lamarckism to explicitly political appeals as compelled by the challenges it faced from selectionist opponents both in and outside of the laboratory at the turn of the century. It marks the moment at which neo-Lamarckian evolutionism shades, via its penetration of the social sciences, into the statist-democratic strain of the "New Liberalism" that took root in US political culture after 1880. New liberals sought to apply social-scientific knowledge in constructing nurturing and uplifting environments and institutions—in the words of one new liberal, to make "the law of love . . . part of the true political economy."[55]

Neo-Lamarckians warned audiences what would become of civilization should selectionism gain hegemony. The choice between mechanisms of evolution, Osborn cautioned in *Atlantic Monthly* in 1891, "profoundly affects our views and conduct of life." Should neo-Darwinism triumph,

> it will be in a sense a triumph of fatalism; for according to it, while we may indefinitely improve the forces of our education and surroundings, and this civilizing nurture will improve the individuals of each generation, its actual effects will not be cumulative as regards the race itself, but only as regards the environment of the race; each new generation must start *de novo*, receiving no benefit of the moral and intellectual advance made during the lifetime of its predecessors. It would follow that one deep, almost instinctive motive for a higher life would be removed if the race would only be superficially benefited by its nurture, and the only possible channel of improvement were in the selection of the fittest chains of race plasma.[56]

The same year, Lester Frank Ward expressed similar trepidation to his audience of biologists:

> If nothing that the individual gains by the most heroic or the most assiduous effort can by any possibility be handed on to posterity, the incentive to effort is in great part removed. If all the labor bestowed on the youth of the race

to secure a perfect physical and intellectual development dies with the individual to whom it is imparted why this labor? . . . In fact the whole burden of the neo-Darwinian song is: cease to educate, it is mere temporizing with the deeper and unchangeable forces of nature.[57]

"Alas," cried Joseph Le Conte in the *Monist* that same year, "for our hopes for race-improvement, whether physical, mental or moral!"[58]

To these commentators' chagrin, scientific authority would increasingly, and then definitively, side with the selectionists over the decades that followed. Nevertheless, the neo-Lamarckian narrative, with its themes of volitional transmutation, the heritability of acquired traits, and the disparate evolutionary viability of the races, persisted in popular understandings of evolution, often complementing the newer narrative that spoke in terms of superior and inferior genes.[59] Most crucially, as evidenced above, neo-Lamarckism informed the worldviews of progressives, socialists, and new liberals—all political orientations that charged the state with "the duty of providing such an environment for individual men and women as to give *all*, as far as possible, an equal chance of realizing . . . a moral and *human* life."[60] The blueprint for an "administrative state" that could discharge this duty emerged from Ward's neo-Lamarckian sociology, which formed the armature of the new liberalism—described by Dorothy Ross as "a revision of classical liberalism that expanded its conception of individual liberty, social conscience, and public powers"—that would dominate US politics in the Progressive Era and beyond.[61]

As late as 1924, the year hard-hereditarian eugenicists secured passage of the Johnson-Reed Act, which throttled immigration to the United States for the next four decades, the Austrian biologist Paul Kammerer made it clear that cleaving to Lamarck meant believing in progress of the most noble sort:

> If acquired characteristics are occasionally inherited, then it becomes evident that we are not exclusively slaves of the past—slaves helplessly endeavoring to free ourselves from our shackles—but also captains of the future, who in the course of time will be able to rid ourselves, to a certain extent, of our heavy burdens and ascend into higher and ever higher strata of development. Education and civilization, hygiene and social endeavors are achievements which are not alone benefiting the single individual, for every action, every word, aye, even every thought may possibly leave an imprint on the generation.[62]

This dispatch from the neo-Lamarckian redoubt betrays a hedging ("occasionally inherited," "to a certain extent," "may possibly leave an imprint") absent from the dauntless rhetoric of earlier neo-Lamarckians. Nevertheless, Kammerer, like other Lamarckian holdouts, conjured a state equipped to shoulder the "intensified responsibility" that came with knowing that the population's upgrades and regressions will deposit in the genetic material of future generations. That responsibility, he asserted, "rests most heavily upon the powers which direct education and government" protecting the population "against misrule, against exploitation."[63]

"It is within our power," declared Charlotte Perkins Gilman, also in 1924, "to make this world such an environment as should conduce to the development of a noble race, rapidly and surely improving from generation to generation." Gilman and other feminist evolutionists condemned the Darwinian narrative of natural selection as a masculinist allegory of combat and conquest—"one universal row," as Gilman described it. By contrast, the evolutionary journey of the white races could be read as a feminist telos: human evolution amounted to progressive acquisition and intensification by the human species as a whole of the care-oriented qualities immanent in women and the suppression of men's "inherently combative" nature. Gilman and others urged their audiences to recognize the evolutionary profits to be gained by feminizing state and society, as "whatever constitutes the distinctive qualities of the species is found fully developed in the female: she is the race type." An ethos of care, feminine in origin but taken up by evolutionarily advanced men, would anchor the coming civilization. Gilman affirmed that evolution "can be greatly assisted by cultivation. . . . One would think that agriculture would long since have taught us the way to improve any living thing is to take care of it."[64]

The protests of the neo-Lamarckians against the selectionist claim that "environment is impotent" should not obscure the fact that the two camps sought the same objective: a national population in perpetual evolutionary ascent.[65] This goal required not the parsimonious, laissez-faire state and society the social Darwinists promoted as preserving natural conditions but robust societal instruments of, in Osborn's words, "civilizing nurture." Yet in their desire to proliferate the "best" of humanity and have the "worst" perish, the neo-Lamarckians stood shoulder to shoulder with the most draconian selectionists. "For the savage," concluded Gunning, "we can do nothing. His opportunity is past. He is chronic."[66] Only whites, they premised, merited a surround of care in which they might leverage their gains for the benefit of the species. Nonwhites, whose arrested development stemmed from, in Samuel Butler's estimation, "the absence of the wish to go further," merited either pity or scorn, but certainly not investment.[67] The neo-Lamarckians' prescriptions amounted to a "soft" eugenics in which the state did its utmost to make the "civilized races ascend into evolutionary perfection" while, offstage, "the primitive fade[d] quietly into extinction."[68] Such were the biopolitics of the twentieth-century liberalism that neo-Lamarckism so profoundly influenced.

Consanguinity and Catastrophe

In the twentieth century United States, neo-Lamarckism seized the state. It had elaborated the population—"a set of coexisting living beings with particular biological and pathological features"—that the new liberalism sought to "make live."[69] Two questions remain as we turn to the biopolitical intervention that the New Deal represented. First, who, specifically, composed this evolutionarily enterprising population, the security, safety, and equilibrium of which emerged as the key function of the state; that is, who counted as "white"? Second, under what circumstances could liberalism, a political philosophy that, as Foucault observed, emerged and flourished "as a critique of the irrationality peculiar to excessive government, and as a return to a technology of frugal government," expand its statist machinery?[70] Both questions merit fuller attention than this conclusion can give, but let me gesture toward "consanguine whiteness" to speak to the question of population and "beset whiteness" as the necessary condition for the reorientation of liberalism.

The US context of mass immigration from Europe between the 1840s and 1924 frames considerations of population as, in Foucault's words, "a problem that is at once scientific and political."[71] As Matthew Frye Jacobson and other scholars have documented, the turn-of-the-century racial imagination envisioned a hierarchy of multiple white races.[72] Evolutionists valorized the Anglo-Saxons as the consummation of the intelligent evolutionary labor of what Cope called "the subspecies caucasian."[73] The differences between the white races were indeed figured as biocultural but never as deep and abiding as those between white and nonwhite. Evolutionary capacities remained vital, as Cope had noted, "even in the most ill-favored of the Indo-European stock."[74]

These "probationary" whites' path to achieving full whiteness, and thus eligibility for care, entailed assimilating to Anglo-Saxon cultural practices and avoiding congenial association with nonwhites. This process of racial (re)formation accelerated as the restrictions on immigration imposed by Congress in 1924 began to ease many white elites' anxieties that recent southern and eastern European immigration would overwhelm them culturally, politically, and genetically. Now that the nativists had triumphed and the golden door had been all but shut, natural and social science, popular culture, and the state began to enfold a wider racial variety into the evolutionarily viable white population. Paul Kammerer proclaimed in 1924 that Anglo-Saxons and the newer immigrants had amalgamated into "color-fast Americans." Even Lothrop Stoddard, erstwhile chronicler of the swamping of "Old Stock America," had by 1927 gladdened at the "increasing number of individuals from the 'New Immigrant' stocks who have been genuinely converted to Americanism."[75]

The white immigrant groups described in 1897 by nativist reformer Frances Willard as "the scum of the Old World" began to garner more flattering representations over the early 1900s.[76] Willa Cather's *My Ántonia* (1918), Al Jolson's *The Jazz Singer* (1927), and Gladys Carroll's *As the Earth Turns* (1933) were among the texts that encouraged those citizens in possession of a "conclusive" whiteness to embrace as full biological kin members of the formerly derogated "other white races." Transfiguring biological difference into the lighter garment of ethnicity, this consanguinizing process enabled people racialized as white to see one another as objects of affective and, consequently, material investment. Kammerer allowed that the prejudice that remains "exists only against the most alien races"; white Americans felt toward one another "the good will to replace the struggle of life with mutual help" and (he quoted Jack London) the "altruism and comradeship that have helped make men the mightiest of animals."[77] Consanguinity established the conditions, in other words, for the growth of a public in whose name care-oriented legislation, institutions, and infrastructure could be initiated and sustained.

Migrant Mother participated in the construction of this robust collectivity by consanguinizing Florence Thompson, whom Oklahoma tribal records document as Cherokee.[78] But Lange's image of Thompson also typified the beset whiteness ubiquitously represented during what Franklin D. Roosevelt described as the Great Depression's "days of crushing want."[79] Building the surround of white care required, given the context of the resolutely antistatist political culture in the United States, a series of traumatic blows to the health and security of white citizens. As the legal historian Michele Landis Dauber has argued, the architects of the New Deal made their case for the transformative program as a large but nevertheless customary response by the federal government to disaster. The economic catastrophe of the Depression resembled the epidemics, floods, fires, and so forth, that had regularly afflicted the population since the founding of the republic; or, rather, the Depression as a painstakingly constructed text was made to resemble catastrophes more generally accepted as natural. Dauber shows how New Deal advocates crafted the Depression as a disaster through the accumulation and careful framing of the testimony and images of its victims.[80]

The political utility of victims' images and stories was tied to the degree to which they rendered the victims blameless, honorable, and redeemable, people suffering a "curious and terrible pain" inflicted by the wanton forces of capital.[81] Victims' embodiment of these qualities authorized, in the eyes of their fellow citizens, their claim on the resources of the state. It was under these conditions that the US state amplified its power to "make live" a valorized portion of its population. For some three decades after 1930, themes of precarity, mutual obligation, and empowerment suffused policy acts, cultural production, and academic inquiry, underwriting an environment of care that sheltered its white charges. This environment included New Deal legislation such as the National Industrial Recovery Act (1933), the Social Security Act (1935), the National Labor Relations Act (1935), and the later GI Bill (1944); bodies such as the Federal Housing Administration (1934), the Resettlement Administration (1935), the Works Progress Administration (1935), and the Federal Security Agency (1939); educational reform initiatives such as the California State Master Plan for Higher Education (1960); and infrastructural projects such as the Tennessee Valley Authority (1933) and the Interstate Highway System (1956).

During the apogee years of white care, roughly 1935 to 1965, state-crafted environments, resources, and institutions elevated the standard of living and material equality of most of the white US population to unprecedented levels. It is true that the American welfare state operated as an emaciated version of the social provision edifices other industrialized societies built for their citizens. Even at its zenith, this surround of care never matched those of postwar Europe, where "homes, health, education, and social security" assumed the status of, in the words of one British health minister, a birthright.[82] Even so, for the consanguine white population of the midcentury United States, never were the benefits of citizenship so bountiful and capacitating. The redistributionist policies and the public things—schools and universities, power, water, sanitation, communications and transport infrastructure, libraries, and parks, to name a few—put in place or augmented by the liberal administrative state equipped the nation to move closer than it ever has to social democracy. The possibility of inducting Americans of color into the population eligible for care, which emerged with antiracist activism, court rulings, and legislation in the decade after 1954, would be foreclosed by an ascendant neoliberalism that would eviscerate all state-superintended care, if it could no longer be white.

Notes

1. Lange, quoted in Goggans, *California on the Breadlines*, 94.
2. Harriman and Lucaites, *No Caption Needed*, 55.
3. Steinbeck, *The Harvest Gypsies*, 3, 33.
4. FSA images of African Americans and other nonwhite groups tended to recapitulate "the white tendency . . . of treating the black millions as a monolithic mass" (Natanson, *Black Image in the New Deal*, 247).
5. Dauber, *Sympathetic State*, 91.
6. See Foucault, *"Society Must Be Defended,"* chap. 11.
7. The historian Jan Goggans has described the progressive economist Paul Taylor as exemplary of "a group of thinkers who emerged from World War I believing that catastrophic devastation could create the hope of a new world order and for

whom the Crash, and the economic, political, and social conditions that followed, became the mechanism by which to achieve it" (*California on the Breadlines*, 13).

8. Agassiz, *Structure of Animal Life*, 118.

9. Darwin, *Origin of Species*, 67.

10. Darwin, *Origin of Species*, 647.

11. See Ellegard, *Darwin and the General Reader*.

12. E. P. Powell, quoted in Stockwell, *New Modes of Thought*, 145.

13. Bowler, *Non-Darwinian Revolution*, 5. "The doctrine of Descent remains," wrote Eberhard Dennert. "Darwinism passes away" (*Deathbed of Darwinism*, 142).

14. Spencer, *Principles of Biology*, 449.

15. Osborn, *From the Greeks to Darwin*, 163

16. Lester Frank Ward observed that, although an entomologist had coined the term *neo-Lamarckism* in 1885, Spencer had articulated the concept much earlier (Ward, *Neo-Darwinism and Neo-Lamarckism*, 53). See also Daniels, *Darwinism Comes to America*. Kyla Schuller writes that "the popular notion of Darwinism in the nineteenth-century United States . . . was notably Lamarckian" (*Biopolitics of Feeling*, 143).

17. Osborn, *From the Greeks to Darwin*, 163.

18. Cope, "Theology of Evolution," 1128; Cope, *Theology of Evolution*, 25. See also Cope, *Origin of the Fittest*. Fellow neo-Lamarckian Alpheus S. Packard observed that Cope surpassed Lamarck in "unhesitatingly attribute[ing] consciousness to all animals" (*Lamarck: The Founder of Evolution*, 353).

19. Darwin to J. D. Hooker, January 11, 1844, in Darwin, *Life and Letters of Charles Darwin*, 384.

20. Cope, *Theology of Evolution*, 26; Stockwell, *New Modes of Thought*, 34. Cope dubbed this force *bathmism*. The German neo-Lamarckian Ernst Haeckel testified to the "primitive form of soul-activity . . . already present even in the lowest animals" (*Monism as Connecting Religion and Science*, 41). And the French philosopher Henri Bergson wrote of the "vital impulse" by which organisms activated their own "creative evolution" (*Creative Evolution*, 133).

21. An animal's "intelligent choice," Cope averred, "may be regarded as the *originator of the fittest*, while natural selection is the tribunal to which all the results of accelerated growth are submitted" (*Origin of the Fittest*, 40). Decades later, Osborn would posit "aristogenesis," in which vanguard elements in an organism's gene plasm effect "the orderly creation of something better" ("Aristogenesis," 700).

22. Le Conte, *Evolution*, 91; Eddy, "Thoughts on Evolution," 464; Gunning, *Life-History of Our Planet*, 357; Fiske, *Destiny of Man*, 107.

23. See, e.g., Nott and Gliddon, *Types of Mankind*; and Nott and Gliddon, *Indigenous Races of the Earth*.

24. Quoted in Ellegard, *Darwin and the General Reader*, 74.

25. Cope, *Primary Factors of Organic Evolution*, 159.

26. Quoted in Ellegard, *Darwin and the General Reader*, 75.

27. Gunning, *Life-History of Our Planet*, 333; Fiske, "Progress from Brute to Man."

28. "The crossing of the Rubicon," observed John Fiske, "was the point at which natural selection began to confine itself chiefly to variations in psychical manifestations" ("Progress from Brute to Man," 283). "Cultural and psychological differences that separate the highest developed European peoples from the lowest savages," insisted Haeckel, "are greater than the differences that separate the savages from the anthropoid apes" (quoted in Gasman, *Scientific Origins of National Socialism*, 134). Cope classified those of African descent as "a species of the genus

Homo, [but] as distinct in character from the Caucasian as those we are accustomed to recognize in other departments of the animal kingdom" (*Origin of the Fittest*, 147). Fiske concurred: "The gulf between the cerebral capacity of the Englishman and that of the non-Aryan dweller in Hindostan is six times greater than the gulf which similarly divides the non-Aryan Hindu from the gorilla" ("Progress from Brute to Man," 280).

29. Osborn, "Present Problem of Heredity." In 1927 Osborn still clung to the belief that "the three or more absolutely distinct stocks" called races could be more accurately "be given the rank of species, if not genera" (*Man Rises to Parnassus*, 201).

30. Schuller, *Biopolitics of Feeling*, 71.

31. Haller, *Outcasts from Evolution*.

32. Butler, *Luck, or Cunning*, 114.

33. Cope, "Inheritence [*sic*] of Subserviency," 254.

34. Cope, "Two Perils of the Indo-European," 2053; "Return of the Negroes to Africa," 2110.

35. Cope, "Two Perils of the Indo-European," 2053.

36. Cope, "Two Perils of the Indo-European," 2053–54.

37. Fiske, "Progress from Brute to Man," 283.

38. Cope, "Ethical Evolution," 1523.

39. Fiske, "Progress from Brute to Man," 312, 316, 319.

40. Spencer, *Illustrations of Universal Progress*, 312–14.

41. Spencer, *Illustrations of Universal Progress*, 236. Cope similarly diagnosed in "the lowest races . . . a general deficiency of the emotional qualities, excepting fear" (*Origin of the Fittest*, 387).

42. Spencer, "Comparative Psychology of Man," 18–19.

43. Salter, "Darwinism in Ethics," 77.

44. Fiske, *Destiny of Man*, 101.

45. Crawley, *Studies of Savages and Sex*, 78, 94. Crawley and other sexologists lauded whites' more evolved, "intense," and "complex" erotics.

46. Carter, *Heart of Whiteness*, 95.

47. Partridge, *Dictionary of Catch Phrases*, 204.

48. Osborn, *Man Rises to Parnassus*, 202. See, e.g., Gilman's 1915 novella *Herland*, Burroughs's Barsoom and Tarzan series of novels (beginning in 1912), and D. W. Griffith's film *Birth of a Nation* (1915).

49. Collins, *Truth about Lynching*, 58.

50. Davenport, *Blood Will Tell*, 250, 265. Intellectuals of color militated against claims that in African Americans' natures "very few of the finer feelings [could] find any lodgment" (William Morrow, quoted in Chas. Carroll, *The Negro a Beast*, 64–65). The mathematician Kelly Miller, for example, denied that there was "a single intellectual, moral or spiritual excellence attained by the white race to which the Negro does not yield an appreciative response" (*As to the Leopard's Spots*, 5–6).

51. Gunning, *Life-History of Our Planet*, 356–57.

52. Stockwell, *New Modes of Thought*, 136.

53. Fiske, *Destiny of Man*, 102–3.

54. Bowler, *Eclipse of Darwinism*, 95.

55. Lloyd, *Men, the Workers*, 263. On new liberalism, see Furner, "Policy Knowledge: New Liberalism."

56. Osborn, "Present Problem of Heredity," 363.

57. Ward, *Neo-Darwinism and Neo-Lamarckism*, 65.

58. Le Conte, "Factors of Evolution," 334.

59. As Bowler has observed, "The development of modern genetics involved

considerable conceptual changes that were not easily popularized" (*Eclipse of Darwinism*, 96). Sigmund Freud, for example, maintained a belief in the transmission of acquired characteristics well into the 1930s, as an explicitly political bulwark against Nazi racialism. See Slavet, "Freud's 'Lamarckism.'" "It may be," observe Milford H. Wolpoff and Rachel Caspari, "that Lamarkism [*sic*] was retained for so long (until the modern evolutionary synthesis of genetics and Darwinism in the 1940s) because of its progressive social implications" (*Race and Human Evolution*, 94).

60. Ritchie, *Principles of State Interference*, 150–51.

61. Ross, *Origins of American Social Science*, 91. The progressive Frederic C. Howe told Ward in 1912 that "the whole social philosophy of the present day is a formative expression of what you have said to be true" (91).

62. Kammerer, *Inheritance of Acquired Characteristics*, 31.

63. Kammerer, *Inheritance of Acquired Characteristics*, 358–59.

64. Gilman, *His Religion and Hers*, 6, 93, 92, 82, 93.

65. Bailey, "Neo-Lamarckism and Neo-Darwinism," 673.

66. Gunning, *Life-History of Our Planet*, 354.

67. Butler, *Life and Habit*, 201.

68. Schuller, *Biopolitics of Feeling*, 145.

69. Foucault, *Security, Territory, Population*, 367.

70. Foucault, *Birth of Biopolitics*, 322.

71. Foucault, *"Society Must Be Defended,"* 245.

72. See Jacobson, *Whiteness of a Different Color*; and Ngai, *Impossible Subjects*.

73. "I felt in my pocket yesterday & ran against these grim molars," Cope wrote his daughter after a visit to the dentist. "On examination I concluded that they belonged to the species *homo sapiens*, and the subspecies *caucasian*, and particular marks show that they belonged to a representative of a civilized branch of that race!" (Box 5, 1889–96, letter 437, April 8, 1889, Edward Drinker Cope Papers, American Museum of Natural History).

74. Cope, "Two Perils of the Indo-European," 2053–54.

75. Kammerer, *Inheritance of Acquired Characteristics*, 272; Stoddard, *Reforging America*, 340.

76. Quoted in Bordin, *Woman and Temperance*, 87.

77. Kammerer, *Inheritance of Acquired Characteristics*, 281.

78. See *Tahlequah Daily News*, "'Migrant Mother' May Be One of Tahlequah's Most Famous."

79. Roosevelt, *Public Papers*, 649.

80. See Dauber, *Sympathetic State*, esp. chaps. 4 and 7.

81. Steinbeck, quoted in Goggins, *California on the Breadlines*, 140.

82. *Time*, "Medicine Man," 29.

References

Agassiz, Louis. *The Structure of Animal Life*. New York: Charles Scribner, 1866.

Bailey, L. H. "Neo-Lamarckism and Neo-Darwinism." *American Naturalist* 28, no. 332 (1894): 661–78.

Bergson, Henri. *Creative Evolution*. 1907; repr., New York: Henry Holt, 1911.

Bordin, Ruth. *Woman and Temperance: The Quest for Power and Liberty, 1873–1900*. Philadelphia: Temple University Press, 1981.

Bowler, Peter J. *The Eclipse of Darwinism: Anti-Darwinian Evolution Theories in the Decades around 1900*. Baltimore: Johns Hopkins University Press, 1988.

Bowler, Peter J. *The Non-Darwinian Revolution: Interpreting a Historical Myth*. Baltimore: Johns Hopkins University Press, 1988.

Butler, Samuel. *Life and Habit*. London: Trubner, 1878.

Butler, Samuel. *Luck, or Cunning, as the Main Means of Organic Modification?* 1887; repr. London: Jonathan Cape, 1922.

Carroll, Chas. *The Negro a Beast; or, In the Image of God*. St. Louis, MO: American Book and Bible House, 1900.

Carter, Julian. *The Heart of Whiteness*. Durham, NC: Duke University Press, 2007.

Collins, Winfield. *The Truth about Lynching and the Negro in the South*. New York: Neale, 1918.

Cope, Edward Drinker. "Ethical Evolution." *Open Court* 3, no. 82 (1889): 1523–25.

Cope, Edward Drinker. "Mrs. Helen Gardener on the Inheritence [*sic*] of Subserviency." *American Naturalist* 31, no. 363 (1897): 253–55.

Cope, Edward Drinker. *The Origin of the Fittest*. New York: Appleton, 1887.

Cope, Edward Drinker. *The Primary Factors of Organic Evolution*. Chicago: Open Court, 1896.

Cope, Edward Drinker. "The Return of the Negroes to Africa." *Open Court* 3, no. 130 (1890): 2331.

Cope, Edward Drinker. "Theology of Evolution." *American Naturalist* 21, no. 12 (1887): 1127–29.

Cope, Edward Drinker. *Theology of Evolution*. Philadelphia: Arnold, 1887.

Cope, Edward Drinker. "Two Perils of the Indo-European" (part 1). *Open Court* 3, no. 126 (1890): 2052–54.

Crawley, Ernest. *Studies of Savages and Sex*. London: Methuen, 1929.

Daniels, George, ed. *Darwinism Comes to America*. Waltham, MA: Blaisdell, 1968.

Darwin, Charles. *The Life and Letters of Charles Darwin*. Vol. 1. Edited by Francis Darwin. New York: Appleton, 1911.

Darwin, Charles. *The Origin of Species*. New York: Modern Library, 2009.

Dauber, Michele Landis. *The Sympathetic State: Disaster Relief and the Origins of the American Welfare State*. Chicago: University of Chicago Press, 2013.

Davenport, Benjamin Rush. *Blood Will Tell: The Strange Story of a Son of Ham*. Cleveland: Caxton, 1902.

Dennert, Eberhart. *The Deathbed of Darwinism*. Burlington, IA: German Literary Board, 1904.

Eddy, T. H. "Thoughts on Evolution: A Theistic View." *Open Court* 1, no. 17 (1887): 463–64.

Ellegard, Alvus. *Darwin and the General Reader*. Chicago: University of Chicago Press, 1990.

Fiske, John. *The Destiny of Man*. Boston: Houghton Mifflin, 1884.

Fiske, John. "The Progress from Brute to Man." *North American Review* 117, no. 241 (1873): 251–319.

Foucault, Michel. *The Birth of Biopolitics; Lectures at the College de France, 1978–1979*. Translated by Graham Burchell. New York: Palgrave Macmillan, 2008.

Foucault, Michel. *Security, Territory, Population: Lectures at the College de France, 1977–1978*. Translated by Graham Burchell. New York: Picador, 2009.

Foucault, Michel. *"Society Must Be Defended": Lectures at the College de France, 1975–76*. Translated by David Macey. New York: Picador, 2003.

Furner, Mary O. "Policy Knowledge: New Liberalism." In *International Encyclopedia of the Social and Behavioral Sciences*, 2nd ed., edited by James Wright, 18:299–306. Amsterdam: Elsevier, 2015.

Gasman, Daniel. *The Scientific Origins of National Socialism*. New Brunswick, NJ: Transaction, 2007.

Gilman, Charlotte Perkins. *His Religion and Hers*. London: T. Fisher Unwin, 1924.

Goggans, Jan. *California on the Breadlines: Dorothea Lange, Paul Taylor, and the Making of a New Deal Narrative*. Berkeley: University of California Press, 2010.

Gunning, William Dickey. *Life-History of Our Planet*. New York: R. Worthington, 1881.

Haeckel, Ernst. *Monism as Connecting Religion and Science*. London: Adam and Charles Black, 1895.

Haller, John S. *Outcasts from Evolution*. Urbana: University of Illinois Press, 1971.

Harriman, Robert, and John Louis Lucaites. *No Caption Needed: Iconic Photographs, Public Culture, and Liberal Democracy*. Chicago: University of Chicago Press, 2007.

Jacobson, Matthew Frye. *Whiteness of a Different Color: European Immigrants and the Alchemy of Race*. Cambridge, MA: Harvard University Press, 1998.

Kammerer, Paul. *The Inheritance of Acquired Characteristics*. New York: Boni and Liveright, 1924.

Le Conte, Joseph. *Evolution: Its Nature, Its Evidences, and Its Relation to Religious Thought*. New York: Appleton, 1898.

Le Conte, Joseph. "The Factors of Evolution." *Monist* 1, no. 3 (1891): 321–35.

Lloyd, Henry Demarest. *Men, the Workers*. 1887; repr., New York: Doubleday, 1909.

Miller, Kelly. *As to the Leopard's Spots*. Washington, DC: Hayworth, 1905.

Natanson, Nicholas. *The Black Image in the New Deal: The Politics of FSA Photography*. Knoxville: University of Tennessee Press, 1992.

Ngai, Mae. *Impossible Subjects: Illegal Aliens and the Making of Modern America*. Princeton, NJ: Princeton University Press, 2004.

Nott, Josiah C., and George R. Gliddon. *Indigenous Races of the Earth*. Philadelphia: Lippincott, 1857.

Nott, Josiah C., and George R. Gliddon. *Types of Mankind*. Philadelphia: Lippincott, Grambo, 1854.

Osborn, Henry Fairfield. "Aristogenesis, the Observed Order of Biomechanical Evolution." *Proceedings of the National Academy of Sciences* 19, no. 7 (1933): 699–703.

Osborn, Henry Fairfield. *From the Greeks to Darwin*. 1894; repr. New York: Charles Scribner's Sons, 1927.

Osborn, Henry Fairfield. *Man Rises to Parnassus*. Princeton, NJ: Princeton University Press, 1928.

Osborn, Henry Fairfield. "The Present Problem of Heredity." *Atlantic Monthly* 67, no. 401 (1891): 353–64.

Packard, Alpheus S. *Lamarck: The Founder of Evolution*. New York: Longmans, Green, 1901.

Partridge, Eric. *A Dictionary of Catch Phrases*. London: Routledge and Kegan Paul, 1985.

Ritchie, David G. *Principles of State Interference*. London: Swan Sonnenschein, 1891.

Roosevelt, Franklin D. *The Public Papers and Addresses of Franklin Delano Roosevelt*. Vol. 1, *The Genesis of the New Deal, 1928–1932*. New York: Random House, 1938.

Ross, Dorothy. *The Origins of American Social Science*. Cambridge: Cambridge University Press, 1991.

Salter, William Mackintire. "Darwinism in Ethics." *Open Court* 1, no. 3 (1887): 77–82.

Schuller, Kyla. *The Biopolitics of Feeling: Race, Sex, and Science in the Nineteenth Century.* Durham, NC: Duke University Press, 2018.

Slavet, Eliza. "Freud's 'Lamarckism' and the Politics of Racial Science." *Journal of the History of Biology* 41, no. 1 (2008): 37–80.

Spencer, Herbert. "Comparative Psychology of Man." *Mind* 1, no. 1 (1876): 7–20.

Spencer, Herbert. *Illustrations of Universal Progress.* New York: Appleton, 1864.

Spencer, Herbert. *The Principles of Biology.* Vol. 1. London: Williams and Norgate, 1864.

Steinbeck, John. *The Harvest Gypsies.* Berkeley, CA: Heyday, 2017.

Stockwell, C. T. *New Modes of Thought.* Boston: James H. West, 1901.

Stoddard, Lothrop. *Re-forging America.* New York: Charles Scribner's Sons, 1927.

Tahlequah Daily News. "'Migrant Mother' May Be One of Tahlequah's Most Famous." April 3, 2016.

Time. "Medicine Man." 53, no. 12 (1949): 29–33.

Ward, Lester Frank. *Neo-Darwinism and Neo-Lamarckism.* Washington, DC: Gedney and Roberts, 1891.

Wolpoff, Milford H., and Rachel Caspari. *Race and Human Evolution.* New York: Simon and Schuster, 1997.

Capitalism's Care Problem

Some Traces, Fixes, and Patches

Micki McGee

Capitalism's Care Problem

That capitalism has a care problem is by no means a new observation. Evidence abounds, and makeshift solutions are everywhere apparent.[1] Here are just a few.

At the university library where I have currently sought a quiet place to work, it's finals week. A set of enormous posters promoting a smartphone app that connects despondent students to phone counselors frame the elevators on the ground floor, where for years the most despairing students would land after leaping from the upper levels of the building to their deaths (fig. 1). The university, contravening the wishes of the building's superstar architect, has installed decorative barriers to prevent the jumping option, but if this signage is any indication, the anguish has not abated.[2] Therapy is expensive and time-consuming, and often out of reach for college students. Campus counseling services are understaffed and overbooked.[3] Perhaps an app can help. For the techno-optimists among (or within) us, algorithmic solutions to social problems are a tantalizing fix.

At another nearby university a multiyear battle over health care benefits resulted in, amid many cuts to faculty and staff medical benefits, the creation of an entirely new administrative position, a wellness coordinator, whose task is to promote faculty and staff well-being so as to decrease the high cost of (dis)stressed faculty and staff who require costly pharmacological interventions and one-on-one treatments for their strained hearts and minds. The person who fills this role, a well-intentioned individual of integrity and good cheer, promotes fitness challenges and provides nutritional newsletters. She works tirelessly to foster a culture of wellness

Social Text 142 · Vol. 38, No. 1 · March 2020
DOI 10.1215/01642472-7971091   © 2020 Duke University Press

Figure 1. The first time I encountered the NYU Bobst Library signage promoting a newly launched mental health mobile application was in early December 2018. These images were captured on February 17, 2019, with more recent adjacent posters for a labor history event. This signage has since been removed. Photographs courtesy of the author.

that includes yoga classes, mindfulness meditation, and other tools touted to promote work-life balance. The wellness coordinator is powerless to demand childcare and eldercare subsidies that might ease the most readily visible stressors among employees. From a managerial point of view, the wellness coordinator position is a reasonable solution.[4] Countless scientific studies tout the benefits of exercises, mindfulness, yoga, prayer, hugs, and vitamins. Yet even when such studies are later discredited, anecdotal accounts rule our discourses: people swear by their own fixes to the care problem.[5]

Some in our academic communities, particularly recent graduate students who face the dismal academic job market, or those on the "alt-ac" (alternative-academic) track (aka jobs with no opportunity for tenure or other forms of long-term job security), may seek the counsel of costly academic coaches who occupy a specialty niche in the burgeoning field of personal coaching.[6] Many report excellent results, but only when they are forthcoming enough to admit retaining such services. The stigma of turning to self-help fixes continues to haunt the halls of academe, where the ghost of the lone scholarly genius still rattles about among fading traditions of professorial mentoring and academic patronage. But for those who dare to recognize their predicament in the neoliberal university—and can afford the investment—they claim a little coaching care can go a long way. The most successful of these academic life coaches have codified their tips in a best-selling volume (i.e., best-selling in the subcategory of academic advice) and adopted the use of online platforms to bring down the price point of providing such care. Wherever you live and work, whether in academe (as I do) or elsewhere, the problem of care or, more accurately, the problem of the lack thereof—the care deficit—can be traced in various fixes and patches.

There are good reasons that examples of capitalism's care problems abound: these sorts of problems are what social theorists call "structural." They are not the sort of problems that individuals bring upon themselves, nor do they yield easily to individual solutions. Instead, structural problems are baked in to the ways we organize production and reproduction.[7] Care labor is simply too expensive when market principles are applied to every aspect of daily life. The peculiar (if shortsighted) genius of capitalism's structures and innovations, among them wage slavery (binding the individual human's survival and well-being to the commodity form, i.e., rendering human labor as a commodity), mass production, automation, and artificial intelligence, simply aren't up to the tasks of providing care.[8]

Part of the trouble with care labor is that it often requires individual attention, often in one-to-one, or one-to-few, ratios. Infant care, childcare, eldercare, medical care for those who are ailing or infirm, and provisions for those who require long-term care and supports (e.g., the disabled or differently abled) are social needs that are not readily resolved in a system that relies on commoditized labor.[9] Economies of scale are notoriously difficult to apply to care work. While capitalism is exceptionally good at producing a surfeit of things, it has yet to provide a system that reduces the labor time required for care.

Lack of scalability leads to cost problems. Since the cost of goods and services is relative, as the cost of mass-producible products drop (due to the aforementioned scalability in mass production), the cost of care, in relative terms, increases. Along with this issue of relative value, corporate capitalism's demand for profit renders health care, rehabilitative care, and long-term care unaffordable. The recurrent stories of adjunct professors dying in the midst of medical crises for lack of health care are compounded crises: a broken for-profit health care system intersects with higher education's cost-reduction strategy of relying on the super-discounted labor of contingent faculty who live in exhaustion and penury.[10]

Even the informal global supply chains that move impoverished women from developing areas of the globe (or from poor populations in the United States) to provide care labor in the homes of affluent families can't resolve capitalism's care problem. Such migrant care labor (which in some respects mirrors the chattel slave trade that built US economic preeminence in the nineteenth century) can't solve the care problem; it can only displace it—who provides cares for your care provider's child while they care for yours? For the word *child* you can substitute anyone in your intimate sphere who requires care around the clock and anyone from the provider's intimate sphere whose care needs are unmet or poorly met.[11] Without the unwaged or discounted wages of women, the care economy would be (and in many cases has been) crashing.

Given the large-scale entry of US women into the paid labor markets that accompanied the second wave of feminism in the 1970s, the care crisis has escalated and has been cast as a work-life balance problem throughout US and western European societies. With the ascendancy of neoliberal market principles over the past four decades, the care crisis, like the global calamity of climate change, has escalated. Political theorist Nancy Fraser observes that capitalism relies on the twin fantasies of boundless supplies of care (traditionally in the form of women's unpaid labor in the home, though more recently in the movement of low-wage care workers from one part of the globe to another) and limitless natural resources on what is now clearly a finite and destabilized planet.[12]

Were our current economic system of patriarchal, racialized capitalism unable to enlist, elicit, or forcibly extract the unwaged labor of women and the many others (typically, but not always, people of color) from whom it has historically demanded uncompensated or barely compensated care work, the so-called care economy, already a patchwork of fragile accommodations, would collapse.[13] That is, were everyone to refuse the discounting of the labor of those who educate our children, care for our elders, and attend to the goods and services that simplify our overworked schedules (from fast food delivery to drop-off laundry), then the capital accumulation in our system of expansive economies would founder and run aground.

But the collapse of this system is not likely to happen anytime soon. For the moment the system responds to these challenges in sometimes unexpected, makeshift ways.[14] Capitalism remains, as Fraser writes elsewhere, a "cunning" system that responds with considerable agility to its own internal contradictions.[15] With its hacks, patches, and other fixes, capitalism rumbles, sputters, and sometimes zooms along toward its own demise.

Some have begun to argue that the ubiquity of capitalism's care problem creates an opening. As an issue that affects nearly everyone, the care crisis provides (as with global climate change) a focal point for political organizing and engagement.[16] My contribution here to this conversation is twofold: I trace the care crisis as it is reflected and refracted in popular self-improvement literature that has emerged in the context of an unfolding neoliberal agenda, and then I offer an example of what I call a "patch": the efforts to remedy an individual care crisis that led to union mobilization at an academic institution.

Neoliberal Self-Improvement Fixes: From Having It All to Not Giving a Fuck

Academic career coaching and the cottage industry of academic advice books provide fine examples of classic American self-help solutions: when a system is straining from the contradictions of capitalism, a standard quick fix is to hold up individual solutions and strategies for problems that are economic and structural. Typically, such remedies harness the can-do spirit of American bootstrapping individualism with tool kits that combine a rhetoric of entrepreneurialism, the routines and regimes of time management, and the latest research from motivational psychology.

Consequent to the technological affordances of one-to-many educational platforms (webinars and various video-streaming services) and the availability of horizontal many-to-many social networking platforms (Facebook is most prevalent, but there are always new, usually short-lived other options, such as mightynetwork.com), academic career and other self-improvement advisers and coaches seek to engage in economies of scale by delivering their advice in the form of a monologue while relying on online communities they foster to provide additional sources of advice, attention, and ongoing care. Critiques of the ethics of such services have emerged in higher education news venues, with some calling academic coaches the "war profiteers of the collapsing academic job market."[17]

This new niche market of academic coaching warrants its own focused consideration but, by virtue of its relatively recent emergence, doesn't provide a long enough historical window to track the unfolding crisis of care as it developed in the wake of second-wave feminism. What serves my purposes more robustly is a look at the mainstream self-improvement literature aimed at resolving the issues of the work-life balance or, as sociologist Arlie Russell Hochschild put it, the "time bind." This is a project that I pursued in greater depth in *Self-Help, Inc.* but will briefly revisit, extend, and update here, as I work toward identifying the outlines of radical care.[18]

Having It All and Loving Too Much: Market Principles Jump the Tracks

When Helen Gurley Brown's 1982 best seller headlined and popularized the phrase *having it all*, she could not have known how deeply this concept—at once capacious and rapacious—would resonate among American women. Published at the outset of the neoliberalist era (under policies that would then be named simply as Reaganomics and Thatcherism) Brown's *Having It All* popularized the notion that hardworking, striving, upwardly mobile women could have it all. In real terms, that continued to mean, for all but those who could afford childcare and housekeeping services, that they would attempt to *do* it all.

Buoyed by the middle-class feminist demand for equal pay and increased opportunities for women's participation in the paid labor force, American women swelled the ranks of the labor market. The trouble was, of course, that the institutional changes that could mitigate the new shortage of labor for care at home were not in place; most still aren't. Affordable childcare and childcare subsidies, flexible work time, paid maternity and family leaves, and other provisions for care were elusive, and they remain so.[19] In what historian Kirsten Swinth recently called "feminism's forgotten fight" and sociologist Lynn S. Chancer names feminism's "stall," feminist scholars have been revisiting how second-wave feminism has not worked out so well for women who struggle to balance second and third shifts at work and at home.[20]

In this context, the audience (or market, in the language of neoliberalism) for Brown's advice was primed. But Brown also had an exceptional talent for assessing the problems American women faced and coming up with remedies that conformed to the work ethic that underpins capitalism while upsetting sexual mores. Her 1962 *Sex and the Single Girl* was part Hugh Hefner, part Moll Flanders. Brown's advice was simple: parlay sexual favors into workplace advantage, work exponentially harder than anyone else, and marry up. Her formula challenged the moral window dressing of gender-based inequality (the "nice girls don't" imperative) while leaving the economic basis of women's exploitation intact.

Two decades after *Sex and the Single Girl*, Brown updated her advice: to the advice of "marry up" and "make as much money as possible," she added, if you can't avoid childbearing, at least avoid child-rearing—by paying someone to take care of them. But perhaps most important for our consideration, Brown counseled her readers to treat time and energy as a kind of currency to be managed in a mental ledger sheet. Brown's advice to women relied on the emerging supply chain of global care labor while advancing the *mentalité* that accompanied and supported the financialization of daily life.[21]

Friendship, Brown advises, calls for "reciprocal trade." She notes that "everything costs something. . . . You may be a friend who gives selflessly, endlessly—money and gifts as well as counsel and cheer, without wanting a thing in return—but hold on a minute—you should want something in return. You hold that person's marker."[22] But while one is supposed to keep a careful accounting of one's emotional investments, particularly in friendships, one ought to be generous and giving in a professional context:

> Being too niggardly and selective about what assignments you'll accept—"but I'm not getting paid to do that!"—is like being too skimpy with how much love you are going to give out in life: it may be better to over invest. It may seem that people are "using you" but actually it's the other way around—you are using them. Do get credit if you can—no use coming in on Saturday to straighten the files if no one ever knows you were there. Just don't be too stingy with your "free labor" for bosses or coworkers.[23]

Only a few years later, in 1989, another best-selling advice author, Stephen Covey, would present a time management system that incorporates Brown's idea of an "emotional bank account" and extend this to an audience of both women and men.[24]

How did Brown arrive at her particular and timely advice to women entering the era of neoliberalism? As a woman from an exceptionally impoverished background, Brown had to navigate the conflicts between professional and personal life rather differently than a man of her generation would have; as such, she represents an advance guard position in the elimination of boundaries between professional and public life. Other circumstances also drove Brown's pragmatic approach. As a young woman she faced the challenge of providing care and resources for both her disabled sister and her unemployed mother. As the sole provider for a relative with a disability, Brown knew firsthand both the urgency and the unremitting necessity of providing care, as well as the temporal and financial costs of meeting that demand.[25] Decades before the passage of the Americans with Disabilities Act (1990) and the provisions of Supplemental Security Income (1974), with extremely limited social and economic supports for persons with disabilities, the demands of caring for a family member with a disability were formidable.[26] (In fact, they still are, even as disability activists have successfully pushed for some advances.) It was in this personal and social context that Brown developed her own no-holds-barred, bourgeois sexual mores be damned, approach to surviving and thriving.

Digging deep into the problem of the commoditized nature of care and challenging that system would not provide her with an immediate solution to her own care responsibilities and financial challenges. But adhering to the ethos of individual upward mobility while challenging the conservative sexual mores (which were beginning to crumble around her) allowed Brown's *Sex and the Single Girl* to appear as a "revolutionary" advice manual for making money and "landing your man" while leaving unchanged the heteronormative and ableist economic norms that led to her own plight. *Having It All* followed the *Single Girl* formula: condemn the restrictive mores that aim to limit sexuality to marriage but leave the economic underpinnings of the care crisis unchanged. While radical feminist social thinkers and activists such as Silvia Federici pushed for wages for housework, universal childcare, and other solutions to the emerging care crisis, Brown pushed against the cultural mores of stay-at-home motherhood while leaving the economic dimensions of the emerging crisis buried.[27]

Contemporaneous with Brown's econometric advice for feminine flourishing in the new regimes of neoliberalism, another thread of advice was emerging: the emergence of the concept of codependence and admonitions to women to avoid "loving too much." If the shift of women's care labor in the home to their "productive labor" at work (i.e., labor that counts in labor statistics) was the economic basis of the emergence of a crisis of care in late twentieth-century America, the rhetoric of codependence and loving too much was part of the propaganda that devalued emotional labor in the intimate sphere.[28] As I've observed elsewhere:

> With codependence the public logic of commercial exchange was proposed as the solution to the private dynamics of personal relationships. Giving to another, viewed as an entry on a ledger sheet, had to be balanced. If one gave with no regard for return, one fell into the trap of codependency. Women who gave too much or "loved too much" could never "have it all." Instead, their generosity—previously a characteristic particularly valued in women—set them up for a negative balance sheet and a life without fulfillment.[29]

Viewed in light of the changes in the economic dynamics of the family, questions emerged about how much women invested in their intimate relationships (which were nearly always imagined as heterosexual). If one was no longer dependent on a male breadwinner, then perhaps the slavish devotion and googly-eyed flirtation in the intimate sphere of dating was wasted energy that could more effectively be directed to the workplace or other pursuits.

Some feminists, such as Susan Faludi, argued that the rise of a literature focused on women's ostensible neediness was part of an orchestrated backlash against women's increased power and prominence in the labor force. In the literature of "loving too much" the portrait presented was that of women who were achieving success in the professional world but (perhaps as a result) whose personal lives were in ruins. Others argued the concept of codependency is little more than the pathologization of a culture of caring in a gendered division of labor where the provision of routine, daily care work has long been delegated to females.[30]

The development of the concept of codependency was determined by multiple factors and underscores the tensions created by the increased emphasis on labor force participation for women. Even as Helen Gurley Brown portrayed a world in which women could have both a successful, usually glamorous career *and* a fulfilling (if childless or nanny-provisioned) personal life, an extensive literature—including Robin Norwood's 1985 *Women Who Love Too Much: When You Keep Wishing and Hoping He'll Change* and Susan Forward and Joan Torre's 1986 *Men Who Hate Women and the Women Who Love Them*—suggested that women's personal lives were in disarray.[31]

Hochschild observed that feminism had been "abducted" to legitimate the encroachment of a market logic on the private sphere. Values from the commercial sector had jumped the tracks, hurling market values into intimate life. The concept of codependency, a construct that reframed generosity in the context of caring as a form of pathology, was little more than the application of market values to one's capacity to care or a further commoditization in the intimate sphere. Hochschild notes that "the authors of advice books act as emotional investment counselors. They do readings of broad social conditions and recommend to readers of various types, how, how much and in whom to 'invest' emotional attention."[32] Hochschild was right, both in her general point regarding the move of market logics and in her apt naming of advice writers as "emotional investment counselors": life coaching does indeed emerge from financial coaching, as I discuss next. Rather than opening the way to radical and capacious forms of care, the financialization of care (both metaphorically and practically) led to the hoarding or stockpiling of care, or what came to be called "extreme self-care."

The Rise of Personal Coaching and the Concept of Extreme Self-Care

Life coaching developed, quite literally, from the rise of personal financial advisers and counselors. Personal financial and retirement advice became necessary as neoliberalist policies regarding retirement shifted from traditional pension retirement benefits managed through unions and large employers to the individually funded and managed 401(k) and 403(b) retirement investment plans that put individual workers, typically untrained in finance and investment strategy, in charge of their own retirement funds. In response to this radically privatized retirement model, a new career path emerged: financial planners to provide advice on self-funding retirement. And from their ranks emerged an even newer personal service industry: personal or life coaching.

The first to make note of this development was personal financial adviser and best-selling author Suze Orman, whose late 1990s best-selling financial planning books provided an insider's take on how to insulate oneself and one's family from financial hardship even in the face of neoliberal structural adjustments. Like many of the successful advice givers, Orman was a keen observer of social trends, and even somewhat self-conscious in her practice: "Like most Certified Financial Planner professionals," she wrote, "I started my practice to help other people with their money, but as time went on, I realized that it was far more than their money (or lack of it) that needed attention."[33]

As rational economistic principles were being applied to the private sphere, as Social Security was raided by Congress in the effort to feign a balanced budget, and as corporations seized upon the new opportunity to off-load their traditional responsibility to retirees by phasing out pensions and introducing riskier individual retirement investments, financial counselors were particularly well positioned to observe the need for personal coaching. As journalist Helaine Olen has chronicled, financial advice guides and wealth accumulation schemes, always a staple of the self-help industry, burgeoned.[34] Orman again: "It's as if the language of money has pervaded our culture in a new way and is imploring us to listen."[35] Neoliberal policies, with an imperative of pushing the principles of market economics into every corner of lives, contributed to the fusion of psychological and financial counseling. Orman could see this unfolding, even if she lacked the political analysis to understand the disastrous effects of this transposition.[36]

While Orman stayed close to her roots in financial advising, a few pathbreaking financial advisers set out to reposition themselves as life coaches. Two of the most successful were Thomas Leonard and Cheryl Richardson. Leonard is widely considered to be the founder of the life coaching industry. In 1992 he created Coach University to establish training programs for individuals who aspired to develop coaching careers. Four years later he founded the International Coach Federation, a membership organization for coaches that provides standards and credentialing for the emergent industry.[37] He was also the original provider of online self-help coaching services through his entity coachville.com.

Leonard introduced the idea of "extreme self-care" in 1996, in an online coaching program that he developed as he attempted to recuperate from the exhaustion he experienced after starting Coach University. While Leonard became a legend in the field of coaching, he never became a household name. Instead, his most successful student, author Cheryl Richardson, delivered the concept of "extreme self-care" to households across the country with a June 12, 2000, appearance on the *Oprah Winfrey Show*'s lifestyle makeover series "Energy Drains" to launch her first book, *Take Time for Your Life*.[38]

Exhausted American women seized on Richardson's idea that they must take care of themselves first, and two of Richardson's books rose to the *New York Times* best-seller list shortly after her Oprah appearance. While extreme self-care is often ridiculed owing to its seemingly ridiculous solutions to the care crisis—take a bubble bath, get a massage, light a candle and have a cup of tea—its popularity was a bellwether for the still unfolding care crisis.

Leonard's premise for his program of extreme self-care is that, when one's needs are met and exceeded, one has reserves, and thus others will find such an individual attractive and appealing, and that individual will have a relatively simple time continuing to meet, and exceed, his or her own needs. Leonard's own practice of extreme self-care advocated an emphasis on the words *extreme* and *radical*, as he wrote in his initial version of the plan:

> The key word in the program title is Extreme. For me, self care was always a good idea, but I couldn't get very interested in it until I could get a picture of how to make a comprehensive—and for me—radical change. During the transition, I was supported by 10 health care professionals—including a physician, coach, nutritionist, therapist, Rolfer and others. Everyone has their own way of working this program, so please adapt it to meet your needs.[39]

Leonard's own iteration of the program—which required a team of ten professionals and others—is something few can afford. Though he is careful to note that users should adapt the program to their needs, he is silent on the need to adapt the program to one's resources. And, as might be expected, Leonard's view of radical change, like most self-improvement advice, focuses exclusively on individual well-being and ignores the social and economic context of radical inequality in the distribution of care resources. Rather than offering a model for genuinely radical care, Leonard expanded the view prevalent in the self-help industry: care should be directed back to the self rather than to those in our communities and those with greater need. When care is a commodity, the trickle-down fantasies of market economics are applied.

In the context of the late 1990s—after the first wave of middle management downsizing and amid the rising availability of internet-based resources—Leonard provided these programs online free of charge at the coachville.com platform he created.[40] Simultaneously, he launched a multimillion-dollar coaching industry that provided downsized professional workers with new entrepreneurial careers in the care economy.

The coaching industry sidestepped the temporal investments typically required of individuals in the care industry (e.g., advanced degrees in psychology or social work) and undermined the value of these professions in a deskilling of those certified and licensed professions. Although Leonard developed training institutes and credentialing programs, life coaching remains an unregulated industry.[41] Its own entities provide certification, but no specific credential or licensure is required to claim the status of life coach.

Life coaching didn't provide radical care, but it set out to provide readily available, scalable programs of care via technological affordances that emerged in this period. It worked with checklists and schemas and in many ways set the stage for self-improvement's more recent iterations in the discourse of life hacking.[42]

Life Hacking and Not Giving a Fuck: Quick Fixes, Cyborg Minds, and Finitude

While life coaching relied on the affordances of an early internet to distribute its ideas and materials, life hacking draws on the language, ethos, and work styles of tech industries to tackle the life problems that have proliferated with the speedups required under contemporary capitalism.

Life hacking deploys approaches from the culture of coding: when a software application has some sort of problem, developers don't start over from scratch; they find the bug, fix the specific issue, and move on to the next crash or fail that needs a fix. Life hacking, like code hacking, isn't focused on overhauling the system; it aims for quick and viable fixes. The iterative culture of technology development provided the context in which productivity consultant David Allen developed his best-selling 2001 time management book, *Getting Things Done*. GTD, as the program has been shorthanded, initially gained popularity in communities of technologists in Silicon Valley before emerging as one of the most influential time management books of the first decade of the new millennium. Allen draws on the popular metaphor of the mind's similarity to the architecture of the computer:[43]

> The short-term-memory part of your mind—the part that tends to hold all of the incomplete, undecided, and unorganized "stuff"—functions much like RAM on a personal computer. Your conscious mind, like the computer screen, is a focusing tool, not a storage space. You can think about only two or three things at one. But the incomplete items are still being stored in short-term memory space. And as with RAM, there's limited capacity; there only so much "stuff" you can store in there and still have that part of your brain function at a high level. Most people walk around with their RAM bursting at the seams. They're constantly distracted, their focus disturbed by their own internal mental overload.[44]

The solution Allen offers is a time-tested one: write a list. List making allows the life hacker to store data and "operating instructions" offline—freeing up neurological RAM and bandwidth for tasks immediately at hand. Habits and routines are understood as neurological automation that saves effort and attention much as subroutines simplify computer code.

In a recently released book on the emergence of the culture of life hacking, communications scholar Joseph Reagle examines this new thread in self-improvement culture. Life hacking, along with relying on the metaphors of the mind as machine and life as a game, takes the infiltration of market values into the most personal and intimate spheres to new levels. Reagle describes the self-improvement software application Beeminder, built to cultivate motivation in its users by creating a system of accountability: wagering against oneself (or rather against the app) that you'll complete some behavior, be it go to the gym five days in a row or do twenty minutes of Zen meditation in the morning.[45] If one "stays on track," not much happens, but if a Beeminder user fails to adhere to a plan, the app collects on the bet. "What is Beeminder?" asks the product's promotional copy: "It reminds you with a sting!" Beeminder makes it possible to outsource ones' motivation to an app; the application monetizes your motivation.

Beeminder's inventors—and the founders of the company that builds its profits on its subscribers' failed willpower—have also created another innovation in the intimate sphere of family life. Bethany Soule and Daniel Reeves, who trained in computational game theory and machine learning and "work[ed] on incentive systems" at a major technology firm, have also set up a system called Yootling, an interpersonal auction system to determine who will take on various tasks, whose preferences will be determinative in a new purchase, or who will tuck their kids in on any given night.[46]

Each player sets up a financial account and bids on the various activities of a shared life. If the trash needs taking out, each player bids secretly on what they'd pay the other to do the task. The "winner" of the auction pays the loser to take on the task. Their economistic approach has, as Reagle notes, also emerged in a marriage self-help book: Paula Szuchman and Jenny Anderson's *Spousonomics: Using Economics to Master Love, Marriage, and Dirty Dishes.*

Life hacking, in this instance, takes the form of a monetizing hack; it "gamifies" the common problem of establishing an equitable household division of labor. That is, it sets out to redistribute care labor by recombining existing social practices (turn taking and the form of the auction) to ensure what appears, at least on the surface, to be an equitable (and perhaps entertaining) distribution of household labor.

Alas, whether and how the Yootling game addresses the longstanding gendered inequities in women's earnings in the labor market remains a question. One wonders how an equitable distribution could be maintained if the reality of women's lower wages were to enter the equation. Perhaps the Yootlers artificially level the playing field by operating with the same starting balance in their accounts, or by employing a ratio to adjust wage disparities, attempting to firewall traditional gendered disparities in wages, salaries, and overall net worth.

One of the innovations of David Allen's *Getting Things Done* was the recommendation that to-do lists not be cluttered with tasks and desires that are not immediately relevant. Allen suggests having a category called "Someday Maybe" on one's list of priorities, a section set aside for desires and plans not immediately on the horizon. Rather than fantasizing about that beach house or year of traveling around the world, those sort of big dreams are not eliminated from one's list but are officially placed on the back burner. Allen's model for a life lived well is grounded in the notion that one's energetic resources and one's life span remain finite.

Elsewhere in the vast landscape of late capitalist self-help literature, another discursive thread refuses notions of finitude. The "dream life" to-do lists and vision boards of New Age self-literature, most clearly exemplified by Australian film producer and writer Rhonda Byrnes's 2006 internationally best-selling video *The Secret*, push against the notions of limits and reason. This particular thread, initially found in American uplift literature but now gone global, emerged in the Gilded Age with "New Thought" spirituality and flourished in the United States from the 1950s through the present in the "prosperity gospels" of both evangelical leaders and self-help writers.[47]

The notion that an inexhaustible supply was available to everyone who could maintain a positive outlook soothed the anxieties of Gilded Age economic volatility and later buoyed those facing Depression-era despair. New Thought and its successors in New Age discourses run counter to the encroachment of market-driven values into self-help discourses and, indeed, into every facet of daily life. At the same time, they extend capitalism's most foundational fantasies, of unlimited growth and infinite supplies of natural resources, including care labor. Thus, as offensive as the application of market-driven principles to personal life may seem (and may be), any insistence on finitude, as in Allen's GTD, affords a counterpoint to the fantasies of ever available supply.

In a literature where time, attention, and care are recognized as finite resources, prioritizing takes on a new importance. This turn is evident in Mark Manson's 2016 best seller *The Subtle Art of Not Giving a Fuck: A Counterintuitive Approach to Living a Good Life*. Building on the life philosophy that he's popularized on his blogging platform (markmanson.net), Manson cuts to the chase: life is short, and you have only so many fucks to give. Choose them carefully, he advises, "because if you go around caring about everything and everyone without conscious thought or choice—well then you're going to get fucked."[48]

Unlike the current US First Lady, who boarded *Air Force One* to depart for a photo-op at a detention center for migrant children seized from their parents wearing her infamous khaki "I really don't care, do u?" jacket from the Zara retail clothing line, Manson is not arguing for not caring. Manson advocates being extremely conscious about what one cares about—after consulting with oneself over one's own misconceptions, misassumptions, and values. While Manson's title certainly resonates with the contemptuous culture of cruelty that characterizes our current moment, he's actually making the case for finitude. There's no mystical source of limitless abundance in this worldview.

A year before Manson's book launched, author and longtime book industry professional Sarah Knight launched her book series No Fucks Given with the 2016 best-selling *The Life-Changing Magic of Not Giving a Fuck*. The title's reference to Marie Kondo's 2014 international bestselling decluttering guide, *The Life-Changing Magic of Tidying Up*, coupled with the self-help publishing industry's recent embrace of attention-grabbing expletives, positioned the book for easy reception. Kondo has been the industry's most prominent advocate of finitude, promoting the notion that one should carefully curate one's belongings, as having more things brings "less joy." Finitude is finally in fashion.

Self-improvement trends that eschew the fantasy of endlessly renewable resources require readers to imagine that care requires time and energy and that human time and energy are likewise bounded. The market-driven image of the emotional ledger sheet, the idea of "holding someone's tab," the social acceptability of saying one has "no more fucks to give" offend traditional sentiments about intimate life and friendship. But in bringing these terms into the intimate sphere or emotional sphere, they chip away at the fantasy that care, love, and attention are in infinite supply. Perhaps with an equitable distribution of resources—care, attention, and material resources—there would be no need for a fantasy of infinite supply.[49]

Radical Care: From Patches to Self-Renewing Forms of Social Solidarity

Capitalism's care problem leaves anticapitalists and other social justice advocates with an even more difficult problem: how to develop new forms of care provision that refuse racist, patriarchal, capitalist schemes for supply. How do we create new forms of relationship or, as Donna Haraway would say, new forms of kinship?[50] What new forms of sociality and care might be possible? How do we ensure that we do not rely on the discounting of labor based on the traditional gendered and racial social hierarchies, on the fantasies of self-sufficient individuals whose self-making work of maximizing capacities and potential will insulate them from a devastating lack of community, or on the fantasy of an "infinite supply" for those who stay positive? Examples of these new types of relationships, these patches to the care problem, are emerging continuously.[51]

And imagining and creating those forms of interrelationship and social solidarity is the larger project of this issue of *Social Text* and the work ahead. This work can be guided by following Haraway's advice of "staying with the trouble." It will demand both improvisation and ingenuity, and at the same time it promises to be what fully engaged, unalienated labor can be: exuberant, demanding, exhilarating, and, often, simply fun. If it is not all of these things, it will fail.

I have no secret recipe, or five-point plan, or seven habits for this undertaking. Chance and improvisation, careful observation and the willingness to act on principle, and a sense of community or solidarity can all be key to the success of any such undertaking. What I do have is an anecdote about radical care from the intersection of the most traditional forms of reproduction, childbearing and -rearing, and the world of social reproduction, in contingent faculty labor, where I once ran into some trouble.

Conceiving (in the biological sense) at what was then called an advanced maternal age had its challenges, and when my partner and I had arrived to a viable pregnancy, we had not concealed our happiness. Thus, this pregnancy was common knowledge in the university setting where my adjunct faculty income had long supplemented the salary of my full-time nonprofit day job. I had been a part-time faculty member for nearly a decade; my courses were set and routine. The compensation for the courses was so low that I did not rely on the income.

In retrospect, mine seemed (inaccurately) to be an unusual context: work in this setting was not alienated, and my engagement, while not protected by the affordances of tenure, had gradually become what Karl

Marx would call a "realm of freedom": a social location removed from economic necessity and thus unmarked by alienation.[52] For me, teaching was a pleasure.

And as the income from my day job increased and teaching wages were stagnant (and thus ever more nominal), the compensation for teaching became less and less relevant. Labor wasn't being extracted for subsistence.[53] Luc Boltanski and Eve Chiapello's term "the new spirit of capitalism" characterizes such shifts: the meaningfulness of the work itself provides motivation that had once been compelled by economic necessity.[54]

Capitalism's contradictions, in particular its catastrophes, can yield these sorts of inadvertent spaces of generativity, akin to the landscapes that anthropologist Anna Lowenhaupt Tsing chronicles: sites of ecological devastation where sought-after delicacies, Matsutake mushrooms, flourish among the pine tree ruins of clear-cut old-growth forests.[55] And as the university is notably its own sort of ruins, teaching in this context was so poorly compensated that the fundamental arrangement that ties labor to employment—that the labor should support a livelihood—had fallen away.[56] Teaching had become less a profession or labor than an avocation. But as is so often the case under capitalism, even exploitation has its limits.

Although time-intensive parenting was close on the horizon, I had no plans of giving up my space of freedom; I fully intended to keep teaching for pleasure (for wages that would not have even approached the cost of even the lowest-wage childcare). Of course, this was an unsustainable fantasy. I had perhaps also fallen under the spell of some of the fantasies of infinite supply and miraculous maternal capacity that our cultural industry churns out. Surely it would all simply work out, and I would continue to enjoy the pleasures of teaching unencumbered by the temporal, physical, and thus economic demands of caring for an infant.

Given this, you might imagine my surprise when a colleague and friend, another female part-time faculty member, called me one evening near the end of what was my third trimester to share with me that all my spring courses had been offered to her. When she'd asked the faculty administrator who had scheduled the courses if I was okay with not teaching in the spring, she was told, "Of course, she's having a baby—she won't be able to teach anymore; she won't have any time for it." Of course, I paraphrase now, but all of this was news to me. I'd never had a conversation about dropping my courses. But fortunately for me, the friend who phoned to share this had declined to step into my courses without first consulting with me.

The surprises on this phone call kept on coming. My friend offered what was momentarily a riddle: "Isn't it hilarious that the university has just offered the courses of one pregnant woman who is about to deliver to another pregnant woman who'll be delivering just six weeks later?"

Yes, my friend was also pregnant—nearly as advanced in her pregnancy as I was in mine—but she had been a good bit more realistic about institutional paternalism and pregnancy discrimination. She had concealed her pregnancy. Just days earlier she had slipped into a faculty meeting in an oversize man's coat and kept her file folders over her lap to ensure that her pregnancy would go unnoticed until the last possible moment. Yes, in the late 1990s women were still concealing pregnancies in the workplace to protect their livelihoods. I'm quite sure that many still do.

When our laughter subsided, a problem remained. Now there were two pregnant faculty members who had each expected to be teaching two courses, but only two courses in total were scheduled in their areas of expertise. This was a problem for us and also for our administrative colleague who had made the decision to reassign my classes. The administrator of the program was a feminist and usually an ally. The planned handoff of my usual teaching schedule to my colleague was well intentioned, even if the lack of consultation made for a good bit more than bad optics.

The problems, these troubles, were solved in something that might look like some feminist inversion of the parable of the loaves and fishes. In a rare moment of administrative improvisation, our program's director devised a patch: my colleague and I would coteach the courses at our usual levels of compensation. Two teachers, two courses, four salaries—and, given adjunct compensation levels, still a bargain for the university in question.

Although this was the late 1990s, thirty years into the second wave of feminism, we had no access to anything approaching maternity leave, and that situation has scarcely changed for US American women. What we had was the possibility of an accommodation, a prepolitical solution to the problem born of one pregnant woman's unwillingness to poach the courses of another pregnant woman, and of a feminist program administrator's willingness to remedy a lapse in judgment. We had our own fix, an instant iron-on patch held in place by the invisible adhesive of feminist solidarity. Add a little heat and the patch sticks.

There were fascinating unintended consequences from this fragile fix. Few activities are more effective in fostering social solidarity than coteaching with infants in tow. The friendship that my colleague and I shared started to jump the traditional kinship boundaries. Each of our biological families were hundreds (in my case, thousands) of miles away. Sororal affiliation (aka sisterhood, as we once said), without biological kinship, is a formidable and scalable force.

But the patch peeled off quickly. The following semester, my colleague found her own teaching swiftly downsized: a course she was scheduled to teach was canceled less than three hours before she was slated to take the subway into Manhattan to teach it. Her childcare arrangements for the evening were already in place. Our contracts had no cancellation or "kill" fee, and she'd been counting on the paycheck; teaching had always been a profession and livelihood for her. And in this case, there could be no makeshift fix or patch.

Within our faculty community, in our particular work world, this event was both polarizing and what social movement theorists would call "mobilizing."[57] I resigned when I was asked to no longer use part-time faculty labor conditions as an example of exploitation when teaching sections from Marx's *Capital*. When my tiny realm of freedom and my sense of meaningfulness in the work ceased, so did my reason for remaining on the job. And many part-time faculty, like my colleague and myself, who had embarked on parenting while continuing to teach in untenable conditions, began meeting with union organizers. Several years later, and thanks to the hard work (let's be sure to not call this work "tireless efforts," as it was both exhausting and exhilarating) of many committed faculty members and labor organizers, the institution's adjunct faculty union was certified.

So herein emerges a valuable lesson in the politics of care labor as they unfold under Boltanski and Chiapello's new spirit of capitalism: the meaningfulness of any particular employment can evaporate suddenly in the face of the recognition of inexcusable injustice and inequality (the untenable working conditions of contingent labor) or with the emergence of new care responsibilities. When such meaning evaporates, motivation dissolves just as quickly.

The problem of care (of how adjuncts, who were earning abysmal wages and also embarking on parenting, would make a viable living) precipitated a long overdue faculty labor organizing campaign. Friendship, nonbiological sisterhood, social solidarity—the intersubjectivity that makes one person's canceled class everyone's canceled class—precipitated an institutional shift. Certainly, other conditions were in place that made this mobilization possible, perhaps most important, the already existing labor organizing of the graduate teaching assistants at this institution. But what sparked the organizing of an adjunct faculty union at a major institution was a crisis of care.

And therein lies the good news. The ubiquity of personal care catastrophes—and most are vastly more disastrous than the ones my colleague and I encountered—can and do open spaces for political mobilization, and sometimes for legal recourse.[58] If, as feminist and critical disability scholars Faye Ginsburg and Rayna Rapp argue, a burgeoning population of persons with disabilities promises that capitalism's care problem will only continue to grow and thus create even more opportunities for political mobilization, then the care crisis is an opportunity.[59]

Tracing capitalism's unfolding care problem—looking at its failed fixes and our own improvised patches—can offer a space of hope. For as wily (to borrow from Nancy Fraser's useful description[60]) as capitalism and its systems of fixes and patches can be, they also inevitably fail. And in the process, when the fixes are revealed as contradictory and our one-off patches no longer adhere, these failures can and must be met by the principled refusals and ingenuity of our communities. Challenging the fixes, making the patches, and most important, finding, opening, and cultivating the spaces for mobilizations are the only sort of self-care that can help any of us. Self-care turns radical when it's turned inside out.

Notes

More than a few thanks are due to the people behind the scenes on this article. It would not have occurred to me to revisit my early research on self-help culture if the editors of this issue—Hiʻilei Julia Hobart and Tamara Kneese—had not sent their provocative and timely proposal on radical care to the *Social Text* editorial collective. I am indebted to them for their vision, leadership, and patience. To Anna McCarthy, a longtime *Social Text* collective member and editor, my deepest thanks for both your comments and your encouragement to revisit my work on labor and self-improvement culture and join this endeavor. To the manuscript's reviewers, my huge thanks for the comments and leads that have enhanced the work: they were both generous and capacious. And finally, to *Social Text*'s editor David Sartorious and managing editor Marie Buck, along with Hiʻilei, Tamara, Anna, and the reviewers, my immense gratitude for staying with me as I worked to craft this article while recovering from a concussion. My whack on the side of the head was an emergent bit of trouble, and they stayed with me. Their generosity, evidenced in flexibility and accommodations all along the way, was a model of radical care. Had I thought of it sooner, perhaps I would have simply written about their graciousness as another patch and opening. Once you start looking for it, once you have a name for it, the opportunities for radical care appear everywhere.

1. For an expansive list of feminist theorists exploring various aspects of the care crisis, see Fraser, "Contradictions of Capital and Care," 99–100, esp. 100n2; and Ehrenreich and Hochschild, *Global Woman*.

2. While working at this university in the 1990s, I had heard from a number of librarians that the clarity and placement of something as simple as the library's signage could not be remedied due to very specific stipulations in the university's contract with architects Philip Johnson and Richard Foster. The gravity of a series of student suicides, and perhaps their occurrence after Johnson's 2005 death, resulted in alterations to the interiors. For reflections on the university's architectural remediation of this particular locus of student despair, see Hogarty, "NYU Library's Artful Veil"; Paramaguru, "NYU's Brilliant Design"; and Taylor, "Natural Enemy of the Librarian."

3. My evidence on this emerges from the confidential reports from students where I teach, as well as reports from colleagues I know who work in campus counseling at

other institutions, which are also confidential. While the conservative American Psychological Association downplays the increasing needs for psychological services on campuses by overlooking how short-staffed most college and university counseling centers have become—and how needs have increased in the present political environment—they have at least begun to ask questions about counseling capacity. Xiao, "Are We in Crisis?"

4. Even as this article is in production, the *Journal of the American Medical Association* questions the effectiveness of corporate wellness programs. See Song and Baicker, "Effect of a Workplace Wellness Program"; and Abelson, "Employee Wellness Programs Yield Little Benefit." Those that engage economic incentives are particularly dubious. See Thirumurthy, Asch, and Volpp, "Uncertain Effect of Financial Incentives."

5. The following studies debunk the mythology of positive psychology or religious cures: Coyne and Tennen, "Positive Psychology in Cancer Care"; Sloan, Bagiella, and Powell, "Religion, Spirituality, and Medicine"; and Sloan et al., "Should Physicians Prescribe Religious Activities?" See also the best seller responsible for debunking the positive psychology myth: Ehrenreich, *Bright-Sided*.

6. See, e.g., Karen Kelsky's website The Professor Is In (www.theprofessorisin.com).

7. These are examples of care challenges faced by those privileged enough to occupy spaces in higher education (even if it means accumulating staggering debt to secure that education). Likewise, these examples include those who have access to health care, even if they are enrolled in costly plans with mazes of in- and out-of-network providers, copays and coinsurance, exclusions or denials, or entangled in countless hours of "administrivia." These examples are by no means representative; rather, they are evocative, pulled from my social location and thus readily in mind. I invite you to take a quick look around you, whatever your context, for the signs of the care crisis in your life, family, and community. I'll wager that you don't need to look very far or very hard and that the magnitude of the crises you and your community face is inversely proportionate to the community's level of access to various forms of capital.

8. Fraser, *Fortunes of Feminism*; Ehrenreich and Hochschild, *Global Woman*, 1–15.

9. Likewise, education, another component of the social reproduction of labor, has operated as a form of care labor with somewhat higher ratios, for example, the traditional classroom where one paid teacher sees to the education of twenty-five, thirty, or sometimes more students. The emergence of online and distance learning attenuated these ratios even further, increasing racial and economic inequality. Cottom, *Lower Ed*.

10. For two well-known examples of part-time university faculty dying immiserated, see Anderson, "What Really Happened to Margaret Mary Vojtko?"; Harris, "Death of an Adjunct"; Flaherty, "Newspaper Column on 'Death of an Adjunct'"; and Sanchez, "Sad Death of an Adjunct Professor."

11. Ehrenreich and Hochschild, *Global Woman*; Oishi, *Women in Motion*; Tadiar, *Things Fall Away*.

12. Fraser is particularly clear on this point in an interview in *Dissent*: Leonard and Fraser, "Capitalism's Crisis of Care."

13. Ehrenreich and Hochschild, *Global Woman*, 1–15.

14. In a moving *New York Times* opinion piece, Nona Willis Aronowitz recounts how her father, Stanley, one of this journal's founders, relies on the affordances of Amazon's swift delivery in the wake of a stroke. Capitalism, wily and sticky, catches

us all: few can elude a system that snares us with our own embodied vulnerabilities. Aronowitz, "Hate Amazon? Try Living without It."

15. Fraser, *Unruly Practices*, 71.

16. The care problem affects us all, even if disproportionately, save those who can afford to pay for a staff to attend to their care needs. But sociologist Arlie Russell Hochschild contends that even those who have the resources to manage their own care crises may suffer from a new kind of alienation as they "outsource their lives." Hochschild, *Outsourced Self*.

17. Field, "Academe Is a New Green Pasture for Consultants."

18. While I seldom revisit prior publications, a convergence of circumstances made that appropriate in this instance (see acknowledgments).

19. Swinth, *Feminism's Forgotten Fight*.

20. Hochschild, *Time Bind*; Chancer, *Rise and Stall of American Feminism*.

21. Martin, *Financialization of Daily Life*.

22. Brown, *Having It All*, 307.

23. Brown, *Having It All*, 29.

24. Covey, *Seven Habits*, 177.

25. Scanlon, *Bad Girls Go Everywhere*, 12–14; McGee, *Self-Help, Inc.*, 86.

26. Davis, *Enabling Acts*; Nielsen, *Disability History*, 161, 180–81.

27. Federici, *Wages against Housework*, 74–87.

28. McGee, *Self-Help, Inc.*, 88–91.

29. McGee, *Self-Help, Inc.*, 88

30. Faludi, *Backlash*; Anderson, "A Critical Analysis of the Concept of Codependency"; Hochschild, "Commercial Spirit."

31. See also Cowin and Kinder, *Smart Women, Foolish Choices*.

32. Hochschild, "Commercial Spirit," 12.

33. Orman, *Nine Steps*, 2.

34. Olen, *Pound Foolish*.

35. Orman, *Nine Steps*, xi.

36. Orman attempts to soften her financial focus by counseling her readers to "put people first," followed by things, and only then money (*Nine Steps*, 131).

37. CoachInc.com, "CoachInc.com Accredited Programs Information"; International Coach Federation, "History of ICF."

38. For a closer analysis of this *Oprah Winfrey Show* episode, see McGee, *Self-Help, Inc.*, 104–7.

39. Leonard, "Extreme Self Care Program."

40. At this point the coachville.com domain leads to the practice of another coach, but poorly maintained remnants of Leonard's work can be found there and on the International Coach Federation website (www.coachfederation.org).

41. Indeed, the unregulated nature of the self-improvement industry has led to the deaths of individuals seeking personal improvement or transformation. The 2009 deaths of Kirby Brown, James Shore, and Liz Neuman in a pseudo-Native American "sweat lodge" ritual led to the trial, conviction, and prison term of New Age motivational entrepreneur James Arthur Ray (Lovett, "James Ray, Self-Help Guru, Is Sentenced to Prison"). The family of sweat-lodge victim Kirby Brown has initiated a move for state regulation of the self-improvement industry. See www.seeksafely.org (accessed April 18, 2019).

42. If space allowed I would guide the reader through some of my favorite documents from these programs, including the list of 1,001 "tolerations" that Leonard asks his readers to review and, if relevant, eliminate from their lives. The list of tolerations is no longer easy to find on the internet, as the list of Leonard's programs

on the International Coach Federation site is a graveyard of broken links, but it's well worth a read as a startling array of what we would now dismiss as "First-World problems." One of the last places online that this artifact can be found is Leonard, "1001 Tolerations."

43. Maltz, *Psycho-Cybernetics*.

44. Allen, *Getting Things Done*, 22.

45. Reagle, *Hacking Life*, 57.

46. Reagle, *Hacking Life*, 119–21.

47. See, e.g., Hill, *Think and Grow Rich*; or Ponder, *Dynamic Laws of Prosperity*. One of the best examples of the nineteenth-century roots of the prosperity Gospel is Conwell, *Acres of Diamonds*.

48. Manson, *Subtle Art of Not Giving a Fuck*, 15.

49. One endeavor that aimed to find an egalitarian form to remedy inequities and shortages of caring attention is Harvey Jackins's reevaluation cocounseling movement. Jackins and his organization had aimed to accomplish this by creating one-on-one and small-group counseling settings where individuals trained in the cocounseling method each counseled one another and thus aimed to solve the shortage of attention or emotional recognition that Jackins contends most of us experience under capitalism. This organization continues its work under the leadership of Tim Jackins, the founder's son. See the Re-evaluation Counseling website (www.rc.org) and Jackins, *Fundamentals of Co-counseling Manual*.

50. Haraway, *Staying with the Trouble*.

51. For example, Lisa Duggan and Anna McCarthy's 2018 essay "Cancer Twins" chronicles their new kinship formation forged amid concurrent cancer diagnoses and treatment. Leah Lakshmi Piepzna-Samarasinha demonstrates the vitality of queer-crip communities of care in *Care Work: Dreaming Disability Justice*, where she describes the emergence of the Creating Collective Access project and the work of Sins Invalid, which are both queer, crip, and antiracist spaces of mutual support and recognition. New forms of sociality emerge from both emergent and transient increased care requirements and from the ongoing and individual care needs of all kinds of body-minds.

52. As Marx notes: "In fact, the realm of freedom actually begins only where labour which is determined by necessity and mundane considerations ceases; thus in the very nature of things it lies beyond the sphere of actual material production" ("Capital Vol. III").

53. Citing Luc Boltanski and Eve Chiapello, in *Work's Intimacy* Melissa Gregg observes that some workers, in particular creative workers working "flexibly"—from their homes or coffee shops—experience their labor as unalienated, as work is tied to identity.

54. Boltanski and Chiapello, *New Spirit of Capitalism*, 76.

55. Tsing (*Mushroom at the End of the World*) tells the story of how the industrial clearing of old-growth forests gave way to pine forests, which in turn are an ideal site for the flourishing of prized matsutake mushrooms.

56. Readings, *University in Ruins*.

57. While many social movement theorists are working on resource mobilization theories, some of the most instructive work concerns the mobilization of emotion and aesthetics. See Jasper, *Art of Moral Protest*; Jasper, *Emotions of Protest*; and Boyd and Mitchell, *Beautiful Trouble*.

58. As one example, in the recent class action lawsuit against UnitedHealth Group for denial of mental health benefits, UnitedHealth Group lost the case. Abelson, "Mental Health Treatment Denied."

59. Ginsburg and Rapp, "Disability Publics."

60. Fraser's description of capitalism's versatility as "wily" first appears in her essay questioning deconstruction's role in diminishing the impact of the political ("The French Derrideans," 131). More recently, this apt language resurfaces in a recent manifesto of which Fraser is a coauthor (Arruzza et al., *Feminism for the 99 Percent*, 61).

References

Abelson, Reed. "Employee Wellness Programs Yield Little Benefit, Study Shows." *New York Times*, April 18, 2019. www.nytimes.com/2019/04/16/health/employee -wellness-programs.html.

Abelson, Reed. "Mental Health Treatment Denied to Customers by Giant Insurer's Policies, Judge Rules." *New York Times*, March 6, 2019. www.nytimes.com /2019/03/05/health/unitedhealth-mental-health-parity.html.

Allen, David. *Getting Things Done: The Art of Stress-Free Productivity*. New York: Penguin, 2001.

Anderson, L. V. "What Really Happened to Margaret Mary Vojtko, the Duquesne Adjunct Whose Death Became a Rallying Cry?" *Slate*, November 17, 2013. www .slate.com/articles/news_and_politics/education/2013/11/death_of_duquesne _adjunct_margaret_mary_vojtko_what_really_happened_to_her.html.

Anderson, Sandra C. "A Critical Analysis of the Concept of Codependency." *Social Work* 39, no. 6 (1994): 677–85. www.jstor.org/stable/23717128.

Aronowitz, Nona Willis. "Hate Amazon? Try Living without It." *New York Times*, December 14, 2018. www.nytimes.com/2018/12/08/opinion/sunday/hate-amazon -try-living-without-it.html.

Arruzza, Cinzia, et al. *Feminism for the 99 Percent: A Manifesto*. London: Verso, 2019.

Boltanski, Luc, and Eve Chiapello. *The New Spirit of Capitalism*. London: Verso, 2005.

Boyd, Andrew, and Dave Oswald Mitchell. *Beautiful Trouble: A Toolbox for Revolution*. New York: OR Books, 2016.

Brown, Helen Gurley. *Having It All*. New York: Pocket Books, 1982.

Chancer, Lynn S. *After the Rise and Stall of American Feminism: Taking Back a Revolution*. Stanford, CA: Stanford University Press, 2019.

CoachInc.com. "CoachInc.com Accredited Programs Information." Coach U. www .coachinc.com/CoachU/Programs%20and%20Services/Overview/default.asp (accessed December 15, 2018).

Conwell, Russell H. *Acres of Diamonds: Our Every-Day Opportunities and Their Wondrous Unsuspected Riches*. Philadelphia: Bishop, 1893.

Cottom, Tressie McMillan. *Lower Ed: The Troubling Rise of For-Profit Colleges in the New Economy*. New York: New Press, 2018.

Covey, Stephen R. *The Seven Habits of Highly Effective People: Powerful Lessons in Personal Change*. New York: Simon and Schuster, 1989.

Cowan, Connell, and Melvyn Kinder. *Smart Women, Foolish Choices: Finding the Right Men, Avoiding the Wrong Ones*. New York: Signet, 1986.

Coyne, James C., and Howard Tennen. "Positive Psychology in Cancer Care: Bad Science, Exaggerated Claims, and Unproven Medicine." *Annals of Behavioral Medicine* 39, no. 1 (2010): 16–26. doi.org/10.1007/s12160-009-9154-z.

Davis, Lennard J. *Enabling Acts: The Hidden Story of How the Americans with Disabilities Act Gave the Largest US Minority Its Rights*. Repr. ed. Boston: Beacon, 2016.

Duggan, Lisa, and Anna McCarthy. "The Cancer Twins." *Avidly*, December 14, 2018. avidly.lareviewofbooks.org/2018/12/14/the-cancer-twins.

Ehrenreich, Barbara. *Bright-Sided*. New York: Metropolitan Books, 2009.

Ehrenreich, Barbara, and Arlie Russell Hochschild. *Global Woman: Nannies, Maids, and Sex Workers in the New Economy*. New York: Metropolitan Books, 2002.

Faludi Susan. *Backlash: Undeclared War against American Women*. New York: Crown, 1991.

Federici, Sylvia. *Wages against Housework*. Bristol, UK: Falling Wall, 1975.

Field, Kelly. "Academe Is a New Green Pasture for Consultants." *Chronicle of Higher Education* 64, no. 38 (2018): 12.

Flaherty, Colleen. "Newspaper Column on 'Death of an Adjunct' Prompts Debate." *Inside Higher Ed*, September 19, 2013. www.insidehighered.com/news/2013/09/19/newspaper-column-death-adjunct-prompts-debate.

Forward, Susan, and Joan Torres. *Men Who Hate Women and the Women Who Love Them*. New York: Bantam Books, 1986.

Fraser, Nancy. "Contradictions of Capital and Care." *New Left Review*, no. 100 (2016): 99–117.

Fraser, Nancy. *The Fortunes of Feminism*. London: Verso, 2013.

Fraser, Nancy. "The French Derrideans: Politicizing Deconstruction or Deconstructing the Political?" *New German Critique*, no. 33 (1984): 127–54. doi.org/10.2307/488357.

Fraser, Nancy. *Unruly Practices: Power, Discourse, and Gender in Contemporary Social Theory*. Minneapolis: University of Minnesota Press, 1989.

Ginsburg, Faye, and Rayna Rapp. "Disability Publics: Toward a History of Possible Futures." Paper presented at the Fordham Distinguished Lecture on Disability, Fordham University, New York, April 27, 2017.

Gregg, Melissa. *Work's Intimacy*. Cambridge: Polity, 2011.

Haraway, Donna Jeanne. *Staying with the Trouble: Making Kin in the Chthulucene*. Durham, NC: Duke University Press, 2016.

Harris, Adam. "The Death of an Adjunct." *Atlantic*, April 8, 2019. www.theatlantic.com/education/archive/2019/04/adjunct-professors-higher-education-thea-hunter/586168/.

Hochschild, Arlie Russell. "The Commercial Spirit of Intimate Life and the Abduction of Feminism: Signs from Women's Advice Books." *Theory, Culture, and Society* 11, no. 2 (1994): 1–24. doi.org/10.1177/026327694011002001.

Hochschild, Arlie Russell. *The Outsourced Self: Intimate Life in Market Times*. New York: Metropolitan Books, 2012.

Hochschild, Arlie Russell. *The Time Bind: When Work Becomes Home and Home Becomes Work*. New York: Henry Holt, 2001.

Hogarty, Dave. "NYU Library's Artful Veil of Suicide Prevention." *Curbed NY*, August 20, 2012. ny.curbed.com/2012/8/20/10338040/see-nyu-librarys-artful-veil-of-suicide-prevention.

International Coach Federation. "History of ICF." www.coachfederation.org/history (accessed April 19, 2019).

Jackins, Harvey. *Fundamentals of Co-counseling Manual (Elementary Counselors Manual for Beginning Classes in Re-evaluation Co-counseling)*. Seattle: Rational Island, 1970.

Jasper, James M. *The Art of Moral Protest: Culture, Biography, and Creativity in Social Movements*. Chicago: University of Chicago Press, 1997.

Jasper, James M. *The Emotions of Protest*. Chicago: University of Chicago Press, 2018.

Leonard, Sarah, and Nancy Fraser. "Capitalism's Crisis of Care." *Dissent* 63, no. 4 (2016): 30–37. www.dissentmagazine.org/article/nancy-fraser-interview-capitalism -crisis-of-care.

Leonard, Thomas. "Extreme Self Care Program." Version 1.0. CoachVille, August 1996. www.coachville.com/tl/thomasleonard/cli/assess/12.html.

Leonard, Thomas. "1001 Tolerations." www.upliftcoach.com/documents/197tolerations 1001.pdf (accessed April 18, 2019).

Lovett, Ian. "James Ray, Self-Help Guru, Is Sentenced to Prison in Sweat Lodge Deaths." *New York Times*, November 18, 2011. www.nytimes.com/2011/11/19 /us/james-ray-self-help-guru-is-sentenced-to-prison-in-sweat-lodge-deaths .html.

Maltz, Maxwell. *Psycho-Cybernetics: A New Way to Get More Living out of Life*. Engle-wood Cliffs, NJ: Prentice-Hall, 1960.

Manson, Mark. *The Subtle Art of Not Giving a Fuck: A Counterintuitive Approach to Living a Good Life*. New York: HarperOne, 2016.

Martin, Randy. *Financialization of Daily Life*. Philadelphia: Temple University Press, 2002.

Marx, Karl. "Capital Vol. III; Part VII. Revenues and Their Sources; Chapter 48. The Trinity Formula." 1844. Marxists Internet Archive. www.marxists.org /archive/marx/works/1894-c3/ch48.htm.

McGee, Micki. *Self-Help, Inc.: Makeover Culture in American Life*. New York: Oxford University Press, 2005.

Nielsen, Kim E. *A Disability History of the United States*. Boston: Beacon, 2012.

Norwood, Robin. *Women Who Love Too Much: When You Keep Wishing and Hoping He'll Change*. New York: Pocket Books, 1985. archive.org/details/womenwholove toom00norw_0.

Oishi, Nana. *Women in Motion: Globalization, State Policies, and Labor Migration in Asia*. Stanford, CA: Stanford University Press, 2005.

Olen, Helaine. *Pound Foolish: Exposing the Dark Side of the Personal Finance Industry*. New York: Portfolio/Penguin, 2013.

Orman, Suze. *The Nine Steps to Financial Freedom: Practical and Spiritual Steps So You Can Stop Worrying*. New York: Three Rivers, 2000.

Paramaguru, Kharunya. "NYU's Brilliant Design Solution to a Building's Suicide Problem." *Time*, August 26, 2012. newsfeed.time.com/2012/08/26/nyus-brilliant -design-solution-to-a-buildings-suicide-problem/.

Piepzna-Samarasinha, Leah Lakshmi. *Care Work: Dreaming Disability Justice*. Van-couver, BC: Arsenal Pulp, 2018.

Ponder, Catherine. *The Dynamic Laws of Prosperity: Forces That Bring Riches to You*. Englewood Cliffs, NJ: Prentice-Hall, 1962.

Readings, Bill. *The University in Ruins*. Cambridge, MA: Harvard University, 1999.

Reagle, Joseph Michael. *Hacking Life: Systematized Living and Its Discontents*. Cam-bridge, MA: MIT Press, 2019.

Sanchez, Claudio. "The Sad Death of an Adjunct Professor Sparks a Labor Debate." NPR, September 22, 2013. www.npr.org/2013/09/22/224946206 /adjunct-professor-dies-destitute-then-sparks-debate.

Scanlon, Jennifer. *Bad Girls Go Everywhere: The Life of Helen Gurley Brown*. New York: Oxford University Press, 2009.

Sloan, R. P., E. Bagiella, and T. Powell. "Religion, Spirituality, and Medicine." *Lan-cet* 353, no. 9153 (1999): 664–67. doi.org/10.1016/S0140-6736(98)07376-0.

Sloan, Richard P., Emilia Bagiella, Larry VandeCreek, Margot Hover, Carlo Casalone, Trudi Jinpu Hirsch, Yusuf Hasan, Ralph Kreger, and Peter Poulos. "Should Physicians Prescribe Religious Activities?" *New England Journal of Medicine* 342, no. 25 (2000): 1913–16. doi.org/10.1056/NEJM200006223422513.

Song, Zirui, and Katherine Baicker. "Effect of a Workplace Wellness Program on Employee Health and Economic Outcomes: A Randomized Clinical Trial." *JAMA* 321, no. 15 (2019): 1491–1501. doi.org/10.1001/jama.2019.3307.

Swinth, Kirsten. *Feminism's Forgotten Fight: The Unfinished Struggle for Work and Family.* Cambridge, MA: Harvard University Press, 2018.

Tadiar, Neferti X. M. *Things Fall Away: Philippine Historical Experience and the Makings of Globalization.* Durham, NC: Duke University Press, 2009.

Thirumurthy, Harsha, David A. Asch, and Kevin G. Volpp. "The Uncertain Effect of Financial Incentives to Improve Health Behaviors." *JAMA* 321, no. 15 (2019): 1451–52. doi.org/10.1001/jama.2019.2560.

Tsing, Anna Lowenhaupt. *The Mushroom at the End of the World: On the Possibility of Life in Capitalist Ruins.* New York: Oxford University Press, 2017.

Taylor, Marvin J. "The Natural Enemy of the Librarian." With Andrea Geyer. *Triple Canopy*, April 3, 2018. www.canopycanopycanopy.com/contents/the-natural-enemy -of-the-librarian.

Xiao, Henry. "Are We in Crisis? National Mental Health and Treatment Trends in College Counseling Centers." *Psychological Services* 14, no. 4 (2017): 407–15. doi.org/10.1037/ser0000130.

Deviant Motherhood

House Arrest and Social Belonging in Argentina

Leyla Savloff

> Freedom is not a static condition we achieve once and for all. Nor is it
> something absolutely foreclosed to us by male domination. Instead, it is
> a process of struggle we engage in, in part by resignifying the personas
> of femininity, and the meanings given to our "sex," so to express and
> represent who we are in singularity, and in the complexity of our other
> basic identifications.
> —Drucilla Cornell, *Beyond Accommodation*

On October 27, 2009, a symposium titled "Arrest Sweet Arrest" was
held at the Centro Cultural Rojas, a center created in 1984 as part of
the Outreach Program of the Universidad de Buenos Aires. The cultural
center, located in a historically diverse neighborhood of Buenos Aires,
was established as a permeable entity between community and higher
education. At a walking distance from the theater district, the neighborhood of Balvanera is usually the home of artists, brothels, and cumbia
night clubs. It is filled with cafés and small businesses, covered in murals,
and traditionally inhabited by Armenian and Jewish communities, as well
as Koreans and Bolivians. The "Arrest Sweet Arrest" symposium exam-
ined a recent policy that extends the "benefit" of house arrest to incarcerated women who are pregnant, mothers, or the primary caregivers of
small children. Before this extension of house arrest, incarcerated women
who were pregnant or had children under the age of four were assigned
with their children to special units in the penitentiary, often referred to as
"prison nurseries."[1] Policy makers, journalists, women under house arrest,
and neighborhood collectives all gathered to analyze what this new alter-

Social Text 142 · Vol. 38, No. 1 · March 2020
DOI 10.1215/01642472-7971103   © 2020 Duke University Press

native to incarceration entailed and to raise urgent questions about how this new form of care actually domesticates imprisonment. As Drucilla Cornell suggests in the epigraph above, freedom in this particular context is an unresolved struggle that women engage in, not only to negotiate what alternatives to incarceration mean but also to construe ways of interrelating to one another that disrupt the "hegemonic story of how femininity is mapped onto femaleness within patriarchal cultures."[2]

This research focuses on YoNoFui, a collective that since 2002 offers art-related workshops both inside and outside prisons to women who have been released, community members, and incarcerated women (both in prison and under house arrest) with once-a-week permits to attend the workshops. Feminist interventions have long critiqued the dichotomy between the public and the private, showing that the home is often a site of abuse as much as of care.[3] YoNoFui emerged out of these broader movements, taking particular inspiration from the actions of Argentina's Madres de Plaza de Mayo, an association comprising mothers whose children were "disappeared" in the late 1970s. According to prominent geographer and prison abolitionist Ruth Wilson Gilmore, "In Argentina, under the fascist military government (1976–1983), Las Madres de Plaza de Mayo defied the presumption that women should not meddle in affairs of the state—which is to say the male, or public, sphere—by organizing on the basis of a simple and culturally indisputable claim that mothers ought to know where their children are."[4] Las Madres are a constant collective reminder of the power that organized women can garner to challenge institutional and state violence.[5]

The juxtaposition presented at "Arrest Sweet Arrest," of carceral logics moving into the domestic sphere and women's collectives organizing against them, embodies the larger stakes for prison abolition and collective liberation under neoliberalism. If we account for the gendered politics of prison, of motherhood, and of women's labor, house arrest can operate as a cruel mechanism that expands the social control of women. House arrest in the contemporary Latin American context reveals much about the gendered character of the prison industrial complex and the erosion of social policies of the welfare state. As historian Premilla Nadasen explained, "Neoliberalism's dismantling of the economic safety net, trend toward privatization, and rise of the security state have increased the burden on women."[6] Through this framing, I consider state-based care practices as inevitably entangled with the profit-making, social control techniques that characterize contemporary prisons in Argentina and beyond. I argue that house arrest, portrayed in state policy as a form of care for children of incarcerated mothers, in fact relocates punitive methods of the carceral system into the home. I contextualize the ways motherhood substantially challenges ungendered, unraced constructions of the prison by redirecting individuality toward an interrelated and intersubjective construction of the self.

To seriously examine alternatives to incarceration for women, one must look to more radical forms of care, such as those created by YoNoFui, the women's collective that was the focus of my ethnographic research in Buenos Aires from 2014 to 2017. YoNoFui does not just offer educational spaces in women's prisons; as a workers' cooperative YoNoFui also sells the handcrafts from the workshops, such as clothing, notebooks, their magazine *YoSoy*, and carpentry items, to become a self-sustainable collective. This is not a job-training program. The work of these women is presented as a tool to carve out new practices for new social roles. Their objective is to make visible the continuum of institutional violence women endure, both inside and outside of prisons, and to strengthen the constitution of collective subjects. They put together photo exhibits and poetry readings and organize protests against institutional violence and campaigns for prisoners' rights, providing care on a broader spectrum. In addition to spending time at YoNoFui, I also interviewed legislators behind this new house arrest policy, as well as social workers, lawyers, women under house arrest, and incarcerated women whose applications for house arrest had been denied. This ethnographic work unveils how the practice of house arrest informs broader national anxieties around women's maternal responsibilities and the constitution of a desired "feminine" citizen. It also emphasizes the carceral system as one drenched in discriminatory and punitive practices toward women who defy conventional ideas of motherhood and find themselves outside heteronormative middle-class values.[7] YoNoFui illustrates the increasing organized political power of formerly and currently incarcerated people, women under house arrest, artists, scholars, and community members who work to provide the radical care that the state fails to provide.

The rise in the criminalization of poverty follows a global trend in the expansion of the carceral state. Anthropologist Carolyn Sufrin, in her ethnographic account of pregnant women in a San Francisco jail, exposes how care that emerges behind bars is a symptom of broader social and economic failures to care for society's most marginalized people.[8] For example, marginalized women in jail receive medical care behind bars that they cannot access on the outside. Care, in this instance, is not only about controlling and governing subjects but also about fostering everyday affective relationships. Mahuya Bandyopadhyay, while not focused on women's prisons, also offers a sociological analysis that emphasizes the everydayness of prisons as social sites that allow for negotiation, resistance, and subversion.[9] Despite these and other important studies on women's incarceration, care practices regarding women in prison have remained peripheral, dispersed, and outside critical anthropological debates.[10] In the case of YoNoFui, everyday affective relationships are also paramount, but what makes their care distinct and radical is that they attend to the bureaucratic procedures that are necessary to improve the living conditions of women involved in the carceral system. By tracing how processes around punishment and social control affect understandings of gender norms and family ideals, I investigated the ways women reimagined their lives under such constraints.

One of my research participants, Sabrina, offers a sobering example of how the prison provides basic services unavailable to women outside.[11] Sabrina's parents never registered her birth, so Sabrina never had a formal identity document to apply for jobs and benefits. As a young woman she began the process in 2003 and only received her document in April 2018, after YoNoFui assisted her with the manifold required bureaucratic procedures. During that time, Sabrina was formally recognized only by the penitentiary, where she completed her elementary education. When I met her in 2014, she was in her midtwenties and a single mother of an eighteen-month-old daughter. As her release date approached, she was more afraid of her life on the outside than in prison. Instances of care such as this complicate depictions of prisons as dehumanizing punitive institutions while also underscoring the cruelty in having prison be the first horizon of inclusion for people living at the margins of the state.

In Argentina, the vast majority of incarcerated women are located in Buenos Aires, and over 80 percent of them are mothers. Between 1989 and 2008, women's incarceration increased 271 percent while men's incarceration increased 112 percent.[12] Neoliberal policies that marginalized the urban poor, along with the implementation of a war on drugs modeled after that in the United States, help explain these increases. Since the 1990s, harsher punishment and longer sentences have been applied to deter drug trafficking. Such punishment has fallen disproportionately on minor actors, overrepresented by women and foreigners.[13] Anthropologist Aihwa Ong insists we understand neoliberalism not as an economic doctrine but as an extraordinarily malleable technology of governing that is taken up in different ways by different regimes: "Neoliberal governmentality results from the infiltration of market-driven truths and calculation into the domain of politics."[14] Further, neoliberal technologies are inextricably linked to the biopolitical mode of governing that views the population as living resources to be harnessed and managed by governing regimes.[15] In January 2009, as women's incarceration grew to exponential numbers and penitentiaries proved ill-equipped to manage prison nurseries, the Argentine state extended house arrest to pregnant women and women who were the main caregivers of small children and/or disabled family members.

The Neoliberal Prison

While recent prison studies have focused on disrupting the prison setting as a rigid and impervious site, house arrest as an alternative to incarceration and an instance of state care should be interrogated as well.[16] In 2018, Michelle Alexander wrote about house arrest in the United States as "e-carceration." She warned that "if the goal is to end mass incarceration and mass criminalization, digital prisons are not an answer. They're just another way of posing the question."[17] In Argentina, house arrest constitutes a site of neglect where women must fend for themselves. Rather than offer caregiving support, the state abandons incarcerated women by placing them in the domestic sphere to perform reproductive labor as a way to complete their sentence.

The prison system is designed to promote individualism and isolation rather than strengthen community and familial ties.[18] Prison nurseries were introduced as a benevolent measure to keep mother and child together. However, the institutionalization of children provides a new array of challenges. In 2008 and 2013, women in prison nurseries in Buenos Aires staged hunger strikes to protest the penitentiary's failure to provide enough food for the children, the presence of rats and insects, and the deplorable infrastructure. According to official reports, prison conditions for mothers and their children were highly inadequate in terms of diet, clothing, medical care, and the physical and emotional development of children. Transitioning to life outside of prison is especially traumatic for children who have only experienced life behind bars and are suddenly separated from their mothers when they reach the age of four.[19] House arrest emerged as a more humane alternative to the institutionalization of children. Discourses on the rights of children were at the forefront of the legislative project to extend house arrest to women. Such discourses, however, and the sanctions for women to mother "appropriately," follow women throughout their carceral experience as a constant threat to lose their children or the benefit of house arrest.

From a historical perspective, the prison has always been considered a masculine space and continues to be so today, partly because women worldwide comprise around 5 percent of the prison population. Taking motherhood as a lens to understand punishment and social control foregrounds the masculinist frameworks that penal institutions rely on. Because women are a minority in institutions of punishment, women's issues have been largely ignored, silenced, and poorly addressed.[20] Motherhood as a category of analysis brings to light the multiple contradictions and heteronormative expectations that society places on women.[21] Understood as a social and historical construct, motherhood reveals itself as a highly political and contested site of inquiry.

Before the 2009 extension of this "benefit" to mothers, house arrest was limited to the elderly and terminally ill, suggesting and reinforcing the home as a preferred location for care practices. When "Arrest Sweet Arrest" was held in October 2009, there were only a few dozen women who could provide testimony. Marcela Trujillo was one of these women, with children ages five and three. While providing testimony at the symposium, she noted: "I have to request permission for everything. If my son is dying, what do I do? I am locked up, I cannot take him to the doctor. I have the same issue with food. In prison, I was locked up but I had a job. If I had a headache, I could go to the infirmary and ask for ibuprofen. Now I have to put up with terrible headaches because I cannot afford it."[22] Her statement expressed some of the concerns women face as they are granted house arrest, considering that most of them are unmarried and single heads of households.[23] According to the 2001 national census, 81.75 percent of single-parent households in Argentina were headed by women, while only 18.25 percent were headed by men.[24] As the main providers for their families, women face the difficult decision to stay in prison with steady employment or apply for house arrest, where work opportunities are slim. The lack of public policies to address the myriad situations women face under home confinement is another symptom of broader social and economic failures to care for society's most marginalized people.[25]

House arrest, a seemingly more humane alternative to incarceration, not only fails to address the needs of women and children but also reconfigures the flawed logic of the prison system in the domestic sphere. For example, in 2015, the Patronato de Liberados, the official entity in charge of overseeing parole, conditional release, and house arrest, was on strike for several months. This meant that visits from social workers ceased, and women under house arrest had no contact with the criminal justice system for several months. Such was the case for Amalia, whom I met in October 2014 at a book-binding workshop in YoNoFui where participants learn how to make notebooks for retail. When Amalia joined the workshop (weeks after it had begun, as often happened with women under house arrest, whose permits were always delayed), she was asked to introduce herself. Amalia was unafraid and outspoken: "I've been hungry. I lost a lot of weight after I left the penitentiary. I am not ashamed anymore. I am as poor as they come, and it is just me and my daughter."

House arrest as a site of neglect punishes women even more harshly when they are migrants, Indigenous, and/or survivors of abuse. Amalia had come to Argentina from Peru for surgery after a bus accident left glass shards in her arm. Since she could not afford the surgery in Peru, Amalia traveled to Argentina, where public hospitals provide medical care to everyone. When I visited Amalia at her home I did not ask why she had been incarcerated. As a rule, I never asked women why they were in prison. Early on I learned this was simply not a polite question to ask, nor did it elicit the most interesting conversations. Amalia told me about her time in prison prior to being granted house arrest, during which she discovered she was pregnant. Her first missed period coincided with her time of arrest, so Amalia attributed her missed periods and fatigue to the stresses of prison life. Though she had been told in Peru that she was infertile, she found herself pregnant at age forty-two. She gave birth to a daughter behind bars, with a lot of pain and poor medical treatment. When her daughter was about a year and a half, Amalia was granted house arrest and moved to a rented room with a shared outdoor bathroom and no support system. A neighbor was willing to sign the papers saying he would support her, but soon after that he moved away. The federal legislation that extended house arrest to mothers offered no suggestions or solutions to the economic uncertainties that incarcerated single mothers face. Amalia never told her family in Peru that she was incarcerated. When they called her urging her to visit as her father was dying, she said work prevented her from returning.

YoNoFui's book-binding workshop allowed Amalia to focus on handmade objects made with recycled materials and invited her to visit once a week. They offer a safe space where women can interact with others while also engaging in cultural productions, such as photo exhibits and poetry readings, and considering alternative ways of thinking of themselves. In doing so, YoNoFui provides the actual care that the state takes credit for. This alternative care model, which exists outside the state system, offers a sense of belonging and creates communal ties that were not always there.

Writing about neoliberal governmentalities, James Ferguson and Akhil Gupta argue that, by focusing on the ways in which states are spatialized, an analysis of the legitimacy of the state gives way to understanding the particular practices, ideologies, and experiences that shape such legitimacy. They introduce the term *vertical encompassment* to illustrate how state power works: on the one hand, by naturalizing the notion that the state finds itself above society implementing policies in a top-down fashion while, on the other hand, by revealing that the multiple scales of state power comprise family dynamics, the community organization, the nation, its geopolitical location, and its relation to globalization.[26]

Despite this vertical encompassment that defines governmentality (processes in which the conduct of the population is governed through institutions, discourses, norms, identities, etc.), Ferguson and Gupta suggest that with neoliberalism "the logic of the market has been extended to the operation of state functions, so that even the traditionally core institutions of government, such as post offices, schools, and police, are, if not actually privatized, at least run according to an 'enterprise model.'"[27] This remark is also shared by political scientist Wendy Brown in her description of neoliberalism as a political rationality that renders every human being and institution, including the state, on the model of the firm, supplanting democratic principles with entrepreneurial ones in the political sphere.[28]

After spending time with women under house arrest who participated in YoNoFui's workshops, the humane practice described in the the legislative proposals was not evident to me. Sweet it was not, nor was it homey. The ongoing neglect and bureaucratic contradictions that characterize the experience of women under house arrest reflect how prisons are organized with men as the model prisoner, failing to address the gendered dimensions of childcare. House arrest relieves the state from providing food, shelter, and care. This shift, from government to maternal responsibility, uses symbolic and discursive tools that assume that women are the ideal caregivers of children and that the domestic space is their ideal site of belonging. Women under house arrest are subjected to the intersection of two institutions: motherhood and the criminal justice system. As institutions of social control, they make the state an active participant in engendering specific habits and ideologies for incarcerated mothers. Using the domestic space to complete the prison sentence works to socialize these women into the citizens and mothers they are supposed to be, imposing habits and ways of being that were "lacking" in the past.

House Arrest in Praxis

House arrest is still filled with ambiguities and contestations from the judges who have the authorization to grant it. Judges rely on reports from social workers who assess the woman's neighborhood, living space, and support network to determine how feasible home confinement would be. The confusion arises from misguided beliefs that house arrest offers a form of freedom when in fact it is another way to complete a sentence. Judges vary in their interpretations of what is allowed under home confinement. Some judges might grant permissions for daily leaves or to work from home, while others do not. Mariluz, a young mother from the Dominican Republic, requested permission to drop her son off at school; her permit was approved quickly with no questions asked. But for Denise, the request to drop her daughter off at school was approved only after she drew a detailed map of the route between her home and the school. Judges often scrutinize the most intimate aspects of a woman's life, including how she handled herself during her pregnancy, her socioeconomic standing or neighborhood, and the number of children she has ("too many" is frowned upon and constitutes a failed character).

After I interviewed women who immigrated to Argentina from Peru, Dominican Republic, Bolivia, and Spain, I found state bureaucracies that included embassies and consulates even more confusing. Camila had arrived from the Dominican Republic, and as a single mother of twins, she found herself at the prison nursery. When her twins approached the age of four, she decided to apply for house arrest to avoid separation from them. She had a cousin on the outside who agreed to help her out, and a *comadre* (comother), a term I heard many women use to refer to close friends that help raise the children. Camila described the weeks leading up to the judge's decision as incredibly grueling. She was depressed and anxious at the possibility of losing her children. When her house arrest was approved and she left prison, she suffered from panic attacks and dizziness. The city, with its buses, people, and cacophonic sounds, was overwhelming and difficult to manage. Even though the surveillance mechanisms under house arrest are not comparable to the constant visibility that women are subjected to in their cells, the prohibition of leaving the home is still a very distressing factor for women under house arrest, particularly when they have to care for small children.

While most women were diligent about the restrictions that house arrest imposed, a few tested the limits of their confinement. Claudia was under house arrest after a brief stint in prison when she arrived at the documentary workshop riding a motorcycle. Within minutes of arriving, she mentioned that after the workshop she was heading to the cinema school to post fliers renting her home to students for their movie projects. Claudia was the main caregiver of her three grandchildren and thought this would be a good way to make some money from home. Claudia struggled to understand our concern that she could lose the benefit of house arrest if found riding a motorcycle around the city and that YoNoFui could lose the ability to offer workshops to women under house arrest if women went to other places on the days of the workshop. Even though she was used to disregarding rules except her own, with time she embraced the collective and continued to attend workshops even after completing her sentence. To Claudia, this had become a space for herself.

After being part of the collective for a few years, the day came when Claudia was stopped on the streets and asked for paperwork for her motorcycle. Since she could not produce the required paperwork, the police took the motorcycle away. At the workshop, she confessed that she did not recognize herself when she chose to stay calm and let them take the motorcycle. But she kept thinking about the collective and how she was not alone. The care that Claudia found with YoNoFui was not just about healing and providing a sense of belonging. It was also about building strategies for how best to deal with the patriarchal defilement of the state. This form of radical care is unlike the care of the state: while public policies aim to domesticate women, YoNoFui offers political imaginaries that encourage women to engage in self-management practices and collective endeavors. Workshop participants collaborated, selling food staples at popular events. The textile design workshop and the book-binding workshop received orders from buyers, and in supporting women under house arrest, YoNoFui created opportunities for them to work from home and earn an income.

In November 2014, I attended another house arrest symposium. This time it was held at the Bauen Hotel, a recuperated business run collectively by its workers in the financial district of Buenos Aires. Self-management practices were precipitated after Argentina's 2001 financial crisis, during which neoliberal policies disfavored national factories and small businesses for large transnational corporations. Facing the closure of the factory they worked for, workers chose to organize among themselves and continue to run the factory in a collective manner. Veronica Gago has elsewhere called these practices baroque economies, that is, the articulation of economies that mixes logics and rationalities that tend to be portrayed (in economic and political theories) as incompatible.[29] With a similar DIY philosophy, YoNoFui emerged in 2002, first as a poetry workshop inside prison and later adding more programs both inside and outside prisons.

As with the early symposium, this event gathered judges, lawyers, social workers, women under house arrest, formerly incarcerated individuals, neighborhood collectives, and organizations against state violence to search for better answers for women under house arrest. As the concerns discussed that day began to multiply, government officials were heard whispering, "Don't complain too much or the benefit will be removed altogether," revealing how the state's care of the children had slowly morphed into a threat used against criminalized women.

One of the main sources of distress was the denial of permits women requested and the subsequent isolation they suffered. Examples of permit requests included dropping off/picking up their children from school, going to therapy or a doctor's appointment, and taking a class or workshop. Incarcerated mothers are often single heads of households, and being unable to work, to leave for grocery shopping, or to make trips to the pediatrician when the children's health is at stake is a constant source of affliction. The nominal stipend women get from the state not only reflects that women's lives are devalorized but also manifests the lack of consideration toward single mothers, who often do not rely on other sources of income. Women are faced with impossible choices: remain in a violence-stricken, drug-fueled prison nursery that provides diapers, shelter, and food, or accept the alternative of house arrest, even if that involves, at least for some, going back to an abusive household. Once under house arrest, the threat of losing this benefit if found outside the home is a very powerful and cruel tool for social control.

Immersed in a heavily male-oriented criminal justice system, incarcerated women, both in prison and under house arrest, face myriad challenges in which the patriarchal control that dictates many societal norms is indisputable.[30] Constructions of motherhood are critical sites where the sexual division of labor becomes explicit and reproductive labor is revealed as undervalued yet vital sustenance of the state. The constructions of dominant normative constraints create certain categories of mothers deemed "bad" or "inadequate" because they fail to live up to ideals of motherhood imposed through public policy.[31] These categories, however, are not reflective of the care that the children receive but are actually used to reinforce normative values of family making.

Motherhood as Institution

I met Ana in a journalism workshop, where she wrote a chronicle to make sense of her ever-confounding experience with the Argentine justice system. Her son, Bautista, born in 2012, was the first baby in Argentina registered with two mothers. In a drastic turn of events, when Bautista was six months old Ana was incarcerated, and they ended up in a prison nursery. Ana had worked for the government granting permits to nightclubs. On December 30, 2004, there was a fire at República Cromañón, a cumbia nightclub in the Balvanera neighborhood, and 194 people died. Over 1,400 people were injured, largely because some of the emergency exits were locked. Ana had been demoted from inspector to desk clerk because she had repeatedly warned her superiors that understaffing prevented the city government from ensuring venues were safe. Regardless of the mountains of paperwork that proved she was not responsible for this systemic oversight, Ana was found guilty of neglect and sentenced to two years of incarceration. Her application for house arrest was denied on the basis that her son had another mother, Gabriela, who could take care of him. But Bautista went to prison, incarcerated as an infant, because Ana was breastfeeding him, and Gabriela and Ana, despite both being his mother, were not interchangeable caregivers.

With this particular case, the court, as an institution, proved to be ill-equipped to understand mothering outside of a heterosexual framework. Here, the study of motherhood is relevant in two important ways: on the one hand, it exposes assumptions that women, and not men, are the individuals who should be in charge of child-rearing, and on the other hand, it proves that behaviors that challenge institutions, such as same-sex marriage, are still considered deviant, or criminal, despite their legalization.[32] Had Ana been married to a man, not a woman, the assumption that the baby could stay at home with the dad would not have been made, and Ana would most likely have been granted house arrest.

While incarcerated, Ana participated in YoNoFui's pinhole photography workshop, which collectively produced a photo exhibit titled *Iluminaciones*. During this time, Ana also appealed the rejection of her house arrest application and won. Under house arrest, Ana joined the journalism workshop in YoNoFui, offered in the central neighborhood of Palermo. The radical care YoNoFui offers, aimed at changing the structural conditions under which criminalized women reimagine their lives, is relevant not only to social movements in Latin America but also to discourses of alternatives to incarceration worldwide. Care, in this women's collective, involves the reliance on others to inform the process of self-determination.

As others have shown, alternatives to incarceration can often expand rather than contract the net of social control.[33] The fact that prison nurseries exist only in women's prisons reinforces the misconception that reproductive labor is a predominantly women's enterprise. It also points to the need to make visible the ways in which "institutional motherhood revives and renews all other institutions," so that those aspects of women's lives that contribute to patriarchal structures can be identified.[34] Carol Smart argues that motherhood is an institution that *presents* itself as a natural outcome of biologically given gender differences, as a natural consequence of (hetero)sexual activity, and as a natural manifestation of an innate female characteristic: the maternal instinct.[35] By paying attention to the expectations attached to mothering, the material conditions and constraints placed on women as they carry the responsibility of bearing and rearing children become more apparent.[36] As Adrienne Rich points out, "The experience of maternity and the experience of sexuality have both been channeled to serve male interests."[37] Smart provides a revisionary history of motherhood, writing that there has been "such a heavyweight machinery brought to bear on women to force them into motherhood [that] we must ask why these measures were necessary if motherhood itself was simply a biological process like aging."[38] Smart presents a Foucaldian analysis that connects the naturalization of motherhood as an institution with the institutionalization and criminalization of sexual norms as techniques of power.

In *The History of Sexuality*, Foucault traces how reproductive intercourse was actively "naturalized" during the Victorian era and how other forms of sexual activity became defined as unnatural and perverse.[39] Alongside this particular construction of sexuality, pregnancy and motherhood were equally "naturalized" to satisfy very particular ideals. While folk knowledges of contraceptive and barrier methods were commonly and widely used, during the Victorian era these folk knowledges were "forgotten," and "English upper-class brides of the late eighteenth century, trained to hide any interest in sexuality, warned not to listen to the gossip of servants, and cut off from the larger female community, were probably more ignorant of the workings of their bodies than their grandmothers had ever been."[40] Working-class women, on the other hand, were being forced to interrupt their breastfeeding as it clashed with the demands of labor. With the suppression of contraceptives and the criminalization of abortion, motherhood became increasingly unavoidable while at the same time hailed as a woman's greatest achievement. Unsurprisingly, women who deviated from these Victorian ideals were criminalized, pathologized, or both.[41]

Anthropologist Lynn M. Morgan recounts how, throughout the late nineteenth century and early twentieth century, the collection of embryos created a further categorization of human development that redefined when human life begins.[42] This new conception of human development interpellated women to care for the fetus from the moment of conception. The scrutiny of women expanded not only to monitor women's behavior but also to introduce techniques of monitoring into women's bodies. A contemporary example that illustrates this dimension of policing was reported recently in Wisconsin when, according to the "fetal protection" law, a pregnant woman can be arrested at a health clinic during a prenatal checkup and convicted if she has a past history of drug addiction.[43] Motherhood highlights the normative constraints that affect women's lives today, and the carceral system enforces these constraints even more firmly. As the criminal justice system administers punishment on mothers who break the law, motherhood as a category of social analysis makes explicit the punitive consequences for deviating from a dominant view of gender roles.

Sociologist Lynne Haney explored the practices and uses of motherhood in a prison designed for mothers and children in the United States. In her study she concluded that, when implemented in this particular institutional space, this promising alternative ended up undermining, subsuming, and punishing motherhood, often in quite contradictory ways. Women were instructed on specific ways to reprimand their children and on specific rules on when to allow children to snack between meals and when to watch television. Troubled by their constant exposure, women "surrounded their bunk beds with sheets, creating a cave-like area where they could retreat with their children."[44] The institutional processes of control and domination that operate in traditional prisons do not vanish in prison nurseries. Rather, they are reconstituted to reflect dominant ideas about gender, race, and class.[45] Motherhood in this prison was an expression of true intimacy and a sign of potential pathology, a model of selflessness and a sign of selfishness. It was represented both as a way to absolve oneself of those crimes and as a symptom of those crimes.[46] These contradictions draw attention to a need to revisit motherhood as an institution that is often naturalized and romanticized but also very much punitive.

While these interventions and critiques of motherhood emerged from groups of women belonging to distinct socioeconomic and racial backgrounds in the United States, in Argentina Las Madres de Plaza de Mayo were highly influential in symbolizing the political terrains of motherhood. Las Madres have historically been regarded as beacons of human rights while at the same time been referred to as *las locas* who would not compromise under the terrorism of a dictatorial regime. Their work was not meant to eradicate motherhood from women's lives but, rather, to change the conditions under which motherhood was being conceived while holding the state accountable for its terrorism.

Stratifying Motherhood

Broad concepts such as motherhood that engage a wide variety of ideologies, experiences, and practices run the risk, if uncontextualized, of rendering issues of power invisible.[47] The social context of motherhood can reveal the often unequal relations of power between men and women, dominant and subordinate groups, colonizers and colonized.[48] To understand the practice of motherhood, it is relevant to first understand that "a feminist praxis is not limited to gender issues, but rather sees gender as part and parcel of a number of contingent issues, such as race, sexuality, class, and able- and disabled-bodiness, insisting that these cannot be viewed in isolation."[49] Indigenous social movements have been pivotal in addressing how colonial violence is always entwined with the carceral state, making prisons necessary institutions to maintain settler sovereignty.[50]

The house arrest of Milagro Sala is an exceptional case that makes evident the unequal power relationships between the Argentine state and Indigenous communities. Milagro Sala is an Indigenous leader and activist who founded the collective Túpac Amaru in the northern province of Jujuy. In 2016 she was detained on the grounds of inciting social unrest and has been incarcerated ever since. In July 2017 she was hospitalized after carrying out a hunger strike for being placed in solitary confinement in a cell without a window. In 2018 she was granted house arrest due to concerns for her declining health. Adding to the arbitrariness that characterizes house arrest, police constantly surveil the house where Milagro is serving time, and she has a strict schedule for visiting hours, two regulations that are not part of the stipulations of house arrest. While the decisions of who is approved for house arrest are discretionary to each judge, there is a pattern of harsher punishment for women who deviate from middle-class values (homeowners in a heterosexual marriage), such as migrant, transgender, and Indigenous women. Further, persecutions of political leaders that contest neoliberal policies are not unique to

Argentina. In Brazil it was Marielle Franco, a Black feminist and socialist leader, who was punished by the mandates of the neoliberal state; she was shot multiple times and died in March 2018. Berta Cáceres, an environmentalist and Indigenous leader in Honduras, was also shot to death in March 2016. These persecutions across Latin America bring to light the continuum of institutional and gender-based violence that women experience, as well as the historical linkages between settler colonialism and the carceral state. Milagro Sala's life is endangered. She embodies the way that interlocking systems of power impact the bodies of Indigenous women, who are surveilled and punished more harshly for their condition of being women, Indigenous, and poor.

Mothers of all races, classes, and ages are subjected to patriarchal control, however differently they may experience this control.[51] Poor women and women of color are particularly subjected to invasive forms of control and assaults on their rights to mother. For example, between 2006 and 2010, 150 incarcerated women in California were unlawfully sterilized.[52] Middle-class women face other hurdles: lack of access to legitimate family planning technologies, such as abortion services, or lack of accommodations in their workplace for breastfeeding. Faye D. Ginsburg and Rayna Rapp discuss "stratified reproduction," originally coined by Shellee Colen, as "the power relations by which some categories of people are empowered to nurture and reproduce, while others are disempowered."[53] This stratified reproduction sheds light on which lives are privileged and whose futures are discouraged. Situating motherhood in prisons highlights the current workings of stratified reproduction and the ways in which institutions are complicit in this process. Further, it also reveals new expressions of neoliberal governmentalities that not only execute violence on women's bodies but also redefine the ways in which the state, implementing cost-effective policies, cares for incarcerated women.

Sociologists Constanza Tabbush and Maria Florencia Gentile describe in their study of Argentine prisons how mothering is a key aspect of many incarcerated women's emotional lives, shaped and constrained by prison regulations as well as cultural expectations. Prison cultures themselves are rife with emotions attached to mothering, positioning it as one of the main social objects that regulate a prison's informal moral economies. For instance, in women's prisons, infanticide, the killing of a child, is considered to be the worst crime a woman can commit (in men's prisons, sex offenders are similarly maligned). As such, other women informally penalize it in the form of verbal abuse or mistreatment in everyday exchanges. In the context of prison, as in the world outside its walls, motherhood distributes specific material and symbolic resources, whether in the form of rewards or as negative sanctions.[54]

Motherhood is central to the critical inquiry of prisons, not peripheral, invisible, or an afterthought in a system created for men, because the production of knowledge is in itself gendered. Dominant systems of knowledge used for the design of prisons and policy making reflect masculine views of the social world that leave out the richness and complexities involved in child-rearing practices. Michelle Rosaldo warned anthropologists that ignoring gender asymmetry blinds us to the sorts of facts we must understand and change and instead proposed that what appears as "natural" must be understood as a by-product of "non-necessary institutional arrangements that could be addressed through political struggle and, with effort, undermined."[55]

Concluding Remarks

Institutional confinement extends beyond the prison and has taken various forms, such as homeless shelters, the asylum, detention centers, and prison camps. As women and children move from the institution into home detention, certain legacies of the penal system move into the home as well.[56] However, other types of institutions, such as neighborhood and women's collectives, offer new forms of sociality that redefine imprisonment, family, and care. YoNoFui promotes solidarity and acknowledgment of differences in their community-led space, allowing for alternative subjectivities to prosper. More important, the collective contests house arrest as a condition of isolation and instead cares for a community that reconfigures the notion of neoliberal governmentality as an enterprise in the search for profit. As Veronica Gago has explained, the informalization of the economy emerges primarily from the strength of the unemployed and of women, who enact from below the potentials found in the receding effects of neoliberalism.[57] Rather than coexisting in isolation, YoNoFui is interested in developing communal ties and strengthening collective efforts against institutional violence.

Still, the violence that characterizes the carceral state has impacts that defy the imagination. Mariela was a member of YoNoFui who participated in the textile design workshop. She and her two adult daughters, one of whom had a newborn, were under house arrest. In 2016, a van from the penitentiary picked them up to take them to court to sign an *abreviado*, a legal agreement similar to a plea bargain. Mariela and her daughters were part of the nearly 50 percent of incarcerated women who are pretrial, that is, detained without a conviction. Women sign *abreviados*, relinquishing the right to go to trial, in the hope of accelerating the process. When the van that was taking them to court crashed, Mariela died, and her two daughters, including the newborn, were hospitalized. The baby died some days later. The delivery of Mariela's body was delayed because they had to wait for the judicial order to remove her ankle bracelet. The penitentiary stated that the women had some sort of metal baton, and the van crashed as the women executed an attack. Everybody who knew Mariela insisted this could never be the case. Yet this is one of many instances in which the criminal justice system favors the interests of the penitentiary over the welfare of incarcerated women. The stigma and invisibilization that incarcerated people endure made her death just one more of the many bureaucratic procedures that legitimize the carceral state.

While it is uncertain how the praxis of house arrest will develop in the coming years, certain constraints are already easily identifiable. Instances of radical care that work to compensate for the erosion of the welfare state are not found in the public policies addressed to care for women and children. Instead, it is through grassroots efforts and collectives, such as YoNoFui, that women create a supportive environment where they can advocate for their futures. What could be defined with further detail and more precision are the specific transactions in which the state punishes through neglect while labeling this management of social control a humane form of sentencing that protects the interests of children. The institutional violence that incarcerated women endure, whether in prison or under house arrest, replicates, albeit in alternative forms, the gender-based violence that is prevalent in the Argentine state and much of Latin America today. While prison strikes and feminist social movements can change the conditions under which women live, it is ultimately the public policies put in place, such as house arrest for women, that can shed light on the material consequences that ideologies of gender and motherhood have on women's lives. Attending to those who push the boundaries of such ideologies, the deviant mothers themselves can provide much foresight when considering alternatives to incarceration, gender roles, and family ideals.

Notes

I am indebted to the generosity of YoNoFui and all their participants who contributed to my research. This work was funded by the American Association of University Women's American Dissertation Fellowship, the Dr. Clyde Snow Fund for Latin American Studies, and the Latinx Scholars Graduate School Fellowship. I extend my gratitude to editors Hi'ilei Julia Hobart and Tamara Kneese for their labor in producing this special issue. To the anonymous reviewers who carefully commented on earlier versions of this article, I am thankful for your suggestions. To Maria Elena Garcia, Danny Hoffman, Ann Anagnost, and Janelle Taylor, I thank you for your guidance and support. Any oversights or mistakes are my own.

1. In the United States, for example, eleven states provide prison nurseries: California, Delaware, Illinois, Indiana, Nebraska, New York, Ohio, South Dakota, Texas, Washington, and West Virginia.

2. Cornell, *Beyond Accommodation*, xxvii.

3. Barrancos, *Mujeres, entre la casa y la plaza*; Federici, *Caliban and the Witch*; Tarducci, "Hitos de la militancia lesbofeminista."

4. Gilmore, *Golden Gulag*, 194.

5. Fisher, *Mothers of the Disappeared*.

6. Nadasen, "Domestic Work, Neoliberalism, and Transforming Labor."

7. Carlen, *Women's Imprisonment*.

8. Sufrin, *Jailcare*.

9. Bandyopadhyay, *Everyday Life in a Prison*.

10. Aretxaga, *Shattering Silence*; Pemberton, "Enforcing Gender"; Rhodes, "Towards an Anthropology of Prisons."

11. Except for Ana, all names of research participants have been changed.

12. Corda, *Encarcelamientos por delitos relacionados*, 29.

13. Belknap, *Invisible Woman*; Corda, *Encarcelamientos por delitos relacionados*.

14. Ong, *Neoliberalism as Exception*, 4.

15. Ong, *Neoliberalism as Exception*, 6.

16. Feldman, *Formations of Violence*; Garland, "Sociological Perspectives on Punishment"; Law, *Resistance behind Bars*; Rius, "Pedagogy of the Spiral."

17. Alexander, "Newest Jim Crow."

18. Bernstein, *All Alone in the World*; Comfort, *Doing Time Together*.

19. UNICEF, *Mujeres privadas de libertad*.

20. Howe, *Punish and Critique*.

21. Smart, "Deconstructing Motherhood," 37.

22. Vallejos, "Los dramas del arresto domiciliario."

23. For more details on mothers' incarceration in Argentina, see Tabbush and Gentile, "Emotions behind Bars." For more details on poor women in Buenos Aires, see Geldstein, "Working-Class Mothers as Economic Providers."

24. Centro de Estudios Legales y Sociales (CELS), *Mujeres en prisión*, 27.

25. Sufrin, *Jailcare*.

26. Ferguson and Gupta, "Spatializing States," 982–83.

27. Ferguson and Gupta, "Spatializing States," 989, quoting Burchell, "Liberal Government and Techniques of the Self."

28. Brown, "We Are All Democrats Now."

29. Gago, *Neoliberalism from Below*.

30. Haney, *Offending Women*; McCorkel, *Breaking Women*.

31. Smart, "Deconstructing Motherhood," 39.

32. Same-sex marriage was legalized in Argentina in July 2010. It was the first country in Latin America and the second in the Americas to allow same-sex marriage nationwide.

33. Platt, *Beyond These Walls*.

34. Rich, *Of Woman Born*, 45.

35. Smart, "Deconstructing Motherhood."

36. Federici, *Revolution at Point Zero*.

37. Rich, *Of Woman Born*, 42. In this work, Rich describes how during the 1970s feminists in the United States perceived motherhood as a burden that contributed to the oppression of women while also considering it a source of power and a way to engage with communal ties and activism. See also Chase and Rogers, *Mothers and Children*, 6–8. For example, *Mom's Apple Pie* is a documentary that recounts the struggles and hardships that lesbian women faced in the 1970s in the United States as they were stripped of their parental rights due to their sexual orientation. It also features interviews with founders of the Lesbian Rights Project (now the National Center for Lesbian Rights) and the Seattle-based Lesbian Mothers' National Defense Fund who throughout these years organized, assisted, counseled, and supported hundreds of women facing custody battles (Laine and Reinstein, *Mom's Apple Pie*).

38. Smart, "Deconstructing Motherhood," 38.

39. Foucault, *Introduction*.

40. Smart, "Deconstructing Motherhood," 40.

41. Ehrenreich and English, *For Her Own Good*; Smart, "Deconstructing Motherhood," 42.

42. Morgan, *Icons of Life*.

43. Alicia Beltran was arrested after admitting a past struggle with Percocet. The fact that she was clean at the time was not enough proof that she could control herself. Silva, "Shackled and Pregnant."

44. Haney, "Motherhood as Punishment," 116.

45. Dillon, *Fugitive Life*.

46. Haney, "Motherhood as Punishment."

47. Butler, *Gender Trouble*; Foucault, *Order of Things*.

48. Chase and Rogers, *Mothers and Children*.

49. Dubrofsky and Magnet, "Feminist Surveillance Studies," 3.

50. Dhillon, "Indigenous Girls and the Violence of Settler Colonial Policing."

51. Ortner, "Is Female to Male as Nature Is to Culture?"

52. Dr. James Heinrich defended the sterilizations as "cost-effective" by stating, "Over a 10-year period, that isn't a huge amount of money, compared to what you save in welfare paying for those unwanted children." However, victims stated otherwise: "He made me feel like a bad mother if I didn't do it" ("California Prisons Were Illegally Sterilizing Female Inmates").

53. Ginsburg and Rapp, introduction, 3; and Colen, "With Respect and Feelings," 46–70.

54. Tabbush and Gentile, "Emotions behind Bars."

55. Rosaldo, "Use and Abuse of Anthropology," 11–12.

56. Caimari, "Whose Criminals Are These?"

57. Gago, *Neoliberalism from Below*.

References

Alexander, Michelle. "The Newest Jim Crow." *New York Times*, November 8, 2018. www.nytimes.com/2018/11/08/opinion/sunday/criminal-justice-reforms-race-technology.html.

Aretxaga, Begoña. *Shattering Silence: Women, Nationalism, and Political Subjectivity in Northern Ireland*. Princeton, NJ: Princeton University Press, 1997.

Bandyopadhyay, Mahuya. *Everyday Life in a Prison: Confinement, Surveillance, Resistance*. Hyderabad, India: Orient Blackswan, 2010.

Barrancos, Dora. *Mujeres, entre la casa y la plaza* (*Women: Between the House and the Square*). Buenos Aires: Editorial Sudamericana, 2008.

Belknap, Joanne. *The Invisible Woman: Gender, Crime, and Justice*. 2001. 3rd ed. Belmont, CA: Thomson/Wadsworth, 2006.

Bernstein, Nell. *All Alone in the World: Children of the Incarcerated*. New York: New Press, 2005.

Brown, Wendy. "We Are All Democrats Now." *Kettering Review* 29, no. 1 (2011): 44–52.

Burchell, Graham. "Liberal Government and Techniques of the Self." In *Foucault and Political Reason: Liberalism, Neoliberalism, and Rationalities of the Government*, edited by Andrew Barry, Thomas Osborne, and Nikolas Rose, 19–36. Chicago: University of Chicago Press, 1996.

Butler, Judith. *Gender Trouble: Feminism and the Subversion of Identity*. 1990; repr., New York: Routledge, 2006.

Caimari, Lila M. "Whose Criminals Are These? Church, State, and Patronatos and the Rehabilitation of Female Convicts (Buenos Aires, 1890–1940)." *Americas* 54, no. 2 (1997): 185–208.

Carlen, Pat. *Women's Imprisonment: A Study of Social Control*. London: Routledge, 1983.

Centro de Estudios Legales y Sociales (CELS), Ministerio Público de la Defensa de la Nación, Procuración Penitenciaria de la Nación. *Mujeres en prisión: Los alcances del castigo (Women in Prison: The Scope of Punishment)*. Buenos Aires: Siglo Veintiuno, 2011.

Chase, Susan E., and Mary F. Rogers. *Mothers and Children: Feminist Analyses and Personal Narratives*. New Brunswick, NJ: Rutgers University Press, 2001.

Colen, Shellee. "'With Respect and Feelings': Voices of West Indian Child Care Workers in New York City." In *All American Women: Lines That Divide, Ties That Bind*, edited by Johnnetta B. Cole, 46–70. New York: Free Press, 1986.

Comfort, Megan. *Doing Time Together: Love and Family in the Shadow of the Prison*. Chicago: University of Chicago Press, 2008.

Corda, Raul Alejandro. *Encarcelamientos por delitos relacionados con estupefacientes en Argentina. Sistemas sobrecargados. Leyes de drogas y cárceles en América Latina (Imprisonment for Drug-Related Crimes in Argentina: Overloaded Systems: Drug Laws and Prisons in Latin America)*. Transnational Institute, 2010. www.wola .org/sites/default/files/downloadable/Drug%20Policy/2011/Spanish/sistemas _sobrecargados-resumen_argentina-web.pdf.

Cornell, Drucilla. *Beyond Accommodation: Ethical Feminism, Deconstruction, and the Law*. 1991; repr., New York: Routledge, 1999.

Dhillon, Jaskiran. "Indigenous Girls and the Violence of Settler Colonial Policing." *Decolonization: Indigeneity, Education, and Society* 4, no. 2 (2015): 1–31.

Dillon, Stephen. *Fugitive Life: The Queer Politics of the Prison State*. Durham, NC: Duke University Press, 2018.

Dubrofsky, Rachel E., and Shoshana Emielle Magnet. "Feminist Surveillance Studies: Critical Interventions." In *Feminist Surveillance Studies*, edited by Rachel E. Dubrofsky and Shoshana Amielle Magnet, 1–17. Durham, NC: Duke University Press, 2015.

Ehrenreich, Barbara, and English Deidre. *For Her Own Good: One Hundred Fifty Years of the Experts' Advice to Women*. 1978; repr., New York: Anchor Books Doubleday, 1989.

Federici, Silvia. *Caliban and the Witch: Women, the Body, and Primitive Accumulation*. Brooklyn, NY: Autonomedia, 2004.

Federici, Silvia. *Revolution at Point Zero: Housework, Reproduction, and Feminist Struggle*. Oakland, CA: PM, 2012.

Feldman, Allen. *Formations of Violence: The Narrative of the Body and Political Terror in Northern Ireland*. Chicago: University of Chicago Press, 1991.

Ferguson, James, and Akhil Gupta. "Spatializing States: Toward an Ethnography of Neoliberal Governmentality." *American Ethnologist* 29, no. 4 (2002): 981–1002.

Fisher, Josephine. *Mothers of the Disappeared*. Boston: South End, 1989.

Foucault, Michel. *An Introduction*. Vol. 1 of *The History of Sexuality*, translated by Robert Hurley. London: Penguin, 1990.

Foucault, Michel. *The Order of Things: An Archaeology of the Human Sciences*. New York: Vintage Books, 1973.

Gago, Veronica. *Neoliberalism from Below: Popular Pragmatics and Baroque Economies*. Durham, NC: Duke University Press, 2014.

Garland, David. "Sociological Perspectives on Punishment." *Crime and Justice* 14, no. 14 (1991): 115–65.

Geldstein, Rosa N. "Working Class Mothers as Economic Providers and Heads of Families in Buenos Aires." *Reproductive Health Matters* 2, no. 4 (1994): 55–64.

Gilmore, Ruth Wilson. *Golden Gulag: Prisons, Surplus, Crisis, and Opposition in Globalizing California.* Berkeley: University of California Press, 2007.

Ginsburg, Faye D., and Rayna Rapp. Introduction to *Conceiving the New World Order: The Global Politics of Reproduction,* edited by Faye D. Ginsburg and Rayna Rapp, 1–17. Berkeley: University of California Press, 1991.

Haney, Lynne. "Motherhood as Punishment: The Case of Parenting in Prison." *Signs* 39, no. 1 (2013): 105–30.

Haney, Lynne. *Offending Women: Power, Punishment, and the Regulation of Desire.* Berkeley: University of California Press, 2010.

Howe, Adrian. *Punish and Critique: Towards a Feminist Analysis of Penality.* London: Routledge, 1994.

Laine, Jody, Shan Ottey, and Shan Reinstein, dirs. 2006. *Mom's Apple Pie: The History of the Lesbian Mother's Custody Battle.* Narrated by Kate Clinton. San Francisco: Frameline USA.

Law, Victoria. *Resistance behind Bars: The Struggles of Incarcerated Women.* Oakland, CA: PM, 2009.

McCorkel, Jill. *Breaking Women: Gender, Race, and the New Politics of Imprisonment.* New York: New York University Press, 2010.

Morgan, Lynn M. *Icons of Life: A Cultural History of Human Embryos.* Berkeley: University of California Press, 2009.

Nadasen, Premilla. "Domestic Work, Neoliberalism, and Transforming Labor." In "Gender, Justice, and Neoliberal Transformations," edited by Elizabeth Bernstein and Janet R. Jakobsen. Special issue, *Scholar and Feminist Online* 11, nos. 1–2 (Fall 2012/Spring 2013). sfonline.barnard.edu/gender-justice-and-neoliberal-transformations/domestic-work-neoliberalism-and-transforming-labor/.

Ong, Aihwa. *Neoliberalism as Exception: Mutations in Citizenship and Sovereignty.* Durham, NC: Duke University Press, 2006.

Ohlheiser, Abby. "California Prisons Were Illegally Sterilizing Female Inmates." *Atlantic,* July 7, 2013. www.theatlantic.com/national/archive/2013/07/california-prisons-were-illegally-sterilizing-female-inmates/313591/.

Ortner, Sherry B. "Is Female to Male as Nature Is to Culture?" In *Woman, Culture, and Society,* edited by Michelle Z. Rosaldo and Louise Lamphere, 68–87. Stanford, CA: Stanford University Press, 1974.

Pemberton, Sarah. "Enforcing Gender: The Constitution of Sex and Gender in Prison Regimes." *Signs* 39, no. 1 (2013): 151–75.

Platt, Tony. *Beyond These Walls: Rethinking Crime and Punishment in the United States.* New York: St. Martin's, 2018.

Rhodes, Lorna. "Towards an Anthropology of Prisons." *Annual Review of Anthropology* 30 (1991): 65–83.

Rich, Adrienne. *Of Woman Born: Motherhood as Experience and Institution.* 1976; repr., New York: Norton, 1995.

Rius, Marisa Belausteguigoitia. "The Pedagogy of the Spiral: Intimacy and Captivity in a Women's Prison." In *The Global and the Intimate,* edited by Geraldine Pratt and Victoria Rosner, 243–66. New York: Columbia University Press, 2012.

Rosaldo, Michelle Z. "The Use and Abuse of Anthropology: Reflections on Feminism and Cross-Cultural Understanding." In *Feminist Anthropology: A Reader,* edited by Ellen Lewin, 107–28. Malden, MA: Blackwell, 2006.

Silva, Daniella. "Shackled and Pregnant: Wis. Case Challenges 'Fetal Protection

Law.'" NBC News, October 24, 2013. usnews.nbcnews.com/_news/2013/10/24/21117142-shackled-and-pregnant-wis-case-challenges-fetal-protection-law.

Smart, Carol. "Deconstructing Motherhood." In *Good Enough Mothering? Feminist Perspectives on Lone Motherhood*, edited by Elizabeth Bortolaia Silva, 37–57. London: Routledge, 1996.

Sufrin, Carolyn. *Jailcare: Finding the Safety Net for Women behind Bars*. Oakland: University of California Press, 2017.

Tabbush, Constanza, and Maria Florencia Gentile. "Emotions behind Bars: The Regulation of Mothering in Argentine Jails." *Signs* 39, no. 1 (2013): 131–49.

Tarducci, Mónica. "Hitos de la militancia lesbofeminista de Buenos Aires (1984–1995)" ("Hits of Lesbofeminist Activism in Buenos Aires (1984–1995)"). In *Feminismo, lesbianismo y maternidad en Argentina (Feminism, Lesbianism, and Motherhood in Argentina)*, edited by Mónica Tarducci, 37–59. Buenos Aires: Librería de Mujeres Editoras, 2014.

UNICEF. *Mujeres privadas de libertad: Limitaciones al encarcelamiento de las mujeres embarazadas o con hijas/os menores de edad (Women Deprived of Freedom: Limitations to Women's Imprisonment Pregnant or with Small Children)*. 2009. www.academia.edu/8158095/Mujeres-presas.

Vallejos, Soledad. "Los dramas del arresto domiciliario" ("The Dramas of House Arrest"). *Página 12*, October 31, 2009. www.pagina12.com.ar/diario/sociedad/3-134423-2009-10-31.html.

Suspicion and/as Radical (Care)

Looking Closer at Vaccine Hesitancy
in Postcolonial Barbados

Nicole Charles

This article embraces care's historically antithetical meanings as it examines the caring work of human papillomavirus (HPV) vaccination delivery and suspicion toward it in contemporary Barbados. Looking closer at care, the impetus to care, and the consequences of refusing that care, it wrestles with the (risks of) not-doing and the affective feelings of suspicion that exist for Afro-Barbadian parents who might refuse the care of the HPV vaccine for their adolescent children amid an epidemic of cervical cancer in the developing world. How might the rationale, or perceived rationale, behind care affect the ways that care is both offered and received? What can suspicion toward biomedical and technological forms of care teach us about histories of risk, biotechnologies, and the imperative to care in the postcolonial world? What might it mean to embody protection by means of suspicion toward these very medicotechnological deployments of care and risk? What are the stakes of affective attachments that refuse this care? I offer these as framing questions to contextualize the following discussion on Afro-Barbadian parents' suspicion around the HPV vaccine in postcolonial Barbados.

Before exploring parents' suspicions, this piece begins with a technological history of the HPV vaccine and the socioeconomic context in which it was introduced in Barbados in 2014. I then provide a brief genealogical overview of the language of risk and the use of statistical risk assessment in the history of health care to map how risk logics and the bio-logic of biopower have contentiously coincided around the technology of vaccines and the care they espouse to provide. Highlighting the manifold politics of Black female sexuality, medical imperialism, care, and

Social Text 142 · Vol. 38, No. 1 · March 2020

DOI 10.1215/01642472-7971115 © 2020 Duke University Press

protection that inhere within Afro-Barbadian parents' claims to suspicion around the HPV vaccine, I then offer a reconsideration of what it means to both care and be suspicious of (the care from) this vaccine in a place such as Barbados and amid popular understandings of vaccination refusal in the western world.

The HPV Vaccine in Barbados

With over one hundred different strains, HPV is a species-specific DNA virus and the most common sexually transmitted disease worldwide. While most HPV infections are asymptomatic and clear without treatment, persistent infection with high-risk strains of HPV can develop into precancerous lesions, cervical cancer, head and neck cancers, and genital cancers.[1] The Caribbean is currently among the top four highest subregions in the world with respect to the incidence of cervical cancer and has the highest burden of HPV in the Americas.[2] In Barbados specifically, cervical cancer is the second most common female cancer in women fifteen to forty-four years of age, and it is estimated that forty-four new cervical cancer cases are diagnosed annually in a population of less than three hundred thousand persons.[3]

As a medical technology invested in protecting against HPV and its associated diseases, the HPV vaccine Gardasil is both a profit-making and a risk-managing device. At US$150 per shot, it provides a lucrative market for the pharmaceutical company Merck while also representing a scientific breakthrough as one of the first-to-be-developed preventive cancer vaccines.[4] Often referred to as the cervical cancer vaccine, it is most popularly advertised as providing protection for young women against HPV and the risks of cervical cancer posed by the virus. But because HPV is a sexually transmitted disease, the vaccine further participates in an economy of biopolitical surveillance concerned with caring for and managing the risks of sex itself and thus should also be understood to prevent disease while constituting markets of risk and risk management and the surveillance of those to whom this risk attaches. In the context of Barbados, as articulated to me by Afro-Barbadian parents, nurses, and teenagers alike, these risks appear to attach disproportionately to Black adolescent girls' bodies and their sexuality.

Through the combined efforts of pharmaceutical organizations, international public health organizations, philanthropic agencies, and the Barbadian government, the HPV vaccine was introduced in Barbados as part of a national vaccination program in January 2014 for girls ten to twelve years old.[5] According to senior medical officers at the Barbadian Ministry of Health, dismal uptake rates of just below 20 percent at the end of 2014 alongside growing public commentary and concern over the vaccine quickly indicated the prevalence of HPV vaccine hesitancy across the island. In Barbados, both within and outside the biomedical community, much speculation has since existed around the reasons for parents' hesitancy, from theories about parents' ignorance, miseducation, and/or distrust in science to the widespread belief that it is a pervasive cultural concern around respectability, premature adolescent (female) sex, and the immunization's relationship to sex that dissuades many from accepting it for their children, and specifically for their daughters. Rather than seeking to determine the underlying factors behind Barbadian parents' hesitancy toward the HPV vaccine, the research from which this article derives sought to understand how Barbadians expressed their ambivalence toward the vaccine. This brought insight into some of the histories that comprised parents' concerns and emphasized the affective nature of suspicion, that is, less an active form of resistance and more an embodied response to the vaccine and its complex entanglements within global biomedical, pharmaceutical, and state assemblages.[6]

Suspicion that surrounds the HPV vaccine and its administration in Barbados, I argue, converges on the entangled factors of care, profit, science, Black female sexuality, and risk. Conjoined through colonial and postcolonial biopolitical techniques and technologies, these are factors that, in the colonial history of the Caribbean, have long warranted suspicion. Contextualizing Barbadian parents' suspicion toward the HPV vaccine and its administration thus requires an understanding of how these fraught politics of risk, care, and biotechnologies like vaccines have come into being in coconstitutive ways that underlie the capitalist economy within which the HPV vaccine and the caring work of HPV vaccine delivery exist today.

A Brief History of Risk, Care, and Vaccination

In the 1980s, sociologist Ulrich Beck famously coined the term *risk society* to refer to the widespread social preoccupation with and intensive management of risk across industrial societies.[7] As a modern concept, risk refers to "calculating the incalculable, colonizing the future," in which danger and peril are associated less with demons, nature, and gods and more with "*un*natural, human-made, manufactured uncertainties and hazards."[8] The history of risk, however, precedes these contemporary understandings, originating within the financial realm of transnational maritime insurance and commercialism. Within seventeenth- and eighteenth-century maritime history (and, indeed, maritime slavery), risk referred to a material and corporeal "financial instrument for coping with the mere *possibility* of peril, hazard or danger."[9] To cope with the natural "perils of the seas" and/or an "act of God," colonial merchants would purchase financial compensation or insurance on their risks (including human risks of the enslaved) in an effort to manage the uncertainties of their futures.[10]

As the concept of risk became popularized in the English language from the late eighteenth century (coinciding with rise of capitalism), so too did understandings of risk as something at once material, extreme, immaterial, and in need of quantification and management. Across Europe and the United States, risk management mushroomed in the form of new financial institutions, stock markets, savings accountants, and insurance companies, the latter of which eventually began adopting statistical approaches to mathematically predict chronic disease susceptibilities of prospective policyholders.[11] During this time, risk discourse and theorization also entered into the arena of medicine, with statistical aggregations increasingly being used to scientifically and mathematically quantify uncertainty around disease transmission. By the 1830s, statistics had entered squarely into the field of public health, drawn upon for its ability to evaluate and diagnose the efficacy of medical treatment and, for the first time in modern history, to enable doctors, hygienists, and medical administrators to transcend a long-standing reliance on individual cases to attend to those of the population deemed most at risk. Moreover, statistics enabled doctors to quantify, calculate, and control probabilities around diseases and to advise on the impact of social and environmental factors and sanitation measures.[12]

By the nineteenth century, risk assessment was also prevalent within the realm of biomedicine, where it was used to evaluate the potential dangers of new medical innovations that themselves have always spawned their own risks, questions about efficacy, and social understandings of how these risks might be mitigated.[13] Medical historians have detailed how these multiple configurations of risk, probability, and care and competing beliefs about a progressive modernity illustratively converged across class around interventions such as the selective use of anesthesia in Europe in the 1840s, the contraceptive pill, and vaccines—disputes over which can be traced as far back as eighteenth-century debates over smallpox inoculation in England.[14] Indeed, while public health concerns around vaccination refusal have heightened within the past decade, especially with regard to the resurgence of vaccine-preventable communicable diseases in North America and Europe, as Nik Brown incisively notes, "vaccination [was] from its very incipient opening moments . . . inherently a precarious political affair underpinning a new biopolitics of population vitality, statehood and colonialism."[15] In addition to early European concerns around smallpox variolation, skepticism over the clinical evidence for the bacille Calmette-Guerin (BCG) tuberculosis vaccine in France and Germany and related concerns around the role that public BCG vaccination campaigns in the 1950s and 1960s British Caribbean played in reinvigorating the British Empire exemplify the continued tenuous history of vaccination through the twentieth century.[16] Across these examples, the rights of scientists, medical professionals, and/or states to subject individuals to the risks of vaccination is rationalized by diminishing risk at the level of the population, and the construction of social risk factors and "at-risk" groups is drawn on to justify the then unknown risk of vaccines.[17]

Central to these aforementioned logics of risk reduction is the biologic of biopower, described by Foucault as the power over life. Vaccines, like other reproductive technologies, act simultaneously on biopower's two poles, in that the anatomopolitics, or the disciplining and objectifying of individual bodies, is articulated alongside the biopolitical collective regulation of populations.[18] Public resistance to vaccination emphasizes both the complexity this entwined anatomo-bio-politics presents to the public and the often disconcerting affect embedded within its disciplinary regulation. Indeed, though the utilitarian and population-based public health rationale for vaccination is publicized to both reduce individual risk (even if entailing greater immediate risk) and induce herd immunity (which ultimately reduces individual risk), scientific statements and biopolitical public health policies around vaccination are not neutral, "embody[ing] and at the same time, often obscur[ing] underlying moral values and implicit political decisions."[19] To be sure, as contemporary biopower manifests increasingly through imperatives toward neoliberal self-government, individual choice, freedom, and encouragement to accept biotechnologies like vaccination as a means of caring for oneself and others, there is an increasing slippage between expert scientific, state, and industry knowledge about risk and the moral regulation of health and its relationship to such factors as race, gender, and sexuality.[20]

That public opposition to population-based risk assessment, medical technologies like vaccines, and a preference for individualized knowledge and care for oneself is a growing problem for modern medicine further points to this ambivalent relationship among risk, morality, and care as they converge in the practice of vaccination. Like all (bio)technologies, vaccines are *pharmakons*, fundamentally and irreducibly ambivalent—poison, remedy, or both—and often scapegoats for a plethora of societal problems, values, and understandings about health, morality, risk, responsibility, and care.[21] Insofar as public health discourses surrounding vaccination are often oriented toward a scientific logic of risk reduction as the basis for medical intervention, they effectively obscure these tensions between risk and care. In so doing, they overlook the fundamental ambivalence of technologies like vaccines that are inherent within claims to/of care. Like *pharmakons*, the word *care* similarly exhibits antithetical meanings of "suffering, sorrow, grief, trouble," and efforts to protect/

preserve from or assuage these troubles.[22] Such ambivalences within and between care and risk are amplified within contemporary biopolitical public health campaigns in favor of the HPV vaccine that further articulate the population-risk logic of vaccination with that of sexuality, morality, and gender.[23] In the context of Canada, scholars Erin Connell and Alan Hunt point to an increasing "interconnection between moral discourse and risk discourse" through which accepting the scientific, public health, and pharmaceutical risk-managing strategy/technology of the HPV vaccine becomes doubly tasked a moral imperative to intervene in the sexuality of young females (in particular) to whom the vaccine was initially marketed to prevent cervical cancer.[24] These confluences take on especial significance in the context of postcolonial Barbados, within whose history risk logics and medical logics have notoriously coincided within colonial biopolitics and the surveillance and control of Black female sexuality from the period of slavery across the British Caribbean.

Risk, Hesitancy, and Biopolitical Care in Barbados

As sociologist Mimi Sheller argues, to comprehensively analyze practices of citizenship, self-determination, and politics within the postemancipation Caribbean, one must trace the "political 'mechanisms of life': sex, pregnancy, births, longevity, health," all of which were central to the colonial project.[25] As the predominant colonial tools of classification and spatial governance throughout the colonial period and into the postemancipation period in the British Caribbean, biopolitical initiatives and medicoscientific conceptualizations of racial difference were strategically employed to monitor enslaved peoples' (and especially enslaved women's) health risks so as to maximize their speculative value as laborers and human commodities.[26]

In places like Barbados, "scientifically" racist ideologies of Black people as a socially inferior, immoral species were simultaneously drawn upon by merchant-planters and other white elites as a rationale to withhold and conserve the state's economic, welfare, and biopolitical resources for those deemed worthier of care.[27] Subsequently, whether it was short-lived infant pronatalist campaigns designed to foster optimal conditions for the reproduction of a Black labor supply, contagious disease hospitals deemed necessary to physically and morally regulate promiscuous Afro-Barbadian women's immoral souls and diseased bodies, attempts to examine and study Black women's reproductive labor and heterosexual comportment in the post-WWII period, or birth control campaigns of the 1950s aimed at encouraging their sexual control as a mark of self-governance and civility, biopolitical campaigns in Barbados and across the wider anglophone Caribbean have historically remained entangled with and predicated on this ambivalent relationship between the surveillance and care of Black women and their risky bodies, their reproductive systems, and their sexual activity.[28] These tactics and campaigns were executed and managed through technologies of surveillance, which were at once biopolitical and necropolitical—focused on caring for, optimizing, and controlling the risks of/posed to Black female life, through coercive and often violent, life-threatening measures, and for the purposes of labor. The sustained economic calculus, capitalistic motivations, and rationales for care that undergird these differentially constituted risks and the resultant biopolitical moves enacted in response to them are noteworthy markers of the historically ambivalent manifestation of care and its enmeshment within the bio-logic of slavery's sordid systems.

In postemancipation Barbados, local white elites and professionals who comprised the colonial legislature, as well as British-trained Barbadian doctors who worked alongside philanthropists and colonial officers, dispersed regulations for biomedical care and implemented policies that would save, civilize, and/or reproductively control those perceived to threaten and impede the nation's health and wealth.[29] As the case of Barbados makes clear, these frequently injurious biopolitical projects of "care" that centered on Black female sexuality have also been entwined with conflictual class, economic, and political dynamics that undoubtedly implicate but often transgress race. In addition to white elite suspicions around hyperfecundity and hypersexuality, for example, a different but related set of suspicions around race and sexuality became apparent for the rising Black middle class hoping to assume their place as nationalist leaders in the preindependence period.[30] Here it was specifically the working-class Black woman's sexuality that was in need of regulation into civility and respectability by educated middle-class Black men and women in the name of nation building.[31] By the turn of the twenty-first century, like many other societies, Barbados was facing rapid globalization reflected in the increased commercialization, foreign investment, and technological development within many sectors, including public health.

The 2014 introduction of the HPV vaccine campaign in Barbados reflects one of many biopolitical endeavors historically produced and organized across these aforementioned racialized, gendered, and classed lines, public health discourses of risk reduction and care, and shifting socioeconomic state-industry alliances. As previously noted, HPV vaccination delivery in Barbados was made possible through an assemblage that includes a network of state resources, international public health organizations, and pharmaceutical and philanthropic agencies. These include the Barbadian Ministry of Health, the World Health Organization, the Pan American Health Organization, pharmaceutical company Merck, and the Barbados Cancer Society, which have undertaken various

efforts to reduce the high cost of the vaccine, build Barbados's infrastructure to deliver the vaccine, and drive advocacy campaigns that make
possible new promissory ideals of what it means to be protected from the
sexually transmitted diseases of HPV and its associated cancers. Indeed,
the very existence of the HPV vaccine in Barbados and elsewhere remakes
the idea of risk (and what it means to be risk-free) into a form of capital,
creating new markets for private companies to profit from. Although the
vaccine is heavily subsidized by this nexus of state, nongovernmental, and
humanitarian organizations, that Gardasil is the most expensive childhood vaccine to have ever been marketed worldwide makes the biocapi-
talistic motivations of the pharmaceutical company perhaps impossible
to disentangle from the medical advances that its vaccine promises.[32] In
the wake of these fraught convergences among history, surveillance, care,
capitalism, racialization, and risk, it is vital that we question accounts
that conflate Afro-Barbadians' suspicion toward the HPV vaccine with
a uniform and uninformed refusal of care at the expense of this deeply
informative history. As I argue elsewhere, it is through the language of
suspicion that Barbadian parents articulate their contentious feelings
toward the HPV vaccine, less as a form of resistance toward care and
instead as a palimpsestic feeling, one that is sustained cross-temporally
and transnationally across citizens, colonial and postcolonial biopolitical
projects, and the often invasive technologies and techniques these projects
entail.[33]

   This ambivalence toward particular vaccines, or "vaccine hesitancy," as it is commonly referred to within the medical community, is
defined by the World Health Organization as the delay in acceptance or
complete refusal of vaccines in the context of available immunization services.[34] While biomedical literature has acknowledged the complexity of
this phenomenon and its varying sociocultural, religious, political, and
interpersonal constitutive factors, claims to scientific ignorance continue
to headline many discussions of vaccine hesitancy across popular science
books, medical news forums, and newspaper editorials in North America
and the United Kingdom, driving a narrative that often conflates antivac-
cination, hesitancy, and refusal and frames these phenomena as collective
consequences of mis/uninformed, fearful citizens, and public naivete.[35]
But antivaccine sentiment ought to be differentiated from vaccine hesitancy, which, as social science research has consistently shown, is context
specific and more capaciously encapsulates a range of emotions and decisions, from acceptance amid uncertainty to ambivalence and complete
refusal.[36] While vaccine hesitancy might entangle with antivaccine sentiment for some citizens in specific locales, it is not, as a phenomenon,
subsumable to it. To suggest so overlooks hesitancy's multiple constitutive
factors, risks failing to address them (and thus the biomedical problem

that is hesitancy within public health efforts to increase vaccine compliance), and, for my interests in this article, misconstrues hesitancy as but an ignorant refusal of biomedical care.

Rather than reinforcing the assumption that vaccine hesitancy amounts to a blanket refusal of care, my interviews with Afro-Barbadian parents about their suspicion toward the HPV vaccine offer a different starting point from which to think about vaccination, risk, care, and their political predicaments. These parents did not simply detail their differential understandings of risk around vaccination but invoked the aforementioned historicity of the intersections of risk, care, and capitalism, their centrality to the colonial project, and their residues within a landscape of neoliberalism and biocapitalism in postcolonial Barbados.[37] For many Afro-Barbadians, the tropes of hypersexuality and attempts to morally regulate the Black female body and Black women's sexual activity that were perceived to accompany the vaccine's promotion were further cause for suspicion. These historical intersections both called the state's "care" via vaccination into question and were central to the formation of new risk logics rooted in understandings of the past and skepticism over the motives, efficacy, and value of the vaccine for Afro-Barbadian young women.

Looking Closer: Suspicion as Radical (Care)

Pamela A. is an Afro-Barbadian writer/poet and mother of two children for whom she refused the HPV vaccine.[38] In response to my questioning whether she was at all concerned about the vaccine's association with sex, she framed her suspicions around the vaccine's side effects.

> The main [thing] that I'm really concerned about is the side effects and I don't see the reason . . . and nobody haven't convinced me yet why it is relevant to give a ten-year-old, eleven-year-old, twelve-year-old the human papillomavirus vaccine . . . putting that in her system at such a young age. . . . It's not there now, and I don't know if in the future if it would affect her body when she gets to be an adult.

Insinuating that her eleven- and twelve-year-old daughters were not yet sexually active, Pamela claims to be suspicious of the need to expose them to HPV antibodies so early in their lives and is worried about the long-term effects the vaccine could have on her daughters. Pamela's argument about exposing her daughters to the vaccine "at such a young age" was one made by several parents and was especially problematic for medical practitioners seeking to increase compliance toward the vaccine.[39] While Pamela began talking about her suspicions in terms of the vaccine's side effects, the discussion eventually returned to sex:

Because they were saying, I guess what [the nurses] was saying was that, umm, if the child is promiscuous too, then it's important . . . and that's the thing that have me, this idea of the girls as promiscuous. If you raise your daughter . . . yes you can't, you can't predict the future, but if you're raising your child to have morals and standards and stuff like that, then I don't know if my daughter needs this right away. But yes, I know there is a high prevalence of sexual activities in secondary schools now too. So . . . well . . . I just don't think that is up to me to put that HPV in her system when it's not there now.

Here, Pamela suggests that a promiscuous lifestyle is synonymous with adolescent sexual activity itself. Though she incorrectly conflates the two, what she actually appears to struggle with is the idea that her daughters could be sexually active as early as secondary school. Pamela oscillates between a discomfort with the narrative that her daughters are promiscuous—suggesting that she raises her daughters according to a prescribed set of respectable values—and the defeated recognition that secondary school children of her daughters' age are, in fact, engaged in sexual activity across the country. The contradictions within her statements allude to a belief that modesty, morality, and proper sexual comportment could prevent her daughters from being labeled promiscuous and perhaps from contracting HPV. Her comments simultaneously imply that her suspicion is significantly connected to a prescribed labeling of her Black, preteen daughters as sexually promiscuous and in need of this vaccine. In arguing "that's the thing that have me," Pamela delineates that it is this characterization of promiscuity, one that reverberates colonial stereotypes, that is so deeply unsettling.

David C., a forty-nine-year-old Black Barbadian, schoolteacher, and father of two, also refused the vaccine for his daughter Daphne. David's articulations of his suspicions extend those expressed by Pamela. Though he acknowledged the potential benefits of the vaccine in light of the prevalence of cervical cancer in places such as Barbados, he framed his ambivalence toward the vaccine in terms of suspicions toward the multinational pharmaceutical industry behind its manufacturing, noting, "At US$450 for the complete vaccine, Big Pharma making a lot of money off this thing. . . . It's not that we never administer drugs to our children, but this particular one though, nah; 200 million vaccines, $150 USD per shot. . . . Big Pharma is making a lot of money out of this thing!" Like Pamela, David was wary that the marketing of a vaccine—one that protects against a sexually transmitted disease—to Black Barbadians such as his daughter evoked disturbing colonial pasts. A self-proclaimed Pan-Africanist, he referenced the long history of racial science and medicine under transatlantic slavery and the influence that such ideologies as Black female hypersexuality held in advancing biopolitical intervention and surveillance upon Afro-Caribbean women's bodies. David was particularly worried, he said, that those promoting the immunization were motivated by a belief that Black women in the Caribbean were "highly sexed" and in need of the salvation, protection, and intervention that this vaccine might afford in regulating the risks of said behavior. Such ideologies and their sordid pasts informed many Afro-Barbadian parents' suspicion, a suspicion that circulates, pulses, and resides in their bodies as an affective intensity—a historical and lived reality that has everything to do with care.[40]

Knitting together legacies of the colonial management of Black female sexuality and suspicions as/and desires to protect their children from these pasts, these and other Afro-Barbadian parents with whom I spoke challenge an understanding of vaccine hesitancy as mere scientific ignorance, mistrust, the antithesis of care, or combinations thereof. Instead, their suspicions at once trouble care's ethics and political commitments and inform and embrace different ethics of care, sometimes manifesting as vaccination refusal. For others, suspicion informed ambivalence and delay in HPV vaccine acceptance, an "in the meantime" politics necessary to ask questions about the Barbadian state, its public health priorities, and the inconsistencies evident within its doing-as-caring paradigm.[41] For such parents, the Barbadian state sat at the interstices of their felt suspicions surrounding the vaccine, its intervention upon adolescents' sexual health, and its enmeshment in neoliberal global circuits of technoscience, ethics, economics, and pharmaceutical exchange.

Selena A., an Afro-Barbadian mother whom I interviewed, was one such parent. Connecting her suspicion toward the HPV vaccine with what she perceived to be the government's strategic and misaligned priorities when it came to the sexual health of Barbadians, Selena questioned the exuberant promotion of the vaccine alongside government mandates that restrict adolescents from accessing sexual and reproductive health technologies like contraceptive pills in Barbados without parental consent. Though the age of consent for sexual activity in Barbados is sixteen, adolescents below the age of eighteen are unable to access such sexual health services and treatment without parental consent because they are considered minors under the Barbadian Minors Act.[42] While there is no concrete legislation preventing adolescents from accessing these services per se, female adolescents in particular are unable to secure birth control pills or information on other contraceptives, safe sex, and sexually transmitted diseases in government clinics or pharmacies unless they have their parents' support and accompaniment.

As Selena made clear, despite there being no specific legal mandate in place, the state's nebulous categorization of adolescents between the ages of sixteen and eighteen holds control over their sexual intimacy, rights, and risks. Regardless of whether it is effective in doing so, the

Barbadian state restricts both adolescent intimacy and adolescents' independent access to prescribed contraceptives for safe sex. Referencing this disparity in the law as a basis to question the appropriateness of the vaccine, Selena asked why ten- and eleven-year-old children were being offered the HPV vaccine by the government when under its same rule they weren't able to access contraceptive pills until they are eighteen years old. Frustrated, she asked, "What are the government's real priorities when it comes to adolescent sex and sexual health? Why the restrictions around sexual health in some areas, and the forceful promotion of other technologies like the vaccine to preteens?" As noted by Darcy B., another mother who described herself as still undecided about the vaccine, the government's stated goal to save lives occurs alongside what she perceived to be efforts to fulfill economic allegiances and partnerships with multinational pharmaceutical companies like Merck and the biomedical technologies they manufacture. To be sure, regardless of its (un)stated aims, both these outcomes are likely satisfied in the successful marketing of the HPV vaccine to the Barbadian public. As David, too, incisively claimed, in addition to providing lifesaving technologies to the public, the Barbadian government is also embedded in for-profit pharmaceutical assemblages that profit on the risks of adolescent girls' (sexual) health by marketing technologies like the HPV vaccine.

Parents' suspicion thus attaches not only to biomedical technologies and devices like the vaccine and the presexual adolescent female body upon which the vaccine intervenes but also to wider transnational biopolitical, technoscientific networks or "global assemblages" of exchange in which the Barbadian state has immersed itself since the 1980s and that have become increasingly technologically oriented.[43] Bio-, communication, and information technologies play a pivotal role in mediating and transforming national and transnational economics, health, intimacies, and, I argue, colonial and postcolonial affects of suspicion and the politics and questions such affects engender.[44]

Rather than equating their suspicion with pharmaceutical or government mistrust or the act of refusal, Pamela's, David's, Selena's, and Darcy's claims tell of a careful being with and thinking through of these factors in the present context of HPV vaccination promotion, and in light of the past. As the late Caribbean anthropologist Michel-Rolph Trouillot reminds us, "The past—or, more accurately, pastness—is a position. . . . In no way can we identify the past *as past*."[45] Invoking affective memories of pastness, Afro-Barbadian parents' suspicions ask of the motivations behind care. They reveal care's inequalities and political stakes by mapping how health care work, biomedical authority, state priorities, assemblages, and noninnocent histories of colonial medical injustice often unwittingly intertwine. And yet, understandably frustrating to many,

Afro-Barbadian parents' questions, revelations, and ambivalences, and their often fraught repercussions, exist in a context in which care for and about cervical cancer is urgent.

But perhaps, as Michelle Murphy encourages, we ought to resist the urge to *wholly* conflate understandings of care with positive affects.[46] Indeed, like the "grammar" that has historically overdetermined Black women as hypersexual, deviant, and in need of care and salvation, the dominant grammar of vaccine hesitancy inadvertently and paternalistically naturalizes care via vaccination as uncomplicatedly benevolent.[47] A willingness to interrogate this script might open up space to rewire our approach to the sensibility of hesitancy as something that ought merely to be overcome. This need not conflict with efforts to improve vaccine compliance and prevent cervical cancer but, in fact, might do the opposite. Appreciating and taking parents' suspicions seriously amid efforts to improve HPV vaccine compliance in Barbados means rethinking how we learn to care and what we view as care, so that we might better witness and support the holistic health of our populations. Perhaps, as these interview excerpts suggest, suspicion embodies a radical potential to teach of a care rooted in deep witnessing and reflection as a precursor to prescription, mediation, and medical innovations.

Rethinking suspicion and care calls on medical practitioners and public health workers to release investments in conceiving hesitancy as a refusal of care, in conceiving suspicion and refusal as subsumed by scientific ignorance, and in conceiving vaccine acceptance as a value-neutral willingness to receive care. Further and more challenging still, it requires that social science and scientific researchers/practitioners critically reflect on our conditioned means of studying and offering care; listen more closely to and wrestle with how biomedicine's rationalities around care intersect with histories of injustice, postcolonial state building, and contemporary neoliberal priorities and agendas; and accept the ways in which these rationalities might be understood to inflict more harm than good. Suspicion, suspicious refusals, ambivalence, and hesitancy hold a mirror to the violence often implicit in our caring and naming practices. They unveil the histories of care and, too, the lingering power of historical narratives of ignorance that surface within discourses of vaccine hesitancy and refusal. They necessitate yet again more pause and hesitancy to more ethically revisit the question of care.

Heeding Trouillot's call to shift the lens of analysis inward, to a small place, to capture the "agentive capacities of ordinary people" amid evolving and converging historical and contemporary processes of domination, this article has sought to map the not-so-obvious stakes of biomedical modes of care and suspicion toward that care in the context of postcolonial Barbados.[48] From this perspective, we are faced with care's underbelly. Indeed, as the parents whom I interviewed offered, when framed within a noninnocent history of biomedical experimentation and "care," (post)colonial stereotypes and politics, and pharmaceutical-state assemblages, the historical etymology of the word *care* and its conflation with fear, anxiety, and grief seems more intuitive.

In describing their suspicion, these parents collectively repositioned the crisis of cervical cancer in the Caribbean (indeed, the crisis of caring for this crisis) within and against the anxious paternalism of the postcolonial state and histories of surveillance and neglect, colonialism, biomedical experimentation, and suspicion toward Black women and Black female (hyper)sexuality in Barbados and transnationally. In so doing, they complicate what it means to be suspicious of (the care of) this vaccine in a place such as Barbados and amid popular understandings of vaccine hesitancy and refusal in the Western world. Eschewing the binaries that structure/d both colonial discourse and medical discourse around rationality and irrationality, suspicion implores us to look more closely at the enmeshment of risk, care, and fear in the postcolonial Caribbean and asks that social science and humanities researchers and health-care practitioners alike recognize and accept the histories, ideologies, and practices that we might yet comprehend. To follow suspicion and rethink care is to embrace the ambivalence of care and vaccines, both, and the incomprehensible, seemingly impossible not-doing that hesitancy might constitute in favor of compassionate recognition, close listening, difficult reflection, and cautious pause. And perhaps this is radical.

Notes

This article has evolved over many years of conversation and through the generous feedback of several persons, including Hiʻilei Julia Hobart, Tamara Kneese, Zoë Gross, and the anonymous readers at *Social Text*, to whom I am so grateful.

1. Centers for Disease Control and Prevention, "Human Papillomavirus (HPV) Vaccine Safety."
2. HPV Information Centre, "Human Papillomavirus and Related Diseases in Barbados."
3. HPV Information Centre, "Human Papillomavirus and Related Diseases in Barbados."
4. The other is the hepatitis B virus vaccine that prevents a common form of liver cancer. See Mamo and Epstein, "Pharmaceuticalization of Sexual Risk."
5. While initially targeted to girls in this age group, the vaccine was eventually opened up to preteen boys under the national vaccination program in 2015.
6. See Charles, "HPV Vaccination and Affective Suspicions in Barbados."
7. Beck, *Risk Society*.
8. Beck, "Terrorist Threat," 40–41.
9. Levy, *Freaks of Fortune*.
10. Levy, *Freaks of Fortune*, 3.
11. See Levy, *Freaks of Fortune*; and Schlich, "Risk and Medical Innovation."

12. See Schlich, "Risk and Medical Innovation"; Magnello "Introduction of Mathematical Statistics"; and Zachmann, "Risk in Historical Perspective."

13. See Schlich, "Risk and Medical Innovation."

14. See Marks, "Assessing the Risk and Safety of the Pill"; and Rusnock, "Merchant's Logick."

15. Brown, *Immunitary Life*, 175.

16. See Altink, "'Fight TB with BCG.'" As Henrice Altink notes, while BCG vaccination campaigns against tuberculosis in the mid-twentieth-century British Caribbean were promoted through the lens of public health and its benefits for political, social, and economic advancement, such initiatives ultimately aimed to reinvigorate the British Empire.

17. Bonah, "As Safe as Milk or Sugar Water."

18. Foucault, *History of Sexuality*.

19. Schlich, "Risk and Medical Innovation," 5.

20. See Casper and Carpenter, "Sex, Drugs, and Politics." See also Connell and Hunt, "HPV Vaccination Campaign"; and Lock and Nguyen, "Biomedical Technologies in Practice."

21. I thank this article's anonymous reader for pointing out that vaccines, like all technologies, are inherently *pharmako*-logical in the Derridean sense—that is, both poison and remedy. For more on *pharmakon*, see Derrida, *Dissemination*, 127.

22. *Oxford English Dictionary Online*, s.v. "care," www.oed.com/view/Entry /27899.

23. See Connell and Hunt, "HPV Vaccination Campaign"; Charles, "Mobilizing the Self-Governance of Pre-damaged Bodies"; Mamo, Nelson, and Clarke "Producing and Protecting Risky Girlhoods"; and Polzer and Knabe, "From Desire to Disease."

24. Connell and Hunt, "HPV Vaccination Campaign," 67. Despite the vaccine being offered to preteen boys and girls under Barbados's national vaccination program since 2015, popular and professional discourse around the vaccine and its promotion attaches disproportionately to female sexuality.

25. Sheller, *Citizenship from Below*, 249.

26. De Barros, *Reproducing the British Caribbean*, 35. In the wake of widespread cholera epidemics in the 1850s and resultant labor shortages in such places as Barbados, Jamaica, and Trinidad, a medical tax system was imposed in many islands. British physicians reasoned that, by taxing populations to pay for medical care, they could maintain dominance and economic profit in the colonies and train Black people on the benefits of rational, scientific advice in lieu of irrational, folk, and obeah quackery prescriptions.

27. Browne, *Race, Class, Politics*.

28. See Paton, "Enslaved Women and Slavery"; Challenger, "Benign Place of Healing?"; De Barros, *Reproducing the British Caribbean*; Putnam, "Global Child-Saving"; and Bourbonnais, "Out of the Boudoir."

29. Beckles, "Capitalism, Slavery, and Caribbean Modernity."

30. De Barros, *Reproducing the British Caribbean*.

31. Beyond the racially motivated anxieties and eugenic concerns that undergirded the support of birth control from white elites in places like Barbados and Jamaica, Barbadian middle-class Black politicians, professionals, and reformist elites also advocated for birth control.

32. As Kaushik Sunder Rajan observes, biocapitalism indicates an important shift in the constitution of symptoms to be treated and cared for "away from disease manifestation and toward disease potential" (*Biocapital*, 283). Such a shift neces-

sarily expands the potential market for pharmaceuticals "from 'diseased' people to, conceivably, everyone with purchasing power" (Sunder Rajan, "Subjects of Speculation," 24).

33. Charles, "HPV Vaccination and Affective Suspicions in Barbados."

34. World Health Organization, "Vaccine Hesitancy."

35. Goldenberg, "Public Misunderstanding of Science?"

36. See Hobson-West, "'Trusting Blindly Can Be the Biggest Risk of All'"; Leach and Fairhead, *Vaccine Anxieties*; Lawrence, Hausman, and Dannenberg, "Reframing Medicine's Publics"; and Poltorak et al., "'MMR Talk' and Vaccination Choices." Comparative ethnographies on vaccine hesitancy across the developing world similarly highlight the multifaceted factors that can impact one's hesitancy, including history and politics, religion, mode of vaccine delivery, distrust of the pharmaceutical industry, and the broader health system in which particular vaccines are introduced. See Babalola, "Maternal Reasons for Non-immunisation"; Closser, "Chasing Polio in Pakistan"; and Ghinai et al., "Listening to the Rumours."

37. Parents' excerpts trace what they perceive to be extensions of postcolonial biopolitics through contemporary forms of biocapitalism and its concomitant commodification of care and female sexuality via pharmaceuticals and biotechnologies like the HPV vaccine.

38. I conducted all interviews in Barbados between 2015 and 2018.

39. The rationale for targeting eleven- and twelve-year-old children is based on scientific evidence that indicates increased efficacy of the vaccine if introduced prior to the initiation of sexual contact.

40. Charles, "HPV Vaccination and Affective Suspicions in Barbados."

41. As Sarah Sharma notes, "in the meantime" is an approach to time that captures the minutiae of social politics, control, and coordination between overlapping temporalities (*In the Meantime*, 7).

42. Henry, "Legal Gap Analysis."

43. Collier and Ong, "Global Assemblages," 4.

44 See Collier and Ong, "Global Assemblages"; Horst and Miller, *Cell Phone*; Murray, *Flaming Souls;* and Padilla, *Love and Globalization.*

45. Trouillot, *Global Transformations*, 15.

46. Murphy, "Unsettling Care."

47. I borrow the term *grammar* from Hortense Spillers, who refers to an "American grammar" as the discursive parameters around which understandings of gender and race are constructed and made legible ("Mama's Baby, Papa's Maybe").

48. Agard-Jones, "Bodies in the System," 185.

References

Agard-Jones, Vanessa. "Bodies in the System." *Small Axe* 17, no. 3 (2013): 182–92.

Altink, Henrice. "'Fight TB with BCG': Mass Vaccination Campaigns in the British Caribbean, 1951–6." *Medical History* 58, no. 4 (2014): 475–97.

Babalola, Stella. "Maternal Reasons for Non-immunisation and Partial Immunisation in Northern Nigeria." *Journal of Paediatrics and Child Health* 47, no. 5 (2011): 276–81.

Beck, Ulrich. *Risk Society: Towards a New Modernity*. London: Sage, 1992.

Beck, Ulrich. "The Terrorist Threat: World Risk Society Revisited." *Theory, Culture, and Society* 19, no. 4 (2002): 39–55.

Beckles, Hilary. "Capitalism, Slavery, and Caribbean Modernity." *Callaloo* 20, no. 4 (1997): 777–89.

Bonah, Christian. "'As Safe as Milk or Sugar Water': Perceptions of the Risks and Benefits of the BCG Vaccine in the 1920s and 1930s in France and Germany." In *The Risks of Medical Innovation: Risk Perception and Assessment in Historical Context*, edited by Thomas Schlich and Ulrich Tröhler, 66–86. New York: Routledge, 2006.

Bourbonnais, Nicole. "Out of the Boudoir and into the Banana Walk: Birth Control and Reproductive Politics in the West Indies, 1930–1970." PhD diss., University of Pittsburgh, 2013.

Brown, Nik. *Immunitary Life: A Biopolitics of Immunity*. London: Palgrave Macmillan, 2018.

Browne, David V. C. *Race, Class, Politics, and the Struggle for Empowerment in Barbados, 1914–1937*. Miami: Ian Randle, 2012.

Casper, Monica J., and Laura M. Carpenter. "Sex, Drugs, and Politics: The HPV Vaccine for Cervical Cancer." *Sociology of Health and Illness* 30, no. 6 (2008): 886–99.

Centers for Disease Control and Prevention. "Human Papillomavirus (HPV) Vaccine Safety." June 15, 2017. www.cdc.gov/vaccinesafety/vaccines/hpv-vaccine .html.

Challenger, Denise. "A Benign Place of Healing? The Contagious Diseases Hospital and Medical Discipline in Post-slavery Barbados." In *Health and Medicine in the Circum-Caribbean, 1800–1968*, edited by Juanita De Barros, Steven Paul Palmer, and David Wright, 98–117. New York: Routledge, 2009.

Charles, Nicole. "HPV Vaccination and Affective Suspicions in Barbados." *Feminist Formations* 30, no. 1 (2018): 46–70.

Charles, Nicole. "Mobilizing the Self-Governance of Pre-damaged Bodies: Neoliberal Biological Citizenship and HPV Vaccination Promotion in Canada." *Citizenship Studies* 16, nos. 6–7 (2013): 770–84.

Closser, Svea. *Chasing Polio in Pakistan: Why the World's Largest Public Health Initiative May Fail*. Nashville: Vanderbilt University Press, 2010.

Collier, Stephen J., and Aihwa Ong. "Global Assemblages, Anthropological Problems." In *Global Assemblages: Technology, Politics, and Ethics as Anthropological Problems*, edited by Aihwa Ong and Stephen J. Collier, 3–21. Malden, MA: Blackwell, 2005.

Connell, Erin, and Alan Hunt. "The HPV Vaccination Campaign: A Project of Moral Regulation in an Era of Biopolitics." *Canadian Journal of Sociology / Cahiers Canadiens de Sociologie* 35, no. 1 (2010): 63–82.

De Barros, Juanita. *Reproducing the British Caribbean: Sex, Gender, and Population Politics after Slavery*. Chapel Hill: University of North Carolina Press, 2014.

Derrida, Jacques. *Dissemination*. Translated by Barbara Johnson. Chicago: University Press, 1981.

Foucault, Michel. *The History of Sexuality*. New York: Vintage Books, 1990.

Ghinai, Isaac, Chris Willott, Ibrahim Dadari, and Heidi J. Larson. "Listening to the Rumours: What the Northern Nigeria Polio Vaccine Boycott Can Tell Us Ten Years On." *Global Public Health* 8, no. 10 (2013): 1138–50.

Goldenberg, Maya J. "Public Misunderstanding of Science? Reframing the Problem of Vaccine Hesitancy." *Perspectives on Science* 24, no. 5 (2016): 552–81.

Henry, Ruth. "A Legal Gap Analysis of Adolescent Sexual and Reproductive Health and Rights in Barbados." United Nations Population Fund, 2011. caribbean.unfpa .org/webdav/site/caribbean/shared/publications/2011/Barbados/SRH/Legal%20 Gap%20Analysis%20ASRH%20Barbados.pdf.

Hobson-West, Pru. "'Trusting Blindly Can Be the Biggest Risk of All': Organised

Resistance to Childhood Vaccination in the UK." *Sociology of Health and Illness* 29, no. 2 (2007): 198–205.

Horst, Heather A., and Daniel Miller, eds. *The Cell Phone: An Anthropology of Communication.* Oxford: Berg, 2006.

HPV Information Centre. "Human Papillomavirus and Related Diseases in Barbados." July 27, 2017. www.hpvcentre.net/statistics/reports/BRB.pdf.

Lawrence, Heidi; Bernice Hausman, and Clare Dannenberg. "Reframing Medicine's Publics: The Local as a Public of Vaccine Refusal." *Journal of Medical Humanities* 35, no. 2 (2014): 111–29.

Leach, Melissa, and James Fairhead. *Vaccine Anxieties: Global Science, Child Health, and Society.* Sterling, VA: Earthscan, 2007.

Levy, Jonathan. *Freaks of Fortune: The Emerging World of Capitalism and Risk in America.* Cambridge, MA: Harvard University Press, 2012.

Lock, Margaret M., and Vinh-Kim Nguyen. "Biomedical Technologies in Practice." In *An Anthropology of Biomedicine,* edited by Margaret Lock and Vinh-Kim Nguyen, 15–32. Malden, MA: Wiley-Blackwell, 2010.

Magnello, Eileen. "The Introduction of Mathematical Statistics into Medical Research: The Roles of Karl Pearson, Major Greenwood, and Austin Bradford Hill." In *The Road to Medical Statistics,* edited by Eileen Magnello and Anne Hardy, 95–123. Leiden, Netherlands: Brill Rodopi, 2002.

Mamo, Laura, and Steven Epstein. "The Pharmaceuticalization of Sexual Risk: Vaccine Development and the New Politics of Cancer Prevention." *Social Science and Medicine* 101 (2014): 155–65.

Mamo, Laura, Amber Nelson, and Aleia Clarke. "Producing and Protecting Risky Girlhoods." In *Three Shots at Prevention: The HPV Vaccine and the Politics of Medicine's Simple Solutions,* edited by Keith Wailoo, Julie Livingston, Steven Epstein, and Robert Aronowitz, 121–45. Baltimore: Johns Hopkins University Press, 2010.

Marks, Lara. "Assessing the Risk and Safety of the Pill: Maternal Mortality and the Pill." In *The Risks of Medical Innovation: Risk Perception and Assessment in Historical Context,* edited by Thomas Schlich and Ulrich Tröhler, 170–85. New York: Routledge, 2006.

Murphy, Michelle. "Unsettling Care: Troubling Transnational Itineraries of Care in Feminist Health Practices." *Social Studies of Science* 45, no. 5 (2015): 717–37.

Murray, David. *Flaming Souls: Homosexuality, Homophobia, and Social Change in Barbados.* Toronto: University of Toronto Press, 2012.

Padilla, Mark. *Love and Globalization: Transformations of Intimacy in the Contemporary World.* Nashville: Vanderbilt University Press, 2007.

Paton, Diana. 2007. "Enslaved Women and Slavery before and after 1807." *History in Focus,* no. 12. archives.history.ac.uk/history-in-focus/Slavery/articles/paton.html.

Poltorak, Mike, Melissa Leach, Jackie Cassell, and James Fairhead. "'MMR Talk' and Vaccination Choices: An Ethnographic Study in Brighton." *Social Science and Medicine* 61, no. 3 (2005): 709–19.

Polzer, Jessica C., and Susan M. Knabe. "From Desire to Disease: Human Papillomavirus (HPV) and the Medicalization of Nascent Female Sexuality." *Journal of Sex Research* 49, no. 4 (2012): 344–52.

Putnam, Lara. "Global Child-Saving, Transatlantic Maternalism, and the Pathologization of Caribbean Childhood, 1930s–1940s." *Atlantic Studies* 11, no. 4 (2014): 491–514.

Rusnock, Andrea. "'The Merchant's Logick': Numerical Debates over Smallpox

Inoculation in Eighteenth-Century England." In *The Road to Medical Statistics*, edited by Eileen Magnello and Anne Hardy, 37–54. Leiden, Netherlands: Brill Rodop, 2002.

Schlich, Thomas. "Risk and Medical Innovation: A Historical Perspective." In *The Risks of Medical Innovation: Risk Perception and Assessment in Historical Context*, edited by Thomas Schlich and Ulrich Tröhler, 1–17. New York: Routledge, 2006.

Sharma, Sarah. *In the Meantime: Temporality and Cultural Politics*. Durham, NC: Duke University Press, 2014.

Sheller, Mimi. *Citizenship from Below: Erotic Agency and Caribbean Freedom*. Durham, NC: Duke University Press, 2012.

Spillers, Hortense. "Mama's Baby, Papa's Maybe: An American Grammar Book." *Diacritics* 17, no. 2 (1987): 65–81.

Sunder Rajan, Kaushik. *Biocapital: The Constitution of Postgenomic Life*. Durham, NC: Duke University Press, 2006.

Sunder Rajan, Kaushik. "Subjects of Speculation: Emergent Life Sciences and Market Logics in the United States and India." *American Anthropologist* 107, no. 1 (2005): 19–30.

Trouillot, Michel-Rolph. *Global Transformations: Anthropology and the Modern World*. New York: Palgrave Macmillan, 2003.

World Health Organization. "Vaccine Hesitancy: A Growing Challenge for Immunization Programmes." August 18, 2015. www.who.int/news-room/detail/18-08-2015-vaccine-hesitancy-a-growing-challenge-for-immunization-programmes.

Zachmann, Karin. "Risk in Historical Perspective: Concepts, Contexts, and Conjunctions." In *Risk: A Multidisciplinary Introduction*, edited by Claudia Klüppelberg, Daniel Straub, and Isabell M. Welpe, 3–35. Cham, Switzerland: Springer, 2014.

Beyond Resilience

Trans Coalitional Activism as Radical Self-Care

Elijah Adiv Edelman

Studies of queer and trans suffering, resilience, care, and vitalities are invariably also investigations into the difficult and painful articulations of lives that feel worth living along with deaths that feel okay dying. The notion of resiliency, referring to a conditional state of overcoming difficult situations, neglects to fully encompass our understandings of risk, vulnerability, and life making.[1] Specifically, in this article I explore the ways in which Washington, DC–based trans activists discuss that which renders viable life as being constituted by shared coalitional labor in a contemporary moment that is violently anti-Black, xenophobic, misogynist, and distinctly antitrans. While health researchers have long noted the beneficial role a coalition serves in better representing needs in research,[2] I focus here on how individuals meet their needs not through solitary and normative resilience strategies but within and through spaces of coalitional action. This approach to radical care encourages us to rethink what constitutes livable life. The necropolitics of trans lives—those that get marked as morally suspect and intrinsically disposable, representing "the condition for the acceptability of putting to death"[3]—coexists with what I frame here as trans vitalities, or that which makes lives worth living.

This article, in its exploration of trans activism, coalitional labor, and radical care, is also an exploration of how the production of the "transnormative subject" articulates with notions of resilience as well as spatiality and place.[4] As I discuss here, the ideologies that underlie the notion of trans resilience value a simple "universal trajectory of coming out/transition, visibility, recognition, protection, and self-actualization." However, lived experience does not follow a linear path. The focus on and celebration of the few trans lives that might reproduce this model of

Social Text 142 · Vol. 38, No. 1 · March 2020

DOI 10.1215/01642472-7971127   © 2020 Duke University Press

resilience "remains uninterrogated in [their] complicities and convergences with biomedical, neoliberal, racist, and imperialist projects."[5] In other words, what constitutes valued trans embodiment and practice becomes the template through which resilience imagines both life making and how care is found.

Looking at Life through Death

Barbara, a white trans woman in her early sixties and lifetime local to the Washington, DC, metropolitan area, got involved in trans activism after being told by her therapist that she needed to find a trans support group. Having visited several regional groups and feeling disappointed by what she described as "complaining" by attendees, she found the DC Trans Coalition (DCTC), a trans activist group of which I was also a member. In an e-mail, she explained to me in greater detail what brought her to trans activist work:

> When my therapist told me that I was done, or finished (done makes it sound like I'm a muffin and the timer just went off, time to get out of the oven!) I should seek out a support group. . . . I found out way back then, TEGA was for the crossdressers. Not me. MAGIC was a lot of people who were unhappy that their wives didn't understand them. Umm, not my problem, so I went to the [DCTC] town hall. I was impressed. Here were people who were actually doing something about making life better for everyone. Sure it's about the T, but others benefit also, sort of an ancillary benefit. So I went to my first meeting. . . . My involvement with DCTC has opened doors that I thought were closed to me. Because of the encouragement of its members, I'm in college now. I have met some truly awesome people and have grown so much. I can't imagine my [life] without it.

Barbara was dead several years after getting involved in trans activism and not long after she shared this e-mail with me. Barbara wasn't murdered. She did not commit suicide. She did not die as a result of complications related to living with HIV. She was not homeless or without a source of income when she died. Her funeral, which we did not need to fundraise to hold, was well attended by surviving members of her natal family and of the trans activist communities she was a member of. And members of her birth and trans activist family carried her body to her grave. In many ways, in death just as in life, she provided us with an opportunity to engage in forms of shared radical care. I position the kind of radical care underlying Barbara's activist work, and even within the space carved out by her death, as constituting "vital but underappreciated strategies for enduring precarious worlds," as Hiʻilei Julia Kawehipuaakahaopulani Hobart and Tamara Kneese describe in their introduction to this special issue of *Social Text*. Indeed, while the circumstances surrounding Barbara's life, and death, contrast with that experienced by most trans activists, our coalitional labor, in life and even in death, provided a kind of care that defies conventional descriptions. Our shared labor, as Barbara noted, was not simply about supportive care but, echoing Hobart and Kneese, was constituted by "autonomous direct action and nonhierarchical collective work."

Importantly, the ways in which Barbara's death created desperately needed spaces of radical care and closure does not, in fact, resemble how other activists we worked with died—the murders, the suicides, the premature and likely preventable deaths, the unclaimed bodies, the funerals that never happened because there were no funds to hold them, the natal families that were never involved, and the chosen families that were never invited. Barbara is an outlier. However, I begin this article with her not because her death exemplifies or directly contrasts with trans lives and deaths but because it is often through the messy and frequently traumatic incoherence of death and loss that we experience the full potential of radical care. Moreover, we can striate these forms of radical care with what Sara Ahmed refers to as "desire lines." In thinking about resistance and willfullness, Ahmed reminds us, "when you stray from the official paths, you create desire lines, faint marks on the earth, as traces of where you or others have been. A willfulness archive is premised on hope: the hope that those who wander away from the paths they are supposed to follow leave their footprints behind."[6] When we situate Barbara's life, activist work, and even death within the broader context of what constitutes resilience, radical care, or vitalities, we can imagine those desire lines—the social, political, and personal legacies of our lives—that she both followed and left for others to move over, across, and through. In this article, I explore how radical care and those desire lines structure frameworks of "trans vitalities" as necessary shifts toward disrupting normative expectations of care, resilience, and, ultimately, that which is understood to constitute a life worth living.

Radical Care as Trans Vitalities

Multiple studies of trans health discursively or literally mark particular trans persons or bodies as at risk or as engaging in high-risk activities.[7] While resilience frameworks help us identify structural inequities, particularly among trans women of color, I consider here how we might rethink concepts like risk and care. Specifically, rather than approach risk as something we do, we can view risk as applied to bodies or practices viewed as morally or ethically suspect. Specifically, I focus here on how risk and resilience are constituted and constrained by one's agency or structural limitations. Importantly, situating risk, or the overcoming of risk through resilience, as active behaviors or passive vulnerability erases our complex intertextual subjectivities, as well as the structural and symbolic violence that often results in negative health outcomes for trans persons.[8] As such, a framework of radical care allows us to explore alternative models of trans vitalities for reconfiguring the risk/resilience binary toward models employed by both informal trans social networks and harm reduction agencies in Washington, DC. By focusing on how life making in trans coalitional spaces may very well coexist within spaces heavily marked by death and loss, I document here how these vitalities articulate within and across social justice movements, which ultimately provide alternative models of stability that do not require the kind of normativity a resilience framework demands. In short, I discuss here how the personal and political transformative power of coalition-based trans social justice work functions as a form of radical care and productive life force for many of the participants of the projects explored in this text.

In recent years models of resilience have emerged as a trope within academic fields and activist and social media circles, with calls for self-care and adaptation as a means of resistance. While human and bioecological resilience is certainly advantageous, this article considers implications of resilience as a force that obscures and diverts attention away from relational and structural forms of violence and how directing attention toward self-determined viabilities and vitalities illuminates how communities identify and fill fissures or ruptures in the continuity of oppressive structures, pedagogies, policies, spaces, places, and laws. Indeed, resilience is broadly appealing in that it offers individuals and groups the opportunity to celebrate ingenuity and survival. Yet, resilience is also implicated in the reproduction of one's own subjectification. Rarely is group resiliency prioritized against more individualized forms of adaptation or forms of radical care offered through activist work. However, as discussed here, group resilience is far more "powerful as a buffer for transgender individuals when they are faced with overwhelmingly bleak social and environmental circumstances."[9] Importantly, the fetishization of resilience results in a failure to identify and call for an end to systems that produce the very inequities that some are expected to overcome. In other words, resiliency is an option only for those who are capable of individually overcoming systemic inequity and structures of power.

Trans vitalities, in contrast to concepts like resilience, center an ethics of radical care. I argue that trans vitalities function in three distinct ways: (a) to disrupt and rethink what valuable, viable, or quantifiable quality of life looks like; (b) to shift our understandings of community toward coalition; and (c) to offer a methodological, theoretical, and application-based set of tools that integrates a radical trans politics and a community-based approach to addressing trans lives. Finally, I position trans vitalities as following Lauren Berlant's "cruel optimism" as an "analytic lever" toward an "incitement to inhabit and to track the affective attachment to what we call 'the good life,' which is for so many a bad life that wears out the subjects who nonetheless, and at the same time, find their conditions of possibility within it."[10] Rather, in defining the potential transgression of radical care, this "negates the dictates of the norm and yet paradoxically reinforces the norm's effects (by not simply refusing the norm, but rather negating it, transcending it and completing it). It exceeds a limit but, in its excess, verifies the limit itself."[11] In other words, radical care can be defined as radical only through explaining how it differs from normal care. In effect, definitions of normal care also create the limits for how to define radical care. When applied to normative expectations of viable trans life, as articulated by the capacity to seamlessly integrate oneself into hetero- and cis-normative life worlds, we see that normativity is that which creates—rather than promises relief from—suffering. Barbara, like many of those discussed in this article, was understood to be resilient only as a result of the transformative power of transgressive activist work.

In focusing on trans vitalities, as well as our understandings of standard versus radical care, I find it useful to highlight the ways in which marked and unmarked standards of care provide insight into the limits of the concept of trans community. There is no single, unilateral form of trans experience that can be meaningfully called upon to define all those classified within this community without erasing difference. Rather, those who may identify with or be placed in the trans community range in age and reflect vastly disparate racial, classed, linguistic, sexualized, and educational backgrounds. It is through practices of elision that such issues of inequality, systemic abuse, and violence become invisible. With these concerns of inequity in mind, I identify *community* here to represent a "symbolic totality as well as a practical multiplicity."[12] That is, while there is no singular trans community, the experiences of the participants explored here index the symbolic totality of the phrase and the participants refer to themselves as belonging to a trans community.

Additionally, as noted by scholars engaged in trans-specific academic work, the notion of a cohesive trans community fails to acknowledge that there is no singular kind of trans person.[13] While I continue to utilize the term *trans* here as a gloss for a diverse and complex multitude of expressions and identities, I have chosen to shift away from the artificial boundedness of the term *community*. Instead, I focus here on coalitions as a frame of reference when (re)considering ethnographic depictions of trans lives. As anthropologist Vered Amit cautions, community, as an analytical category, "always require[s] skeptical investigation rather than providing a ready-made social unit upon which to hang analysis"[14] As such, I employ the language of trans *coalitions* in this text as a means to highlight the critical racial, classed, and gendered implications of US historical renderings of trans and queer(ed) bodies in space.

Assessing Trans Needs in Washington, DC

In this article I draw from two distinct but overlapping research projects: (a) a series of community roundtables and mapmaking conducted among trans-identifying persons in Washington, DC, and (b) the design and implementation of a large scale DC-focused trans community needs assessment (DCTNA) survey. Importantly, while I make a point here to critique the use of metrics to inform our understandings of livable life, I include the survey data to highlight the double bind of presenting research on trans communities. Specifically, the impetus behind conducting a survey emerged from a historical pattern of policy makers, governmental official, researchers, and even gender- and sexuality-based community organizations viewing first-hand accounts provided by trans activists in DC as too anecdotal to support legal or structural changes.[15] In many respects the data collected during the community roundtables is both replicated and supported in the DCTNA data and analysis. Moreover, following traditional academic models, the replication of data outcomes in additional studies functions as a validity check, allowing the researcher to emphasize the veracity of the findings. However, as I argue here, metrics overly simplify the enormous complexity of lived experience and, in the absence of the kind of overlapping data sets utilized in this article, often stand in for, rather than support, first-person accounts.[16] Thus, my goal here is not to argue for entirely replacing quantitatively anchored data collection but, rather, to emphasize the danger of overly relying on numbers to measure life. Finally, it is important to note that both the community roundtables and mapmaking research project, along with the subsequent DCTNA, were reviewed and approved by the institutional review board at American University in Washington, DC, where I completed my doctoral work.[17] While institutional review board approval does not inherently translate to degrees of safety for participants, the kinds of information shared in both of these research projects, including providing permissions to reproduce the visual medium of community-centered maps, demand a level of care that requires a system of checks and balances. Additionally, while I functioned as the principal investigator in title, the research process and outcome were guided by a consensus-based coalition of community activists involved in the DCTC, an informal and nonhierarchal trans activist group based in DC, as well as other informal and formal groups.

In early 2010, members of the DCTC, including myself, began what would become a three-stage process to produce the largest US-city-based, trans-specific, community-produced trans needs assessment project. During what would eventually function as the first stage of the project, we held a series of community roundtables. At these roundtables we asked participants to draw a map Washington, DC, as a "trans city." We followed this activity with a discussion about these maps. We closed each roundtable by collecting questions participants wished to see addressed in a larger-format research project. At the close of this phase, occurring in 2010 and 2011, we reached a total of 108 trans-identifying persons.

Importantly, the data collected during the roundtable discussions and mapmaking reflect lived experience—and the centrality of radical care—in ways that neither just interviews nor a survey can capture. This kind of mapping moves away from normative cartographic methods of GIS and objective scientific means and instead utilizes conceptualizations of space and place in which to visualize the city as lived.[18] The act of map production encouraged participants to consider how they fit in within the city, both physically and metaphorically. Additionally, we utilized this notion of "radical cartography" as a means by which to "actively promote social change" with the resulting research.[19] We drew heavily from the central concepts in community-based research, which shifts the goals of traditional research "with the purpose of solving a pressing community problem or effecting social change."[20]

In response to a consistently articulated desire during the round-tables for a larger DC-based, trans-focused project, we chose to implement a large-scale needs assessment in the form of a survey. We based the language of the DCTNA on issues raised during the roundtables, as well as those in nationally used LGBT-specific surveys, such as the joint 2011 survey produced by the National Center for Transgender Equality and the National Gay and Lesbian Task Force, as well as federal census questions and community-produced surveys used in local needs assessment projects, such as the 2007 Virginia Transgender Health Initiative Study and the 2000 Washington Transgender Needs Assessment Survey. After two rounds of internal testing, the survey in both English and Spanish was released in both electronic and paper form in May 2012 and was closed in May 2013. Upon closing, 624 surveys were completed, with a total of 521 surveys qualifying for inclusion in the data analysis. In November 2015 we released *Access Denied*, a 104-page executive summary examining the survey data.[21]

The results from the DCTNA reflected a large cross-section of what trans might look like and provided data that we now had documented in a form more readily acknowledged as valid by policy makers, researchers, and other direct service providers. Approximately 63 percent of survey respondents identified as trans or gender-nonconforming and were assigned male at birth, and approximately 37 percent identified as trans or gender-nonconforming and assigned female at birth. The racial demographic breakdown for the survey was approximately 59 percent respondents of color and 41 percent white respondents. Over 46 percent of respondents reported earning less than $10,000 a year, compared with only 11 percent of Washington, DC, residents as a whole.[22] Trans persons of color, particularly trans women of color, reflected the greatest economic hardships among those we surveyed, with 57 percent making less than $10,000 a year. White trans persons were six times more likely than trans persons of color to have secured a higher education degree. Sixteen percent of white participants reported experiencing financial hardship in higher education, whereas 25 percent of Black participants and 70 percent of Latinx participants reported similar hardships. Seventy-one percent of trans masculine persons reported attaining a higher education degree, compared to only 29 percent of trans feminine individuals.

The survey also reflected disturbingly high rates of assault and harassment. Of those surveyed, 74 percent had been verbally assaulted, 42 percent had been physically assaulted, and 35 percent had been sexually assaulted; 57 percent of trans feminine individuals had been assaulted, compared to 17 percent of trans masculine individuals; and 47 percent of trans feminine individuals had been sexually assaulted, compared to 14 percent of trans masculine individuals. Experiences of assault were more common among trans persons of color compared to white trans persons: 54 percent of Black and 60 percent of Latinx trans persons had been physically assaulted compared to 21 percent of whites; 47 percent of Black and 56 percent of Latinx trans persons had been sexually assaulted compared to 14 percent of whites. Among Black trans persons, 62 percent of trans feminine individuals had been physically assaulted compared to 14 percent of Black trans masculine individuals. Among Latinx trans persons, 70 percent of trans feminine individuals had been physically assaulted compared to 27 percent of trans masculine individuals.

Finally, the survey documented an ongoing health crisis for trans persons living in DC. While 8 percent of the general population of Washington, DC was uninsured in 2012, twice as many trans persons were uninsured during the survey period, and more than one out of every four with insurance relied on public sources, such as Medicare and Medicaid. Although many respondents reported "good to excellent" general health, reporting "poor to fair" health was associated with high rates of poverty and past discrimination. Discrimination from health care providers is particularly important when considering trans health concerns. Among those who had seen a doctor, 19 percent had been denied medical care at least once due to being perceived as transgender. Unlike many other categories of experience, there were no statistically significant differences in denial of medical care based on gender identity or race/ethnicity. However, a significant association was found between medical discrimination and perceived quality of health. Among those who had been medically discriminated against, 24 percent rated their health as poor to fair, compared to 13 percent of those who had not been medically discriminated against.

Importantly, of those surveyed, 65 percent have undergone hormone treatment or body enhancement for the purpose of transitioning. Another 23 percent have not yet had a procedure but wanted to, and 12 percent did not wish to have any procedures. As such, given many of the barriers to accessing treatment through licensed providers, the use of unlicensed care is particularly important when considering trans health needs. Among those who have undergone treatment, 30 percent reported getting procedures from an unlicensed practitioner or source (e.g., internet). Use of unlicensed sources differed significantly by gender identity and race/ethnicity. Trans feminine individuals and persons of color were more likely to use at least one unlicensed source or provider compared with trans masculine individuals and whites.

In addition to physical health, the mental health status of trans populations is often ignored beyond official diagnostic concerns outlined in the American Psychiatric Association's *Diagnostic and Statistical Manual of Mental Disorders*. Suicide remains the tenth most common cause of death in the United States, with roughly 3.7 percent of the general population reporting suicidal ideation in the past year and 0.6 percent having made an actual suicide attempt. In contrast, 60 percent of surveyed individuals report having seriously considered suicide at least once in their lives, and 34 percent had attempted suicide in the past, with 10 percent having attempted within the twelve months prior to the survey—twenty times that of the general population.

Mapping, Big Data, and Coalitional Meaning Making

The community-produced maps collected in the first phase of this project elucidate lived experience in ways that metrics collected from the survey cannot. It should be stressed that, while I make use of data here, I do so while simultaneously critiquing the use of big data to measure a livable life. Indeed, were one to analyze the data collected in this survey in the absence of the roundtable discussions and mapmaking activity, it would seem that, with few exceptions, the trans persons that participated in this survey have a dismal quality of life. However, variables such as yearly income and HIV status are factors that researchers and academics, such as myself, latch on to as a means of providing evidence that all is not equal. This is a point that cannot be emphasized enough: the metrics that are used to define resilience are the same metrics used to define suffering.

In other words, lived experience is not measurable by rates of poverty alone, nor is having class mobility evidence of living a good life. Yet, at the same time, we cannot ignore the materiality of how resources are allocated according to need or how lacking housing, sustainable income, or medical resources is a quality-of-life issue. Rather, data such as those collected in the DCTNA, placed in the context of community-produced maps, would suggest that life is not measured by just income or health but, rather, is marked by where one experiences belonging and where one accesses care and support. Importantly, this is not to suggest that feeling belonging replaces housing, or that experiencing care is static in time or place. Just as space is not inherently safe, care does not exist based solely on the space. In short, my use of these data and mapping in this text is to provide multiple platforms and contrasts toward elucidating livable life and, in multiple contexts, forms of radical care.

Historically, maps have served as a way to silence and erase devalued experience and notions of space.[23] In many ways, mapmaking serves as a way to make visible the felt experiences of negotiating the world as an embodied subject. As Brown and Knopp highlight, Henri Lefebvre—known for his innovations around social space—focuses on the dialectic between space and the body and notes that "the capacity of bodies that defy visual and behavioral expectation to disrupt the shared meaning of public space" reflects the multidirectionality of meaning making.[24] Bodies do not move through vacuums of space but, rather, are always already engaged in and through discourses of power. Here participants were not asked merely to produce a map of the city but, rather, to produce a map from their perspectives as persons with trans identities or subjectivities. Trinh T. Minh-ha situates this kind of "territorialized knowledge" as one that "secures for a speaker a position of mastery: I am in the midst of a knowing, acquiring, deploying world—I appropriate, own and demarcate my sovereign territory as I advance."[25] To claim space, however marginalized or ignored, as one's own is a claim to territorialized and embodied knowledge. Specifically, the maps produced during this project made clear that many spaces of care were measured in terms of trans coalitional labor rather than officially designated spaces of biomedical, psychosocial, or community care.

Moreover, rather than see the map as a "mirror of the world," I situate maps here as forms of power, as well as texts that index somatic and affective experience.[26] Chris Perkins also reminds us that "a focus for cultural research into map use might shift towards participation and observation of real uses, as well as interviews, focus groups and read aloud protocols" in the process of mapmaking and map evaluation.[27] The maps in this project were produced in community roundtable settings, where participants created their own maps and came together at the end of each roundtable to discuss core features of importance. This kind of community mapping represents a "democratized mapping" that "offers new possibilities for articulating social, economic political or aesthetic claims" through shifting knowledge production from the individual to the community.[28]

Building on John Brian Harley's discussion of maps as social texts, I want to stress the utility of community-produced maps as valid data sources.[29] Indeed, maps "actively construct knowledge, . . . exercise power and . . . can be a powerful means of promoting social change"[30] To this I would add that social change can be promoted in the (re)situating of maps and narratives as mutually constitutive of each other. This project attends to space and place as similarly constructed, as real or imagined sites of social interaction. These "spatial forms" that link individuals to "the social world, providing the basis of a stable identity," serve as a basis for understanding lived trans experience in a dynamic fashion.[31]

Finally, while the maps collected here no doubt reflect a prompt to articulate DC through the lens of what constitutes trans experience, these maps nonetheless still confer meaning not only about space and place but also about experience, affect, the body, and power. In this project, these maps serve as visual forms of text as well. Rather than understanding maps simply as forms of direct representation, I consider maps as texts that serve a multitude of projects and purposes, such as giving us visual, textual representations of lived experience.[32] That is, maps provide insight into personal experience but also represent broader sociopolitical discourses of where trans people should or should not go. In many ways we can situate maps as both visual forms of knowledge and experience and as depictions of temporalized embodied movement through space. This depiction then provides us with a dynamic dimension to otherwise relatively static narratives about space and place.

Following the work of Anna Lowenhaupt Tsing, I posit trans coalitional labor as a form of radical care as foregrounded by the knowledge that "collaborations create new interests and identities, but not to everyone's benefit."[33] Rather than solely employing the term *community* to capture the relationships between and across trans-spectrum-identifying persons, I instead use *coalition* here while remaining aware of how even radical forms of care may reproduce inherent inequities across and among different lived experiences. I use *coalition* intentionally as a referent to the relationships between trans experiences or identities of, specifically, those who participated in this project. My use of this term builds from a basic definition provided by Ronda C. Zakocs and Erika M. Edwards, wherein a coalition is composed of people of varied backgrounds, such as "local government officials, non-profit agency and business leaders, and interested citizens who align in formal, organized ways to address issues of shared concern over time."[34] Importantly, Zakocs and Edwards's definition primarily frames difference through one's relative relationship to decision-making power. Additionally, this explanation implies a degree of formality in coalitional structures and goals. In contrast, my use of *coalition* is not to elaborate on particular striations of difference or to identify coalitional goals. Following the claim that "in practice, *coalition* rather than *community* is key to understanding contemporary political movements,"[35] I utilize coalitional spaces as a way to continually bring attention to the differences within, as well as collaborative nature of, community production.

I highlight here three maps collected from the roundtable discussions.[36] Derek, a white trans man in his midtwenties, segregates DC into three different levels of experience: "Virtual Trans DC," "Formal Trans DC," and "Informal Trans DC." Derek's map features many of the organizations other participants included on their own maps (fig. 1). Among the virtual elements, he includes organizations that utilize e-mail correspondence and websites as their primary vector of communication (e.g., DC Area Transmasculine Society and DCTC). His "Formal Trans DC" includes "established orgs" such as Whitman Walker, an-LGBT focused physical and mental health clinic; his personal doctor; HIPS (Helping Individual Prostitutes Survive), a sex worker empowerment organization that uses mobile outreach as their primary method of operation and of which also functions as a place of volunteer work; and a church where the Transgender Day of Remembrance has been held. He qualifies this as the formal elements of a trans city, while the informal elements include his friends' homes and places where he knows trans persons live. Thus, in his map a formal trans city is largely governed by spaces that are accessible and applicable to many within trans coalitions of practice, while an informal trans city is applicable only to him or those within his immediate circle of trans support networks.

In contrast, Joan, a trans woman in her early twenties, does not differentiate between different levels of space in her depictions of community groups. Instead, she links together community organizations and clinics with friends' houses and her home into one seamless web of interconnectivity of "Trans DC safest places" (fig. 2). For Joan, these same community activist organizations exist within a larger network of support. Whitman Walker, which she marks as where she can access hormones, represents a safe place but is located within a web of friends' homes, her gym, and her school. Her map reflects the significance of trans activist work in her trans life as both an embedded element of importance and one that serves a particular function. That is, the safety provided by Whitman Walker may be through the vector of accessible health care, while the safety offered by her gym may be through accessible facilities to work out

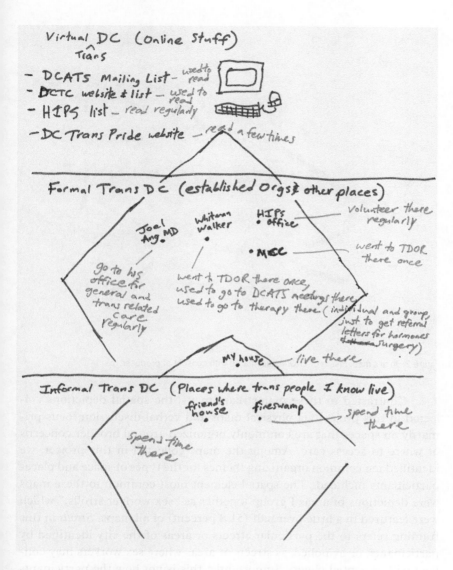

Figure 1. Derek's map. Image of drawn map shared with consent of producer.

in. In turn, these networks function as ways she can gain access to support and mobility but also where she, as a friend or activist, can also provide support and empowerment. A friend's home, in this context, may index broader structures rather than merely where a friend may reside.

Importantly, many maps resemble Naomi's (fig. 3), where a short list of official bars and clubs are provided along with the home of an individual where, in this context, Latinx trans persons new to DC are able to access resources.

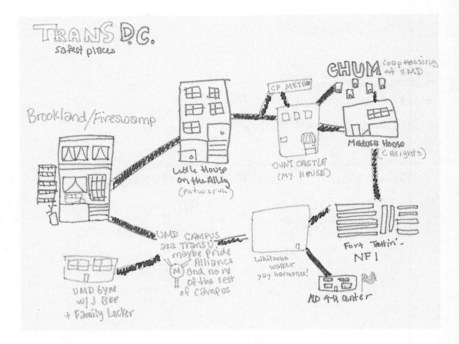

Figure 2. Joan's map. Image of drawn map shared with consent of producer.

Contrasted to these mainstream maps, the spatial depictions collected in this project via physical maps and verbal discussion focus primarily on spaces that are commonly organized around broader concerns of where to access care. Among the maps collected in this project, we identified ten common organizing themes for the types of space and places participants included. The spatial element most common to these maps were depictions of areas I group together as "sex work/er strolls," which were featured in a little over half (51.8 percent) of all maps. *Strolls* in this framing refers to the particular streets or areas of the city identified by participants, or by police, as streets or areas where sex workers may connect with potential clients. Importantly, this is not how the participants of this project solely experienced these areas. Rather, these spaces, while understood to also be areas of sex work, were defined as multilayered, as potentially spaces of care, of where to meet up with or support friends, of police harassment, and of organizational outreach.

The second most common feature that participants included in their maps was health clinics, direct service organizations, and other community organizations, which were featured in roughly a third (36.1 percent) of all maps; 22.1 percent of participants included bars, clubs, and restaurants in their maps, and 15.7 percent included parks and other similar types of spaces for public recreation, such as malls. The home of a friend

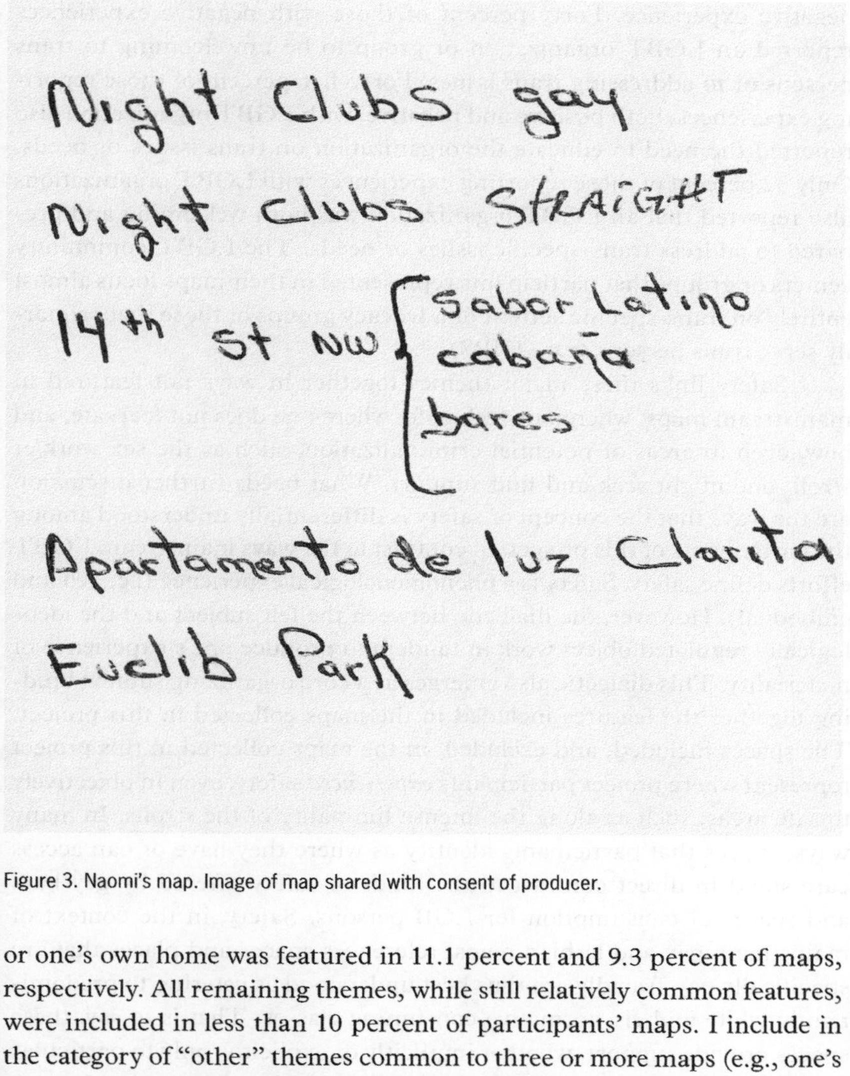

Figure 3. Naomi's map. Image of map shared with consent of producer.

or one's own home was featured in 11.1 percent and 9.3 percent of maps, respectively. All remaining themes, while still relatively common features, were included in less than 10 percent of participants' maps. I include in the category of "other" themes common to three or more maps (e.g., one's gym or school) but not substantial enough to necessitate its own category individually.

Importantly, DC, like many major US cities, is home to a number of LGBT organizations, support groups, and other activist-oriented projects. But focusing only on the organizations and groups included in these maps, trans-spectrum-identifying persons identified care as emerging through spaces with similar social justice, political, or religious practices (e.g., a food co-op or church group). In other words, LGBT rights organizations failed to be included as functional spaces of care. Echoing this sentiment, among those taking the survey, 50 percent who had reported interacting with an LGBT-specific organization reported having had a negative experience. Forty percent of those with negative experiences reported an LGBT organization or group to be unwelcoming to trans persons or to addressing trans issues. Forty-five percent of those reporting experiences, both positive and negative, with LGBT organization also reported the need to educate the organization on trans issues or needs. Only 32 percent of those reporting experiences with LGBT organizations also reported that an LGBT organization was both welcoming and prepared to address trans-specific issues or needs. The LGBT community centers or groups that participants represented in their maps focus almost entirely on trans-specific activist or advocacy groups or those that primarily serve trans persons (e.g., HIPS).

Safety links these major themes together in ways not featured in mainstream maps: where one feels safe, where one does not feel safe, and how, even in areas of potential criminalization, such as the sex work/er stroll, one might seek and find support. What needs further discussion are the ways that the concept of safety is differentially understood among the participants of this project, in contrast to the ways mainstream LGBT efforts define safety. Safety is a phenomenological experience (i.e., felt and embodied). However, the dialectic between the felt subject and the ideologically regulated object work in tandem to produce one's experience of materiality. This dialectic also emerges as a core organizing subtext binding together the features included in the maps collected in this project. The spaces included, and excluded, in the maps collected in this project represent where project participants *experienced* safety, even in objectively unsafe areas, such as along the intense liminality of the strolls. In many ways, spaces that participants identify as where they have or can access care stand in direct contrast to the kinds of safety offered by gay bars and spaces of consumption for LGB persons. Safety, in the context of mainstream gay and lesbian maps, references spaces and places that are specifically gay-friendly are thus best understood as catering to predominantly white and cis-normative consuming classes. That is to say, these spaces provide support, whether implicitly or explicitly, only to particular formations of publicly performed LGB subjectivities and practice. In contrast, safety for the participants in this project often refers instead to areas wherein one's trans history or present is not necessarily at issue, such as at friends' homes.

Notions of safe space that circulate in mainstream LGBT discourses (e.g., the gay bar or the LGBT community center) are often referenced in the maps collected in this project only for their lack of actual safety. Indeed, the processes of deeming safe versus unsafe space are not purely individualistic as much as they are linked to broader discourses and larger organizational efforts with regard to where safety exists. In short, based on the maps collected here, there is no singular, static trans space of care or place of safety. Rather, the maps highlight that care is a contextualized experience that relies on broader social and political interrogations of power rather than simplistic categories of gay space as safe space. As evidenced in these maps, care and support appear to operate not necessarily as a function of being openly trans but, rather, as measured by the capacity to occupy space, if even for brief moments.

Spaces of Care within Death Worlds

As these maps reflect, and to return to Barbara's e-mail, radical care may exist more in contexts wherein the individual's needs are subsumed by the larger project of activism, as transformative and affirmative collaborations redirect support outward. This is not to suggest that activism, or a dismissal of one's individual needs over those of others, is the only form of trans radical care. However, Barbara's narrative about how and why she got involved with DCTC underlies a displacement of normative support models in deference to engaging productively with change to secure a vitality of self. She disregards pathologizing narratives of trans subjectivity and locates empowerment through working for not only the T (trans), as she notes, but also for others. While Barbara never described the work she does, as an active member of the activist community in DC, as a type of radical trans politics, her investment in a trickle-up approach to social organizing articulates a departure from mainstream US LGBT rights discourses that prioritize assimilation and the individual.

Radical care, in this context, may actually more accurately refer to forms of care that are often assumed to exist across our social spaces. In other words, radical care, or the care offered outside, beside, underneath, and perhaps even above normative outlets, is perhaps also the care that refuses a logic of cruel optimism. It is a care that follows desire lines. Barbara's resiliency, as a subject, was not born from support groups, traditional LGBT organizational programming, or even that which she referred to as just the T; instead, the capacity to engage and produce care for others is what she experienced as care for the self.

Trans vitalities is thus not simply a refusal or disavowal of projects of normalization or the commodifiability of trans rights but, rather, a vigilance toward the violently homogenizing expectations of the heterogeneity of lived experience. Trans vitalities calls on those who produce research or provide services, training, or programming on LGBT issues—or even trans-specific practices—to be asked and to answer who benefits from that work. This is not simply a means of identifying lapses in benefits but, rather, is one of the first of many steps to clarify labor and outcomes. However, unlike the cruel optimism promised by resilience or normative models of care, wherein a failure to thrive is the failure of the object of trans bodies to produce ideologically valued forms of production, the subject of trans vitalities is trans lives, and the object is those researchers and metrics that have been empowered with defining life. Within a framework of trans vitalities, the failure is with the measurement; it is not with the body that fails to reify and produce the proper citizen-subject but, rather, with the researcher, the academic, the social service worker, and the LGBT rights organization that have sustained systems of inequity.

Rather than appealing to discourses of success or struggle, trans vitalities and frameworks of radical care call for a rethinking of value and process. Time, space, bodies, and actions are all variables that cannot be overlooked or merged to fit scalable rights frameworks. What this means, logistically, is that projects that seek to attend to trans lived experience must integrate—if not be overtly supportive of—ways of doing and being that go beyond the perceived impacts of gender transgression. Rather, agencies and laws seeking to tend to the imagined trans community and related resilience must simultaneously integrate bodies and practices that mainstream civil right groups abandon. In other words, a framework of trans vitalities, as heavily structured by radical care, that displaces resilience resituates a passive disavowal of bodies that have been marked as disposable toward an intentionally disturbing recognition that we directly facilitate which bodies to dispose of. If we are upfront and foreground the key narratives that guide US sociopolitical discourses of salvage resilience, we will always keep in our analytic that these discourses also prioritize accumulation of capital—social and material—above life. These discourses prevent, rather than facilitate, a grounded celebration of desire lines, of explorations of livable life, of the unimaginable possibilities in approaching all life as sacred. What I am proposing is, instead, a profound and radical disinvestment of hierarchies of worth toward an approach that may very well undermine the appearance of innovation of my own work; however, if my own work can, in some way, render itself useless, I can think of no better outcome or expression of radical care.

Notes

I extend my immense gratitude to Hiʻilei Julia Hobart and Tamara Kneese for their labor, multiple close readings and comments, and extraordinary patience in organizing this volume centered on radical care; to the reviewers of my manuscript and their comments and feedback; to Brooke Bocast for reviewing and providing feedback on multiple iterations of this text; to Elizabeth Pfeiffer, Audrey Cooper, and Emelia Orellana for reviewing and commenting on notions of trans vitalities; and to the organizers and participants of the roundtable discussions and DC-focused trans community needs assessment survey design, implementation, analysis, and write-up. Most important, this text, and all of the discussion, data, and analysis within, is possible only because of the donated labor, time, and shared experiences of trans persons for whom this text has no benefit. As such, the author requests readers view this article as yet another form of unequal labor extraction from lives and bodies that are, far more often than not, valued less than the author's.

1. Harvey, "Ecological Understanding of Resilience," 9.

2. Lechance et al., "Collaborative Design and Implementation," 46; McMillan et al., "Empowerment Praxis in Community Coalitions," 701; Braithwaite, Bianchi, and Taylor, "Ethnographic Approach to Community Organization," 409.

3. Mbembe, "Necropolitics," 17.

4. Snorton and Haritaworn, "Trans Necropolitics," 67.

5. Snorton and Haritaworn, "Trans Necropolitics," 67.

6. Ahmed, *Willful Subjects*, 21.

7. Garofalo et al., "Overlooked, Misunderstood, and At-Risk"; Operario, Tan, and Kuo, "HIV/AIDS in Asian and Pacific Islanders," 375; Poteat et al., "HIV Risk and Preventive Interventions," 274; World Health Organization, "Guidance on Oral Pre-exposure Prophylaxis."

8. Hamilton, Adolphs and Nerlich, "Meanings of 'Risk,'" 163; Hall, "Intertextual Sexuality," 125; Milani, "Queering the Matrix," 59.

9. Breslow et al., "Resilience and Collective Action," 262.

10. Berlant, *Cruel Optimism*, 27.

11. Overboe, "Vitalism," 28.

12. Miller and Slater, *Internet*, 16.

13. Stryker, *Transgender History*, 24; Valentine, *Imagining Transgender*, 22.

14. Amit, *Trouble with Community*; with regard to gender, see Young, "Rawls's Political Liberalism," 189.

15. For a similar rationale guiding their own DC-based, trans-focused research design and intended outcomes, see Alliance for a Safe and Diverse DC, *Move Along*; and Xavier et al., "Needs Assessment of Transgendered People of Color."

16. My appreciation to reviewer comments in pointing out the contradictory nature of using metrics in support of the critique of metrics.

17. My appreciation to reviewer comments recognizing the potential harm either of these projects could enact were they conducted in the absence of institutional oversight and, importantly, protocols that ensure participants' anonymity and rights.

18. Geltmaker, "Queer Nation Acts Up," 234; Bhagat and Mogel, introduction, 6.

19. Bhagat and Mogel, introduction, 6.

20. Strand et al., *Community-Based Research and Higher Education*, 3.

21. See Edelman, *Access Denied*.

22. Edelman, *Access Denied*.

23. Piper, *Cartographic Fictions*, 42.

24. Brown and Knopp, "Queer Cultural Geographies," 315.

25. Minh-ha, "Write Your Body and the Body in Theory," 260.

26. Harley, "Rereading the Maps of the Columbian Encounter," 522; Rocheleau, "Maps as Power Tools," 327–28.

27. Perkins, "Cultures of Map Use," 152.

28. Perkins, "Cultures of Map Use," 154; see also Bhagat and Mogel, introduction.

29. Harley, "Deconstructing the Map," 10.

30. Crampton and Krygier, "Introduction to Critical Cartography," 15.

31. Zukin, "City as a Landscape of Power," 223.

32. Cosgrove and Daniels, "Fieldwork as Theatre," 169.

33. Tsing, *Mushroom at the End of the World*, 13.

34. Zakocs and Edwards, "What Explains Community Coalition Effectiveness?," 351.

35. Walby, "From Community to Coalition,"120; emphasis added.

36. All names used are pseudonyms; participants provided consent for their roundtable maps to be used in analysis and publication of research findings.

References

Ahmed, Sara. *Willful Subjects*. Durham, NC: Duke University Press, 2014.

Alliance for a Safe and Diverse DC. *Move Along: Policing Sex Work in Washington, D.C.* Different Avenues, 2008. dctranscoalition.files.wordpress.com/2010/05/movealongreport.pdf.

Amit, Vered. *The Trouble with Community*. London: Pluto, 2002.

Berlant, Lauren. *Cruel Optimism*. Durham, NC: Duke University Press, 2011.

Bhagat, Alexis, and Lize Mogel. Introduction to *An Atlas of Radical Cartography*, 6–11. Los Angeles: Journal of Aesthetics and Protest Press, 2007.

Braithwaite, Ronald L., Cynthia Bianchi, and Sandra E. Taylor. "Ethnographic Approach to Community Organization and Health Empowerment." *Health Education Quarterly* 21, no. 3 (1994): 407–16.

Breslow, Aaron S., Melanie E. Brewster, Brandon L. Velez, Stephanie Wong, Elizabeth Geiger, and Blake Soderstrom. "Resilience and Collective Action: Exploring Buffers against Minority Stress for Transgender Individuals." *Psychology of Sexual Orientation and Gender Diversity* 2, no. 3 (2015): 253.

Brown, Michael, and Larry Knopp. "Queer Cultural Geographies—We're Here! We're Queer! We're over There, Too." In *The Handbook of Cultural Geography*, edited by Kay Anderson, Mona Domosh, Steve Pile, and Nigel Thrift, 313–24. London: Sage, 2003.

Cosgrove, Denis, and Stephen Daniels. "Fieldwork as Theatre: A Week's Performance in Venice and Its Region." *Journal of Geography in Higher Education* 13, no. 2 (1989): 169–82.

Crampton, Jeremy W., and John Krygier. "An Introduction to Critical Cartography." *ACME: An International E-Journal for Critical Geographies* 4, no. 1 (2006): 11–33. www.acme-journal.org/index.php/acme/article/view/723.

Edelman, Elijah Adiv. *Access Denied: Washington, DC, Trans Needs Assessment Report*. With Ruby Corado, Elena Lumby, Robert Gills, Jona Elwell, Jason Terry, and Jady Emperador Dyer. DC Trans Coalition, November 2015. dctranscoalition.files.wordpress.com/2015/11/dctc-access-denied-final.pdf.

Garofalo, Robert, Joanne Deleon, Elizabeth Osmer, Mary Doll, and Gary W. Harper. "Overlooked, Misunderstood, and At-Risk: Exploring the Lives and HIV Risk of Ethnic Minority Male-to-Female Transgender Youth." *Journal of Adolescent Health* 38, no. 3 (2006): 230–36.

Geltmaker, Ty. "The Queer Nation Acts Up: Health Care, Politics, and Sexual Diversity in the County of Angels." *Environment and Planning D: Society and Space* 10, no. 6 (1992): 609–50.

Hall, Kira. "Intertextual Sexuality." *Journal of Linguistic Anthropology* 15, no. 1 (2005): 125–44.

Hamilton, Craig, Svenja Adolphs, and Brigitte Nerlich. "The Meanings of 'Risk': A View from Corpus Linguistics." *Discourse and Society* 18, no. 2 (2007): 163–81.

Harley, John Brian. "Deconstructing the Map." *Cartographica* 26, no. 2 (1989): 1–20.

Harley, J. Brian. "Rereading the Maps of the Columbian Encounter." *Annals of the Association of American Geographers* 82, no. 3 (1992): 522–42.

Harvey, Mary R. "Towards an Ecological Understanding of Resilience in Trauma Survivors: Implications for Theory, Research, and Practice." *Journal of Aggression, Maltreatment, and Trauma* 14, no. 1–2 (2007): 9–32.

Lachance, Laurie L., et al. "Collaborative Design and Implementation of a Multisite Community Coalition Evaluation." *Health Promotion Practice* 7, no. 2 Suppl (2006): 44S–55S.

Mbembe, Achille. "Necropolitics," translated by Libby Meintjes. *Public Culture* 15, no. 1 (2003): 11–40.

McMillan, Brad, Paul Florin, John Stevenson, Ben Kerman, and Roger E. Mitchell. "Empowerment Praxis in Community Coalitions." *American Journal of Community Psychology* 23, no. 5 (1995): 699–727.

Milani, Tommaso M. "Queering the Matrix? Language and Identity Troubles in HIV/AIDS Contexts." *Stellenbosch Papers in Linguistics Plus* 41 (2012): 59–75.

Miller, Daniel, and Don Slater. *The Internet: An Ethnographic Approach.* Oxford: Oxford University Press, 2000.

Minh-ha, Trinh T. "Write Your Body and the Body in Theory." In *Feminist Theory and the Body: A Reader*, edited by Janet Price and Margrit Shildrick, 258–66. New York: Routledge, 1999.

Operario, Don, Judy Tan, and Caroline Kuo. "HIV/AIDS in Asian and Pacific Islanders in the United States." In *Handbook of Asian American Health*, edited by Grace J. Yoo, Mai-Nhung Le, and Alan Y. Oda, 375–88. New York: Springer, 2013.

Overboe, James. "Vitalism: Subjectivity Exceeding Racism, Sexism, and (Psychiatric) Ableism." *Wagadu* 4 (2007): 23–33.

Perkins, Chris. "Cultures of Map Use." *Cartographic Journal* 45, no. 2 (2008): 150–58.

Piper, Karen Lynnea. *Cartographic Fictions: Maps, Race, and Identity.* New Brunswick, NJ: Rutgers University Press, 2002.

Poteat, Tonia, Andrea L. Wirtz, Anita Radix, Annick Borquez, Alfonso Silva-Santisteban, Madeline B. Deutsch, Sharful Islam Khan, Sam Winter, and Don Operario. "HIV Risk and Preventive Interventions in Transgender Women Sex Workers." *Lancet* 385, no. 9964 (2015): 274–86.

Rocheleau, Dianne. "Maps as Power Tools: Locating Communities in Space or Situating." In *Communities and Conservation: Histories and Politics of Community-Based Natural Resource Management*, edited by J. Peter Brosius, Anna L. Tsing, and Charles Zerner, 327–62. Walnut Creek, CA: AltaMira, 2005.

Snorton, C. Riley, and Jin Haritaworn. "Trans Necropolitics: A Transnational Reflection on Violence, Death, and the Trans of Color Afterlife." In *The Transgender Studies Reader 2*, edited by Susan Stryker and Aren Z. Aizura, 67–76. New York: Routledge, 2013.

Strand, Kerry J., Nicholas Cutforth, Randy Stoecker, Sam Marullo, and Patrick Donohue. *Community-Based Research and Higher Education: Principles and Practices.* San Francisco: John Wiley, 2003.

Stryker, Susan. *Transgender History.* Berkeley, CA: Seal, 2008.

Tsing, Anna Lowenhaupt. *The Mushroom at the End of the World: On the Possibility of Life in Capitalist Ruins.* Princeton, NJ: Princeton University Press, 2015.

Valentine, David. *Imagining Transgender: An Ethnography of a Category.* Durham, NC: Duke University Press, 2007.

Walby, Sylvia. "From Community to Coalition." *Theory, Culture, and Society* 18, nos. 2–3 (2001): 113–35.

World Health Organization. *Guidance on Oral Pre-exposure Prophylaxis (PrEP) for*

Serodiscordant Couples, Men and Transgender Women Who Have Sex with Men at High Risk of HIV: Recommendations for Use in the Context of Demonstration Projects. Geneva: World Health Organization, 2012.

Xavier, Jessica M., Marilyn Bobbin, Ben Singer, and Earline Budd. "A Needs Assessment of Transgendered People of Color Living in Washington, DC." International Journal of Transgenderism 8, nos. 2–3 (2005): 31–47.

Young, Iris Marion. "Rawls's Political Liberalism." Journal of Political Philosophy 3, no. 2 (1995): 181–90.

Zakocs, Ronda C., and Erika M. Edwards. "What Explains Community Coalition Effectiveness? A Review of the Literature." American Journal of Preventive Medicine 30, no. 4 (2006): 351–61.

Zukin, Sharon. "The City as a Landscape of Power: London and New York as Global Financial Capital." In Global Finance and Urban Living: A Study of Metropolitan Change, edited by Leslie Budd and Sam Whimster, 198–226. London: Routledge, 1992.

Solidarity Not Charity

Mutual Aid for Mobilization and Survival

Dean Spade

In the current political moment in the United States, defined by climate crisis, increased border enforcement, attacks on public benefits, expansive carceral control, rising housing costs, and growing white right-wing populism, leftist social movement activists and organizations face two particular challenges that, though not new, are urgent. The first is how to address the actual changing conditions that are increasing precarity and shortening lives. The second is how to mobilize people for resistance. In the face of these conditions, movements might strengthen, mobilizing tens of millions of new people to directly fight back against cops, US Immigration and Customs Enforcement (ICE), welfare authorities, landlords, budget cuts, polluters, the defense industry, prison profiteers, and right-wing organizations. Or, movement organizations could fail to provide any real relief for those whose lives are most endangered and leave newly scared and angry people to the most passive and ineffective forms of expressing their opinions. This article argues that, in the face of these conditions, expanding use of mutual aid strategies will be the most effective way to support vulnerable populations to survive, mobilize significant resistance, and build the infrastructure we need for the coming disasters. Based on my observations participating in policy reform work, public education efforts, and mutual aid projects in movements for queer and trans liberation and prison and border abolition and my study of related and overlapping efforts, I argue that mutual aid is an often devalued iteration of radical collective care that provides a transformative alternative to the demobilizing frameworks for understanding social change and expressing dissent that dominate the popular imagination. I examine the benefits of mutual aid, its challenges, and how those are being addressed by contemporary organizations mobilizing through mutual aid.

Social Text 142 · Vol. 38, No. 1 · March 2020
DOI 10.1215/01642472-7971139 © 2020 Duke University Press

Reformism Is Often Demobilizing

Resistant intellectual traditions have consistently raised the concern that reforms emerge in the face of disruptive movements demanding justice but for the most part are designed to demobilize by asserting that the problem has been taken care of, meanwhile making as little material change as possible. Many reforms provide no material relief and change only what the system says about itself, such as when institutions pass antidiscrimination policies but nothing about the behavior of participants or the outcomes of their operations change. Many reforms, if they do provide any material relief, provide it only to those who are least marginalized within the group of people who were supposed to benefit from the reform. For example, immigration reforms that cut out people with criminal records or who are "public charges," or that make military service or college graduation conditions for relief, are likely to be accessible only to those least targeted by police, those who can pay tuition, those not pushed out of school by ableism and racism. Reforms often merely tinker with existing harmful conditions, failing to reach the root causes.[1] For example, police departments might begin to hire cops of color or gay or trans cops, but the functions of police violence remain the same.[2] A slight procedural change in how people can be evicted, deported, lose their benefits, or be expelled from school will fail to reach the root causes of how these processes target particular populations and shorten their lives. Reforms also sometimes expand the capacity for harm, such as when police reforms include increasing the number or equipment of police.[3] Reforms also reproduce cultural norms that mark some people as disposable by dividing the targeted population into deserving and undeserving categories, such as by lifting up "good" immigrants and arguing that they deserve relief that other immigrants do not deserve.

Social movements have developed criteria for evaluating reforms because of awareness of how they can be inadequate, harmful, and demobilizing. These criteria are not a simple checklist for determining a beneficial reform. Rather, they are bases for engaging in debate and speculation as organizations and coalitions evaluate campaigns and demands. Prison abolitionists, for example, ask, Does the reform in question expand the criminal punishment system? Based on an analysis that prison reforms have tended to expand the reach of policing and criminalization, abolitionists evaluate reforms based on whether they move toward the goal of eliminating the system. Police abolitionist Mariame Kaba offered the following questions as criteria for evaluating police reforms emerging after Mike Brown's murder in Ferguson: "Are the proposed reforms allocating more money to the police? Are the proposed reforms advocating for MORE police and policing? . . . Are the proposed reforms primarily technology-focused? . . . Are the proposed 'reforms' focused on individual dialogues with individual cops?"[4] These criteria address the dangers of police expansion and legitimization through reform.

Peter Gelderloos offers questions for assessing whether a tactic is liberatory: Does it "seize[] space in which new social relations can be enacted"? Does it "spread awareness of new ideas (and . . . [is] this awareness . . . passive or [does] . . . it inspire others to fight)"? Does it "ha[ve] elite support"? Does it "achieve any concrete gains in improving people's lives"?[5] Gelderloos wants to assess how the tactic might allow people to practice new ways of being, such as practicing solidarity across movements, collectively meeting our own needs rather than relying on harmful institutions, making decisions by consensus rather than by following authority, or sharing things rather than hoarding and protecting private property. These criteria suggest that how movements structure participation can give people new skills for practicing democracy, redistributing material resources, and self-defense. Gelderloos's second question focuses on participatory rather than passive awareness. He is not simply asking, Have people heard of it? Rather, he is asking whether people have practiced it, started their own local chapters, or otherwise replicated it. This distinction is important in the context of the demobilizing aspects of social media, where we can be encouraged to solely participate by liking, sharing, declaring, or debating our views within our media silos, without otherwise engaging with others toward change. Further, Gelderloos asserts that "if part of the elite supports a movement it is much more likely that that movement appears to achieve victories, when in fact that victory is insubstantial and supports elite interests."[6] This provides a provocative question about what the interests of any strange bedfellows in a given fight might be, and what that might reveal about the limits of a particular tactic or demand.

In my own work studying and participating in queer and trans liberation projects and in organizations centered on border and prison abolition, I have relied on four primary questions as criteria for evaluating reforms and tactics: Does it provide material relief? Does it leave out an especially marginalized part of the affected group (e.g., people with criminal records, people without immigration status)? Does it legitimize or expand a system we are trying to dismantle? Does it mobilize people, especially those most directly impacted, for ongoing struggle? The first three questions track primary points in the critique of reforms I laid out above. The final question is about how various approaches to political organizing might build greater capacity for the next fight and the next fight. Reforms, especially those forwarded by elite nonprofits with staff invested in lawsuits, policy reform, and lobbying, are often won through conversations behind closed doors with elected officials and heads of administrative agencies or corporations. These "wins" are more likely to be compromised by carve-outs that protect existing arrangements and are more likely to be inadequately or selectively implemented. Reforms won through mobilization, rather than granted through reasoning with elites, are more likely to meet the other criteria described here.

Bottom-Up Strategies for Change

Systems of domination produce routes for channeling dissatisfaction that are nonthreatening to those systems. We are encouraged to bring our complaints in ways that are the least disruptive and the most beneficial to existing conditions. Voting, filing lawsuits, giving money to causes we care about that are properly registered as nonprofits, writing letters to the editor, posting our views on social media, and maybe occasionally attending a permitted march that is flanked by cops and does not disrupt traffic are forms of dissent (as opposed to disobedience) that are tolerable and mostly nondisruptive for existing arrangements. Some of those things can be done as tactics within larger strategies for transformation, but taken alone they are unlikely to cause significant change to existing distributions of wealth and violence. Most of these approved methods of expressing concern are designed to lead to the kinds of limited policy and law reform critiqued in the previous section of this article. However, also by design, most people cannot imagine raising concerns in any way besides these. The central US national fiction about justice and injustice, the story that racism was resolved by civil rights, also rewrites the histories of resistance movements, including the civil rights movement, to tell us that approved tactics are and have been the correct and effective ones for resolving concerns.

Resistant left movements seek to reignite people's imaginations about not just what they can demand but also what tactics they can use to win. Such movements model three kinds of work that change material conditions rather than just winning empty declarations of equality: (a) work to dismantle existing harmful systems and/or beat back their expansion, (b) work to directly provide for people targeted by such systems and institutions, and (c) work to build an alternative infrastructure through which people can get their needs met. Dismantling work includes campaigns to stop the expansion of surveillance, policing, imprisonment, and deportation, to close precincts and prisons, to stop privatization of schools and utilities, to terminate gentrification, pipelines, fracking, mining, and more. This work includes such tactics as pipeline sabotage, direct actions at building sites, training people not to call the cops, divestment campaigns, blocking deportation buses, disrupting city council meetings, door knocking, and working to change state and municipal budgets to defund police and jails. Work to support people impacted by harmful systems can include prison visiting and pen pal programs, rapid response systems for ICE raids, ride sharing, reentry resources, eviction defense, medical clinics, childcare collectives, food distribution, disaster response, and court support efforts. Work to create an alternative infrastructure based in left values of democracy, participation, care, and solidarity includes many of the prior activities, which establish community connections and put in place structures for meeting needs. It might also include things like creating food, energy, and waste systems that are sustainable and locally controlled, building methods of dealing with conflict and harm that do not involve the police or prisons, and building health, education, and childcare infrastructure controlled by the people who use it.

The balance of these three elements is particularly important because of the boldness of working to end capitalism, white supremacy, colonialism, and borders.[7] The three-part framing avoids a purism that would suggest only the most overtly militant actions are valuable, discounting work that directly cares for people made vulnerable by current conditions now, while also avoiding becoming solely focused on providing for people without getting to the root causes of what produces vulnerability. Similarly, building alternatives without also dismantling current systems can lead to utopian projects that can sometimes become exclusive, building a new way of life only for the few who access such projects disconnected from frontline struggles. Acknowledging the necessity of immediate care and defense work alongside work to get at the root causes of harmful conditions and work to build alternative structures allows for a complex, nuanced, and developing imagination of coordinated short- and long-term strategies.

Even within this strategic framework, however, some forms of participation are more valued and more visible than others. In the context of contemporary culture, certain activist and social movement activities align with imperatives of external validation and elitism. Reproductive labor, such as cooking; cleaning; caring for sick people, old people, and children; maintaining one-on-one relationships; visiting prisoners and people in hospitals; providing emotional support to people in crisis; making sure people have rides; and making sure people are included and noticed, is devalued and mostly uncompensated. Social movements reproduce these hierarchies, valuing people who give speeches, negotiate with bosses and politicians, get published, get elected, and otherwise become visible as actors in ways that align with dominant hierarchies. Forms of celebrity similarly circulate within movements. It is glamorous to take a selfie with Angela Davis, but it is not glamorous to do weekly or monthly prison visits. The circulation of dominant hierarchies of valuation inside movement spaces shapes how people imagine what it means to participate in work for change, who they want to meet, and what they want to do and be seen doing. This is especially true for people who have not yet gotten to participate in social movements and have been fed obscuring fictions about social change from misrepresentations of the civil rights movement circulated in school curricula and media. Such representations center charismatic individuals and hide the realities of mass participation and coordination that does not produce careers or notoriety for most participants.[8] For these reasons and others, mutual aid work is one of the least visible and most important forms of work that social movements need to be developing right now.

Mutual Aid

Mutual aid is a form of political participation in which people take responsibility for caring for one another and changing political conditions, not just through symbolic acts or putting pressure on their representatives in government but by actually building new social relations that are more survivable.[9] There is nothing new about mutual aid—people have worked together to survive for all of human history. The framework of mutual aid is significant in the context of social movements resisting capitalist and colonial domination, in which wealth and resources are extracted and concentrated and most people can survive only by participating in various extractive relationships. Providing for one another through coordinated collective care is radical and generative. Effective social movements always include elements of mutual aid. The most famous example on the left in the United States is the Black Panther Party's survival programs, including the free breakfast program, the free ambulance program, free medical clinics, a program offering rides to elderly people doing errands, and a school aimed at providing a liberating and rigorous curriculum to children. The Black Panthers' programs mobilized people by creating spaces where they could access basic needs and build shared analysis about the conditions they were facing. J. Edgar Hoover famously wrote in a 1969 memo sent to all FBI offices that "the BCP [Breakfast for Children Program] represents the best and most influential activity going for the BPP [Black Panther Party] and, as such, is potentially the greatest threat to efforts by authorities to neutralize the BPP and destroy what it stands for."[10] The night before the Chicago program was supposed to open, police broke into the church that was supposed to host it and urinated on and destroyed all the food. The co-optation of the program, with the US Department of Agriculture (USDA) starting a federal free breakfast program that still feeds millions of children today, is evidence of the significance of this mutual aid tactic.[11]

The Black Panthers' survival programs have inspired many other organizations to organize mutual aid efforts to attract people to movements and to build shared analysis of problems as collective rather than individual. People often come to social movement organizations because they need something, such as eviction defense, child care, social connection, health care, or advocacy. Being able to get help with a crisis is often a condition of being able to politically participate. It is hard to be part of organizing when you are struggling with a barrier to survival. Getting support through a mutual aid project that has a political analysis of the conditions that produced your crisis also helps break stigma and isolation. In capitalism, social problems resulting from maldistribution and extraction are seen as individual moral failings of targeted people.[12] Getting support in a context that sees the systems, not the people suffering in them, as the problem can help combat the isolation and stigma. People at the front lines have the most awareness of how these systems harm and are essential strategists because of their expertise. Directly impacted people and people who care about them often join movements because they want to get and give help. Mutual aid exposes the failures of the current system and shows an alternative. It builds faith in people power and fights the demobilizing impacts of individualism and hopelessness-induced apathy.

Mutual aid projects also build solidarity. I have seen this at the Sylvia Rivera Law Project, a law collective that provides free legal help to trans and gender-nonconforming people who are low income and/or people of color. People come to the organization for services but are invited to stay and participate in organizing. Members may have some things in common—being trans or gender nonconforming, for example—but also differ from one another in terms of race, immigration status, ability, HIV status, age, housing access, sexual orientation, language, and more. By working together and participating in shared political education programming, members learn about experiences that are not their own and build solidarity. Doing explicit work around difference within the group builds the skills of members to practice solidarity and build broad analysis. In the context of nonprofitization, organizations are incentivized to be single-issue oriented, aligning with elites rather than with targeted populations, and use palatable tactics.[13] Solidarity is disincentivized, yet solidarity is what builds and connects large-scale movements. Mutual aid projects, by creating spaces where people come together based on some shared need or concern but encounter and work closely with people whose lives and experiences differ from their own, cultivate solidarity.

Mutual aid projects also build skills for collaboration, participation, and decision making. People engaged in a project to help one another through housing court proceedings will learn the details of how the system does its harm and how to fight it, but they will also learn about meeting facilitation, working across difference, retaining volunteers, addressing conflict, giving and receiving feedback, following through, and coordinating schedules and transportation. They may also learn that it is not just lawyers who can do this kind of work and that many people have something to offer. This departs from expertise-based services systems that connect helping one another to getting advanced degrees. Mutual aid is antiauthoritarian, demonstrating how to do things together in ways that we were told not to imagine and how to organize human activity without coercion.[14] Most people in the United States have never been to a meeting where there was not a boss or authority figure with decision-making power over others determining the outcomes. Most people work inside hierarchies where disobedience leads to punishment or exclusion. Of course, we bring our learned practices of hierarchy and (de)valuation with us even when no paycheck or punishment enforces our participation. However, experiences of being in groups voluntarily motivated by shared transformative principles and a sincere effort to practice them can build new skills and capacities.

For example, in Occupy encampments that emerged in 2011, people engaged in skill building about how to resolve conflict without calling the police. Occupy mobilized many people who had never participated in political resistance before, introducing them to practices like consensus decision making, taking public space, and engaging in free political education workshops. Many who joined Occupy did not already have a developed critique of policing. Participants committed to police abolition and antiracism cultivated conversations about not calling the police. This was inconsistent and imperfect, but it introduced many people to new skills about responding to harm, which they took with them in their work after Occupy encampments were dismantled by the police. Mutual aid lets people learn and practice the skills and capacities we need to live in the world we are trying to create—a world shaped by practices of collective self-determination.[15]

Mutual aid can also generate boldness and a willingness to defy illegitimate authority. Taking risks with a group for a shared purpose can be a reparative experience when we have been trained to follow rules. Organizers from Mutual Aid Disaster Relief (MADR), a network organizing to provide mutual aid in the context of disasters, share this story in their 2018 workshop facilitation guide to emphasize their argument that "audacity is our capacity":

> When a crew of MADR organizers travelled to Puerto Rico (some visiting their families, others bringing medical skills), they found out about a government warehouse that was neglecting to distribute huge stockpiles of supplies. They showed their MADR badges to the guards and said, "We are here for the 8am pickup." When guards replied that their names were not on the

list, they just insisted again, "We are here for the 8am pickup." They were eventually allowed in, told to take whatever they needed. After being let in once, aid workers were able to return repeatedly. They made more badges for local organizers, and this source continued to benefit local communities for months.[16]

MADR asserts that by taking bold actions together, "we can imagine new ways of interacting with the world."[17] In the face of disaster, mutual aid helps people survive and builds new social relations centered in solidarity and resistance to illegitimate authority. When dominant social relations have been suspended, people discover that they can break norms of individualism, passivity, and respect for private property above human need and collaborate to meet their needs. MADR asserts that "saving lives, homes, and communities in the event and aftermath of disaster may require taking bold action without waiting for permission from authorities. Disaster survivors themselves are the most important authority on just action."[18] Courageous mutual aid actions of disaster survivors occur against a backdrop of injustice, where government agents primarily show up to lock down cities while failing to provide aid or support recovery.[19]

Mutual aid projects providing relief to survivors of storms, floods, earthquakes, and fires, as well as those developed to support people living through the crises caused by poverty, criminalization, housing costs, endemic gender violence, and other ordinary conditions, produce new systems that can prevent harm and improve preparedness for the coming disasters. In the context of Hurricane Maria's devastation of Puerto Rico, it was the existence of food justice efforts that made it possible for many people to eat when the corporate food system that brings 90 percent of the island's food from off-island was halted by the storm. Similarly, it was local solar that allowed people to charge medical devices when the electrical grid went down. The mutual aid projects that exist before the acute disasters become the alternatives that help people survive when disasters arise. By looking at what still works in the face of disaster, we can learn what we want to build to prepare for the next storm or fire. Naomi Klein argues that locally controlled microgrids are more desirable for delivering sustainable energy, given the failures of the energy monopolies that currently dominate energy delivery.[20] In the wake of the 2018 fires in Northern California, Klein's descriptions of how large energy companies work to prevent local and sustainable energy efforts offer particularly compelling support for her argument that in energy as in other areas of survival, we should be working toward locally controlled, democratic structures to replace our crumbling and harmful infrastructure.[21] In the wake of those fires, as the public learned that they were caused by the mismanagement of PG&E and the state government immediately offered PG&E a bailout while failing to support people displaced by the disaster, Klein asks us to imagine getting rid of the undemocratic infrastructure of our lives and replacing it with people's infrastructure. For social movements working to imagine and build a transition from extractive "dig, burn, dump" economies to sustainable, regenerative ways of living, mutual aid offers a way to meet current needs and prepare for coming disasters.[22]

Pitfalls and Challenges of Mutual Aid

Charity and social services frameworks dominate mainstream understanding of what it means support people in crisis. Mutual aid is not charity. *Charity, aid, relief,* and *services* are terms used in various contexts to denote the provision of support for survival to poor people where that support is governed by rich people and/or government. Charity models promote the idea that most poverty is a result of immorality and that only those who can prove their moral worth deserve help. Charity comes with eligibility requirements that relate to these moral frameworks of deservingness, such as sobriety, piety, curfews, participation in job training or parenting courses, cooperation with the police, or identifying the paternity of children. The determination of deservingness and undeservingness is based in cultural archetypes that pathologize Black families, frame poor women as overreproductive, and criminalize poverty.[23] The conditions of receiving aid are made so stigmatizing that they discipline everyone into taking any work at any exploitative wage or condition in order to avoid the fate of people who must seek relief. Charity makes rich people and corporations look generous and upholds and legitimizes the systems that concentrate wealth.[24]

Charity is increasingly privatized and contracted out to the massive nonprofit sector. Nonprofits compete for grants to address social problems. Elite donors get to decide what strategies should be funded and then protect their money from taxation by storing it in foundations that fund their pet projects, most of which have nothing to do with poor people. Even nonprofits that do purport to address poverty are mostly run by white elites. Nonprofitization has reproduced antidemocratic racist and colonial relationships between the winners and losers of extractive, exploitative economic arrangements.[25]

Mutual aid projects face the challenge of avoiding the charity model. A member of North Valley Mutual Aid, a group working to support people displaced by the Camp Fire in Northern California, described how narratives of deservingness drove the attacks on the tent city that emerged in a Walmart parking lot after the fire.[26] In the days following the fire, as displaced people with more resources began to leave the tent city, city officials and media portrayed the people still living there as not displaced fire survivors but ordinary homeless and itinerant people who did not deserve to remain. The eligibility processes of the Federal Emergency Management Agency (FEMA) exclude people who cannot confirm an address before the disaster, such as homeless people or people living in poor communities where individual dwellings are not given an individual mailing address. The distinction between deserving and undeserving disaster survivors rests on the idea that suddenly displaced renters and homeowners are sympathetic victims, while people who were already displaced by the ordinary disasters of capitalism are blameworthy.

Mutual aid project participants replicate moralizing eligibility frameworks inside mutual aid projects when they require sobriety, exclude people with certain types of convictions, or stigmatize and exclude people with psychiatric disabilities for not fitting behavioral norms. Myrl Beam traces the tension that emerged in an organization founded to support queer and trans youth, and to operate by and for youth, as the organization formalized, diverging from its initial mission and commitments to youth governance. The organization began to participate with the local police to check warrants for youth.[27] This example of departure from mutual aid principles and toward the implementation of eligibility requirements that enforce deservingness highlights the relationship between governance practices and the slide toward punitive charity models. A MADR participant tells a related story:

> After Hurricane Irma, a local sheriff announced that, "If you go to a shelter for Irma and you have a warrant, we'll gladly escort you to the safe and secure shelter called the Polk County Jail." [This] . . . essentially weaponizes aid against the most vulnerable and put numerous lives in danger. . . . There is always a shocking number of guns that show up after a disaster. A dehydrated child without access to electricity or air conditioning in the blazing Florida or Texas or Puerto Rico sun, needs somebody carrying Pedialyte, not an M16. Both the military or police and the nonprofit industrial complex often serve to reestablish the inequitable dominant social order rather than leverage their resources to assist disaster survivors in leading their own recovery.[28]

Mutual aid projects must also be wary of saviorism, self-congratulation, and paternalism. Populations facing crisis are cast as in need of saving, and their saviors are encouraged to use their presumed superiority to make over these people and places, replacing old, dysfunctional ways of being with smarter, more profitable, more moral ways of being. Politicians, nonprofiteers, and business conspire to remake these places, implementing devastating "innovations" that eliminate public housing, permanently displace residents, privatize schools, and destroy public health infrastructure.[29] Mutual aid projects and their individual participants must actively resist savior narratives and find ways to support participants to build shared analysis about the harms of saviorism and the necessity of self-determination for people in crisis.

Mutual aid also faces the challenge of neoliberal co-optation. Neo-liberalism combines attacks on public infrastructure and public services, endorsing privatization and volunteerism. As public services are cut, neo-liberals push for social safety nets to be replaced by family and church, assuming that those who fail to belong to such structures deserve abandonment. Philanthropy and privatization are expected to replace public welfare, and public-private partnerships are celebrated as part of a fiction that everything should be "run like a business." The cultural narrative about social justice entrepreneurship suggests that people who want change should not fight for justice but should invent new ways of managing poor people and social problems. This raises the question, How do mutual aid projects remain threatening and oppositional to the status quo and cultivate resistance, rather than becoming complementary to abandonment and privatization? In the wake of Hurricane Harvey, corporate media news stories on volunteer boats for rescues followed this pattern, neither criticizing government relief failure nor interrogating the causes of worsening hurricanes and whom they most endanger.[30] Stories of individual heroes obscured the social and political conditions producing the crisis.

This danger of becoming a complementary structure to harmful systems pervades debates about restorative justice programs and other alternatives to incarceration. These kinds of programs, including drug treatment programs, programs that divert some arrestees from the criminal system to social service programs, and restorative justice programs where people who have done harm go through a mediated process with those they have harmed, all have the potential to be disruptive mutual aid programs or to be nondisruptive adjuncts and/or expansions of carceral control. Most such programs emerge from communities impacted by racist systems of criminalization, but many formalize and transition to become funded and shaped by police and courts. Minnesota's restorative justice program, one of the earliest examples of a state incorporating a restorative justice approach statewide, has become another site where the same populations already targeted for arrest are processed through a system. Its emergence did not change who is criminalized or disrupt the way policing and criminalization operate; it only added to the existing system and provided legitimacy through the cover of innovation.[31] In Seattle, throughout a seven-year fight to stop the building of a new youth jail, public officials have relentlessly used the small, minimally publicly funded diversion programs operated primarily by people of color as cover to suggest that the county has already addressed concerns about youth incarceration and that the jail construction is actually in line with a county's commitment to "zero youth detention."[32] The co-optation of grassroots projects aimed at supporting criminalized youth to rationalize further investment in caging youth exposes the real dangers facing mutual aid projects.

Mutual aid projects may appear to overlap with neoliberalism in that their participants critique certain social service models and believe in voluntary participation in care and crisis work. But the critiques of public safety nets made by mutual aid project participants are not the same as those of neoliberals. Mutual aid projects emerge because public services are exclusive, insufficient, or exacerbate state violence. Neoliberals take aim at public services in order to further concentrate wealth and in doing so exacerbate material inequality and violence. The difference is visible comparing the trend of privatization of fire services to the work of the Oakland Power Projects (OPP), which seeks to build an alternative to calling 911. Increasingly, public firefighting services are inadequate and also face cuts; meanwhile, the private firefighting business is growing, with wealthy homeowners paying insurers who come to seal their homes, spray fire retardants on the premises, and put owners in five-star hotels while less affluent people struggle in shelters and fight FEMA for basic benefits. The shift toward eroding public firefighting and creating private, exclusive, profit-generating fire services typifies the neoliberal attack on public services that exacerbates the harms of fire and the concentration of wealth.[33] The OPP's critique of public emergency services and efforts to create an alternative differ in origins, aim, impact, and implementation. OPP emerged out of antipolice and antiprison movement organizations that observed that when people call 911 for emergency medical help, the police come along, endangering people who called for help. In response, the OPP is working to train people in communities impacted by police violence to provide emergency medical care for treating conditions such as gunshot wounds, chronic health problems like diabetes, and mental health crises.[34] This strategy is part of broader work to dismantle policing and criminalization, and it works to both meet immediate needs and mobilize people to participate in building an alternative infrastructure for crisis response that is controlled by people with shared commitments to ending racist police violence and medical neglect.

Feminist and antiracist movements building mutual aid projects have disseminated insights gleaned from this work about how co-optation of mutual aid projects happens and what practices might help resist it. In the written resources produced by mutual aid project participants, as well as at gatherings where activists share their work, discussion of the necessity of maintaining community control of mutual aid projects and the dangers of accepting funding that limits activities or eligibility and of collaborating with law enforcement are prevalent.[35] Feminist scholars and activists have traced how the anti–domestic violence movement shifted from centering mutual aid projects, such as community, volunteer-run shelters and defense campaigns for criminalized survivors, to formalizing and taking government money that required collaboration with police and that increased criminal penalties and made arrests mandatory on domestic violence calls. These shifts increased the criminalization of communities of color, made the services less accessible to the most vulnerable survivors of violence, and provided good public relations for police, prosecutors, and courts as protectors of women.[36] This history and others like it highlight the necessity for mutual aid projects to cultivate autonomy from elite institutions and government and accountability to the populations made most vulnerable by the existing systems. Mutual aid projects also work to maintain community control by structuring decision making to avoid concentration and hierarchy. Co-optation of projects and organizations often happens through co-optation of individual people, often charismatic leaders or founders of projects who get bought off by elites through access to increased funding, influence, job security, or other forms of status.[37] When one or a small number of people have the power to shift the direction of a project, it can be hard to resist the incentives that come with co-optation. Often, charismatic leaders are people who are not the most vulnerable inside the participant group, because being regarded as charismatic, persuasive, important, or authoritative relates to hierarchies of valuation and devaluation that also determine vulnerability. As a result, a single individual or small group running a project may not be the same people who would have the most to lose if the project veers toward elite interests. It is those most vulnerable within the participants who are most likely to have objections to the shifts that come with co-optation, such as new eligibility requirements that cut out stigmatized groups. To return to the example of the queer youth center described earlier, the adults who had the power to make decisions about accepting additional funding and agreeing to run warrants on youth were people who would personally gain (with job security and leadership status) from those decisions, while the youth who would no longer be able to use the space without facing arrest were excluded from the decision-making processes that led to the changes. Given these dynamics, many mutual aid organizations work to create horizontal, participatory decision-making processes and to utilize consensus decision making to cultivate meaningful collective control and prevent co-optation. Relatedly, some establish explicit criteria or guidelines about making sure certain perspectives that are often left out or marginalized are heard, including by agreeing that decisions that break down around identity lines will be reevaluated to assess alignment with the group's transformative principles. Some groups establish quotas about members of decision-making bodies within the group, ensuring that groups particularly likely to be left out are well represented in those bodies.[38]

Consensus decision making, in addition to avoiding the problem of having majorities vote down minorities and silence vulnerable groups, establishes an ethic of desiring others' participation. Decision-making systems focused on competition—on getting *my* idea to be the one that wins—cultivate disinterest in other people's participation. Consensus decision making requires participants to bring forward proposals to be discussed and modified until everyone is sufficiently satisfied that no one will block the proposal. This means participants get to practice wanting to hear people's concerns and their creative approaches to resolving them, and not needing the group's decision to be *exactly* what any one individual wants. If the goal of our movements is to mobilize tens of millions of people, we need to become people who genuinely want others' participation, even when others bring different ideas or disagree with us. Most people will not stay and commit to intense unpaid work if they get little say in shaping that work. We need ways of practicing wanting one another present and participating, not just going along with what one charismatic or authoritative person says. Most people have not gotten to practice this, since the institutions that run our lives, like schools, jobs, and governments, are hierarchical. Instead, we get a lot of practice either going along or trying to be the dominant person or people. MADR says, "We all have something to offer."[39] This is a radical idea in a world where help is professionalized and most people are supposed to stay home and passively consume and occasionally make a donation to a nonprofit or volunteer at a soup kitchen on Thanksgiving. To argue that in the context of crisis everyone has something to offer, that we are all valuable and we can work to include us all, is a significant intervention on the disposability most of us are taught to practice toward one another and the passivity we are encouraged to feel about direct engagement to remake the world. MADR offers the slogan, "No Masters, No Flakes."[40] This simultaneous rejection of hierarchies inside the organizing and commitment to build accountability based on shared values asks participants to keep showing up and working together not because a boss is making you but because you are working together on something that matters.

Conflict is part of all groups and relationships, so mutual aid projects need methods for addressing conflict. Working and living inside hierarchies deskills us for dealing with conflict. We are taught to either dominate others and be numb to the impact of our domination on them, or submit with a smile and be numb to our own experiences of domination in order to get by. We learn that giving direct feedback is risky and that we should either suppress our concerns or find sideways methods to manipulate situations and get what we want. We are trained to seek external validation, especially from people in authority, and often have minimal skills for hearing critical feedback, considering it, and acting on what is useful. To survive our various social positions, we internalize specific instructions about when and how to numb our feelings and perceptions, avoid giving feedback, disappear, defend, demand appeasement, or appease. As a result, we are mostly unprepared to engage with conflict in generative ways and instead tend to avoid it until it explodes or relationships disappear. Mutual aid organizations often work to build shared analysis and practices that recognize and address racism, ableism, sexism, classism, and other systems of meaning and control that produce harm between participants and structure interactions, in order to be better prepared to address conflict. Some provide skills-building activities for giving and receiving direct feedback and avoiding gossip. Ensuring that organizations have a clear approach to decision making and that participants understand it can prevent conflicts that tear projects apart. Creating transparency, especially about money, can prevent destructive conflict. Using transformative justice and mediation frameworks for addressing conflict and harm between participants can help address immediate crises and build skills for preventing and addressing harm in the future.[41] Work to address conflict and harm within organizations and projects, like mutual aid work in general, builds infrastructure and capacity for collective self-governance and survival.

Transition to Collective Care

The most visible mutual aid work in contemporary movements for justice is happening on the front lines of storms, floods, and fires. In those locations, people experience failures of dominant infrastructure and the power of helping and sharing with one another. These disasters are, of course, anything but natural. The profound loss, trauma, and violence occurring at their front lines are created by the ways that access to survival is already organized to support exploitation and extraction. MADR writes:

> Neoliberal capitalism and colonization is daily disaster—the meaningless drudgery of the work, the loss of authentic social relationships, the destruction of the water, the air, and everything we need to survive. Even though a hurricane or a fire or a flood is immensely devastating, it also in a sense washes away the unnamable disaster that is everyday life under neoliberal capitalism. Without the coercion from above, most disaster survivors default back to meaningful relationships based on mutual aid. After the 1906 San Francisco earthquake, Dorothy Day said, "While the crisis lasted people loved one another." We want that love to last. We want to stretch out these temporary autonomous zones, where people are able to share goods and

services with each other freely, where we reimagine new social relationships outside of the dictates of the market, where we work for something real and build something together.[42]

MADR's understanding of disaster relief as a moment of production of new social relations is actually not entirely different from that of disaster capitalists, who seek to remake populations and regions in crisis according to neoliberal imperatives. We might understand mutual aid projects as frontline work in a war over who will control social relations and how survival will be reproduced, especially in the face of worsening crises. Will neoliberals come in to further privatize and extract, or will mutual aid projects based in collective self-determination and local control and dedicated to meeting human needs determine emergent social relations in the wake of disaster? MADR writes,

> Think of all the things we rely on our opposition to do for us. Our food, water, energy, transportation, entertainment, communications, medical care, trash pickup. If the political establishment takes care of people's survival needs, they maintain power, but due to capitalism eating itself, the political establishment seems increasingly disinterested and unable to meet those needs. If instead corporations or fascists meet people's needs, people will probably look to them for leadership. But if grassroots movements for collective liberation facilitate the people's ability to meet their own needs, the better world we dream of very well may become a reality.[43]

Mutual aid work is mostly invisibilized and undervalued in mainstream and left narratives about social movement resistance, despite its significance as a tool for opposing systems of domination. The marginalization of care work as uncompensated feminized labor, the mystification of law and policy reform, and the demobilizing liberal mythology of moving hearts and minds that keeps people busy expressing themselves online all impede a focus on mutual aid. However, mutual aid projects are central to effective social movements, and as conditions worsen, mutual aid projects are becoming an even more essential strategy for supporting survival, building new infrastructure, and mobilizing large numbers of people to work and fight for a new world. It is through mutual aid projects that we can build our capacities for self-organization and self-determination.

> There are enough spare rooms and empty houses for everybody who is homeless. There is enough food produced to feed anybody and everybody who is hungry. . . . In order to face the resource depletion and other climate change realities that are just around the corner, we need to be experimenting now with alternative ways of relating to each other that are based on humanity and generosity, rather than self-interest and greed. It is imperative for our collective survival.[44]

Notes

1. Peace, "Desire to Heal."
2. Tan, "NYPD Unveils Rainbow-Themed Vehicle."
3. Davis, *Are Prisons Obsolete?*, 22–39.
4. Kaba, "Police 'Reforms' You Should Always Oppose"; Critical Resistance, "Reformist Reforms vs. Abolitionist Steps."
5. Gelderloos, *Failure of Nonviolence*, chap. 3.
6. Gelderloos, *Failure of Nonviolence*, 15.
7. Walia, *Undoing Border Imperialism*, 12–15.
8. Flaherty, *No More Heroes*, 11–33.
9. Big Door Brigade, "What Is Mutual Aid?"
10. Collier, "Black Panthers."
11. Ealey, "Black Panthers' Oakland Community School"; Nelson, *Body and Soul*, 17; Heynen, "Bending the Bars."
12. Neubeck and Cazenave, *Welfare Racism*, 15–38; Piven and Cloward, *Regulating the Poor*, 3–37.
13. INCITE!, *Revolution Will Not Be Funded*, 21–39, 53–62, 129–49; INCITE!, *Color of Violence*, 53–65, 208–21.
14. Levine, *Resisting Illegitimate Authority*, 5–21.
15. Gitterman and Schulman, "Life Model," 30–31; Caffentzis and Federici, "Commons against and beyond Capitalism," 95–105; Mutual Aid Disaster Relief, "Workshop Facilitation Guide," 26–31.
16. Mutual Aid Disaster Relief, "Workshop Facilitation Guide," 36.
17. Mutual Aid Disaster Relief, "Workshop Facilitation Guide," 36.
18. Mutual Aid Disaster Relief, "Workshop Facilitation Guide," 29.
19. South End Press Collective, *What Lies Beneath*; Banuchi, "Llueven las denegatorias de asistencia."
20. Klein, *Battle for Paradise*, chap. 1.
21. Morris, "California Regulator."
22. Movement Generation Justice and Ecology Project, "From Banks and Tanks to Cooperation and Caring."
23. Neubeck and Cazenave, *Welfare Racism*, 15–38; Piven and Cloward, *Regulating the Poor*, 3–37.
24. Bowman, "Flip Side to Bill Gates' Charity Billions"; Eisinger, "How Mark Zuckerberg's Altruism Helps Himself"; Rhodes and Bloom, "Trouble with Charitable Billionaires"; Savage, "Privatizing Morality."
25. INCITE!, *Revolution Will Not Be Funded*, 21–39, 53–77, 129–49.
26. It's Going Down, "Autonomous Disaster Relief Organizing."
27. Beam, *Gay, Inc.*, chap. 4.
28. Staufer, "Mutual Aid Disaster Relief," 2.
29. Klein, *Shock Doctrine*, 3–25, 409–84, 487–512.
30. Jervis, "Citizens with Boats."
31. Peace, "Desire to Heal"; Minnesota Department of Corrections, "Restorative Justice."
32. Spade, "Faux Progressive Arguments"; King County, "King County Zero Youth Detention."
33. Smiley, "Private Firefighters."
34. Critical Resistance, "Oakland Power Projects."
35. Sylvia Rivera Law Project, "From the Bottom Up," 1–17; Munshi and

Willse, "Navigating Neoliberalism"; Barnard Center for Research on Women, "Queer Dreams and Nonprofit Blues."

36. INCITE!, *Color of Violence*, 1–24, 208–26.

37. INCITE!, *Revolution Will Not Be Funded*, 129–49.

38. Sylvia Rivera Law Project, "From the Bottom Up," 1–17.

39. Mutual Aid Disaster Relief, "Workshop Facilitation Guide," 68.

40. Mutual Aid Disaster Relief, "Workshop Facilitation Guide," 68.

41. Sylvia Rivera Law Project, "From the Bottom Up," 1–17; Alatorre, "From Drama to Calma."

42. Mutual Aid Disaster Relief, "Workshop Facilitation Guide," 81.

43. Mutual Aid Disaster Relief, "Workshop Facilitation Guide," 81.

44. Staufer, "Mutual Aid Disaster Relief," 3.

References

Alatorre, Lisa Marie. "Round 2: From Drama to Calma." May 17, 2018. lisamarie alatorre.com/2018/05/17/round-2-from-drama-to-calma/.

Banuchi, Rebecca. "Llueven las denegatorias de asistencia por parte de FEMA en Puerto Rico" ("In Puerto Rico, It's Raining FEMA Denials of Assistance"). Centro de Periodismo Investigativo, February 5, 2018. periodismoinvestigativo.com/2018/02 /llueven-las-denegatorias-de-asistencia-por-parte-de-fema-en-puerto-rico/.

Barnard Center for Research on Women. "Queer Dreams and Nonprofit Blues." bcrw.barnard.edu/queer-dreams-and-nonprofit-blues/ (accessed July 22, 2019).

Beam, Myrl. *Gay, Inc.: The Non-profitization of Queer Politics*. Minneapolis: University of Minnesota Press, 2018.

Big Door Brigade. "What Is Mutual Aid?" bigdoorbrigade.com/what-is-mutual-aid/ (accessed January 1, 2019).

Bowman, Andrew. "The Flip Side to Bill Gates' Charity Billions." *New Internationalist*, April 1, 2012. newint.org/features/2012/04/01/bill-gates-charitable-giving -ethics.

Caffentzis, George, and Silvia Federici. "Commons against and beyond Capitalism." *Community Development Journal* 49, no. S1 (2014): i92–i105.

Collier, Andrea King. "The Black Panthers: Revolutionaries, Free Breakfast Pioneers." *National Geographic*, November 4, 2015. www.nationalgeographic.com /people-and-culture/food/the-plate/2015/11/04/the-black-panthers-revolutionaries -free-breakfast-pioneers/.

Critical Resistance. "Oakland Power Projects—Health Resources." criticalresistance .org/opphealthresources/ (accessed January 1, 2019).

Critical Resistance. "Reformist Reforms vs. Abolitionist Steps in Policing." static1 .squarespace.com/static/59ead8f9692ebee25b72f17f/t/5b65cd58758d46d34254 f22c/1533398363539/CR_NoCops_reform_vs_abolition_CRside.pdf (accessed January 1, 2019).

Davis, Angela Y. *Are Prisons Obsolete?* New York: Seven Stories, 2003.

Ealey, Shani. "Black Panthers' Oakland Community School: A Model for Liberation." Black Organizing Project, November 3, 2016. blackorganizingproject.org /black-panthers-oakland-community-school-a-model-for-liberation/.

Eisinger, Jesse. "How Mark Zuckerberg's Altruism Helps Himself." *New York Times*, December 3, 2015. www.nytimes.com/2015/12/04/business/dealbook/how-mark -zuckerbergs-altruism-helps-himself.html.

Flaherty, Jordan. *No More Heroes: Grassroots Challenges to the Savior Mentality*. Chico, CA: AK Press, 2016.

Gelderloos, Peter. *The Failure of Nonviolence*. Seattle: Left Bank Books, 2015.

Gitterman, Alex, and Lawrence Schulman. "The Life Model, Oppression, Vulnerability, and Resilience, Mutual Aid, and the Mediating Function." In *Mutual Aid Groups, Vulnerable and Resilient Populations, and the Life Cycle*, edited by Alex Gitterman and Lawrence Schulman, 3–38. New York: Columbia University Press, 2005.

Heynen, Nik. "Bending the Bars of Empire from Every Ghetto for Survival: The Black Panther Party's Radical Antihunger Politics of Social Reproduction and Scale." *Annals of the Association of American Geographers* 99, no. 2 (2009): 406–22.

INCITE!, ed. *Color of Violence*. Durham, NC: Duke University Press, 2016.

INCITE!, ed. *The Revolution Will Not Be Funded*. Durham, NC: Duke University Press, 2017.

It's Going Down. "Autonomous Disaster Relief Organizing in the Wake of the #CampFire." November 26, 2018. itsgoingdown.org/organizing-in-the-wake-of-the-campfire/.

Jervis, Rick. "Voices: Citizens with Boats Filled Rescue Void a Year Ago during Hurricane Harvey Floods." *USA Today*, August 27, 2018. www.usatoday.com/story/news/2018/08/27/boats-rescues-texas-hurricane-harvey-floods-houston/1112146002/.

Kaba, Mariame. "Police 'Reforms' You Should Always Oppose." *Truthout*, December 7, 2014. truthout.org/articles/police-reforms-you-should-always-oppose/.

King County, WA. "King County Zero Youth Detention." Public Health—Seattle and King County, September 19, 2018. www.kingcounty.gov/depts/health/zero-youth-detention.aspx.

Klein, Naomi. *The Battle for Paradise: Puerto Rico Takes on the Disaster Capitalists*. Chicago: Haymarket Books, 2018.

Klein, Naomi. *The Shock Doctrine: The Rise of Disaster Capitalism*. New York: Metropolitan, 2008.

Levine, Bruce E. *Resisting Illegitimate Authority: A Thinking Person's Guide to Being an Anti-authoritarian*. Chico, CA: AK Press, 2018.

Minnesota Department of Corrections. "Restorative Justice." mn.gov/doc/victims/restorative-justice/ (accessed January 1, 2019).

Morris, J. D. "California Regulator Lays Groundwork for PG&E Bailout." *San Francisco Chronicle*, November 15, 2018. www.sfchronicle.com/california-wildfires/article/California-regulator-lays-groundwork-for-PG-E-13397247.php.

Movement Generation Justice and Ecology Project. "From Banks and Tanks to Cooperation and Caring: A Strategic Framework for a Just Transition." November 2016. movementgeneration.org/wp-content/uploads/2016/11/JT_booklet_English_SPREADs_web.pdf.

Munshi, Soniya, and Craig Willse, eds. "Navigating Neoliberalism in the Academy, Non-profits, and Beyond." *Scholar and Feminist Online* 13, no. 2 (2016). sfonline.barnard.edu/navigating-neoliberalism-in-the-academy-nonprofits-and-beyond/.

Mutual Aid Disaster Relief. "Workshop Facilitation Guide." mutualaiddisasterrelief.org/wp-content/uploads/2018/11/MADR-WORKSHOP-FACILITATION-GUIDE-rough-1.pdf (accessed January 1, 2019).

Nelson, Alondra. *Body and Soul: The Black Panther Party and the Fight against Medical Discrimination*. Minneapolis: University of Minnesota Press, 2011.

Neubeck, Kenneth J., and Noel A. Cazenave. *Welfare Racism: Playing the Race Card against America's Poor.* New York: Routledge, 2001.

Peace, Stevie. "The Desire to Heal: Harm Intervention in a Landscape of Restorative Justice and Critical Resistance." In *Uses of a Whirlwind: Movement, Moments, and Contemporary Radical Currents in the United States,* edited by Team Colors Collective, 149–61. Chico, CA: AK Press, 2010.

Piven, Frances Fox, and Richard A. Cloward. *Regulating the Poor: The Functions of Public Welfare.* New York: Random House, 1993.

Rhodes, Carl, and Peter Bloom. "The Trouble with Charitable Billionaires." *Guardian,* May 24, 2018. www.theguardian.com/news/2018/may/24/the-trouble-with -charitable-billionaires-philanthrocapitalism.

Savage, Luke. "Privatizing Morality." *Jacobin,* December 23, 2018. jacobinmag .com/2018/12/privatizing-morality-charity-altruism-tax-deduction.

Smiley, Lauren. "Private Firefighters and Five-Star Hotels: How the Rich Sit Out Wildfires." *Guardian,* September 20, 2018. www.theguardian.com/world/2018 /sep/20/private-firefighters-wildfire-insurance-climate-change-capitalism.

South End Press Collective, ed. *What Lies Beneath: Katrina, Race, and the State of the Nation.* Cambridge, MA: South End, 2007.

Spade, Dean. "How Politicians Are Using Faux Progressive Arguments to Lock Up Young People." *In These Times,* April 30, 2018. inthesetimes.com/article/21097 /seattle-no-new-youth-jail-politicians-faux-progressives-prison-abolition.

Staufer, Jonathan. "Mutual Aid Disaster Relief: An Interview with the MAHB to Discuss Resilience." Millennium Alliance for Humanity and the Biosphere, December 17, 2018. mahb.stanford.edu/library-item/mutual-aid-disaster-relief -interview-mahb-discuss-resilience/.

Sylvia Rivera Law Project. "From the Bottom Up: Strategies and Practices for Membership-Based Organizations." May 2013. srlp.org/wp-content/uploads/2013 /05/SRLP_From_The_Bottom_Up.pdf.

Tan, Avianne. "NYPD Unveils Rainbow-Themed Vehicle before City's Gay Pride March." ABC News, June 23, 2016. abcnews.go.com/US/nypd-unveils-rainbow -themed-vehicle-ahead-citys-pride/story?id=40072112.

Walia, Harsha. *Undoing Border Imperialism.* Chico, CA: AK Press, 2013.

Keep up to date on new scholarship

Issue alerts are a great way to stay current on all the cutting-edge scholarship from your favorite Duke University Press journals. This free service delivers tables of contents directly to your inbox, informing you of the latest groundbreaking work as soon as it is published.

To sign up for issue alerts:

1. Visit **dukeu.press/register** and register for an account. You do not need to provide a customer number.

2. After registering, visit **dukeu.press/alerts**.

3. Go to "Latest Issue Alerts" and click on "Add Alerts."

4. Select as many publications as you would like from the pop-up window and click "Add Alerts."

Printed and bound by CPI Group (UK) Ltd, Croydon, CR0 4YY

13/04/2025

14656479-0003